The **Business**

ADVANCED Teacher's Book

Martin Barge, William Tweddle and Paul Emmerson

MACMILLAN

Contents

The Business

ADVANCED

To the teacher

The objective of *The Business* is to help your students learn two things: how to do business in English and the language they need to do it. The new language and structures are presented in the Student's Book whilst the DVD-ROM provides language practice and extension and this Teacher's Book provides teaching notes and ideas, answers, recordings, subject background notes and additional reading and speaking notes. Below is a description of what you will find in each.

Student's Book

The modules

The Student's Book contains 48 modules in eight units. Each unit deals with a key sector of activity in the business world. There are six different types of module:

1 About business

These modules contain information and language for the topic area of each unit. The focus is on getting students to understand the topic and the general sense of the texts. The key topic vocabulary is dealt with in depth in the vocabulary module, allowing you to concentrate on developing reading comprehension skills here.

2 Grammar

The Grammar modules tackle key structures that advanced-level students should be able to use. *Did you know?* boxes present interesting facts that students may not know about the structures. Controlled exercises allow students to check they can use the forms before being given an opportunity to hear and produce them in realistic business situations in later activities. The Grammar modules are supported by the *Grammar and practice* section at the back of the book.

3 Vocabulary

These modules build on the important words and phrases introduced in the *About business* modules and provide thorough practice. There is a useful focus on phrasal verbs and collocations most commonly used in business.

4 Management skills

These modules develop important skills and techniques for managing business situations. Language is recycled from other modules, but the focus is mainly on functional words and phrases. There are lots of group work and problem-solving tasks to engage students and encourage their fluency in using the target language in realistic situations. These modules contain pronunciation practice too, which is supported by further interactive practice on the DVD-ROM.

5 Writing

These modules provide practice for the most important types of document students will need to write at work. Model texts are examined and used as a basis to write their own. Key writing sub-skills are focused on in the process of the guided writing, such as using appropriate style and register, reformulating, ordering and expanding from notes.

6 Case study

The case studies provide an opportunity for the students to apply all the language, skills and ideas they have worked on in the course of the unit. The case studies present authentic problem-solving situations similar to those encountered in business.

Internet research

Every module includes an Internet research task. The Internet provides almost unlimited resources for students to improve their English and learn more about business. These tasks direct them to interesting background and details on topics related to each module. The tasks can be set as homework and done before or after working on the module.

Note that words to type into the search engine are in *italics*. They should only be entered between quotes (" ") if quotes are used in the rubric.

Other features

In addition to the eight main units, the Student's Book contains the following:

Reviews

These units can be used in three ways: to consolidate language covered in the units, to catch up quickly on any lessons missed, and to revise before tests or exams.

Additional material

This section contains all the extra materials students need to do pair or group work activities.

Grammar and practice

The section gives a very useful summary of grammar rules with clear examples, but also provides further practice of the essential grammar points in this level of the course.

Recordings

Full scripts of all the audio recordings are given for reference, allowing students to check or study the audio dialogues in detail. However, encourage students not to rely on reading them to understand the listenings.

Wordlist

In the modules, key business terms which advanced-level students may not know are in grey. Definitions of grey words are given in the wordlist, with example sentences.

Phrasal verb index

The index lists over 1,000 English verbs along with one or more phrasal verb equivalents. Students can take a verb they already know and find a phrasal verb that they may be able to use instead.

The DVD-ROM

The DVD-ROM empowers students to continue improving their English autonomously, away from the classroom. It contains:

Interactive workbook

This includes everything you would normally find in a workbook, and more; interactive exercises for vocabulary, grammar, writing and listening practice. There are also pronunciation exercises in each unit, which allow students to record themselves and compare the recording with that of a native speaker. Like the *Review* units in the Student's Book, the Interactive workbook can be used in three ways: to improve skills and consolidate language work from the Student's Book; to catch up on missed lessons; to revise for tests and exams.

Video

Each unit includes part of a management-training video illustrating the communication and people skills practised in each unit, with exercises to practise the functional language used in the video.

Business dilemmas

There are four problem-solving games to allow you to review and practise functional language from the Student's Book. You could also try doing these in class with the students working in pairs to practise discussing problems and solutions.

Tests

There are four tests, one for every two units. These allow students to check their progress through the DVD-ROM. If they do well on a test, they get 'promoted'; if they do well on all four tests, they become CEO!

Business documents

There is a model document for each unit, including mission statements, written warnings, letters to shareholders, etc. Each document includes annotations explaining the structure and key phrases, and a follow-up activity tests understanding of this.

Grammar reference

Students can refer to this section any time for helpful grammar rules and examples.

Class audio

This section of the DVD-ROM contains all the audio recordings from the Student's Book, together with scrollable scripts.

Downloadables

The DVD-ROM includes a set of downloadable files for use outside the DVD-ROM or away from a computer. There is a downloadable and printable PDF of the answers to the Student's Book exercises; a Word file containing the text of each Business document; and MP3 files of all the Student's Book audio that can be transferred to an MP3 player or iPod for listening on the move.

Teacher's Book

This Teacher's Book aims to make using *The Business* Student's Book easy. It provides ideas for lead-in activities for each unit, for further practice and for extension / personalization activities, as well as answers and recording scripts and additional, photocopiable reading and speaking activities.

Subject background

Each unit begins with a page of background notes about the sector of activity in the business world that is dealt with in the unit. It also contains a list of useful websites that will provide you and / or your students with more in-depth knowledge and information about the topic of each unit.

Teaching notes

The teaching notes for each module contain the following:
–   Classroom procedure and task management notes.
–   Ideas for lead-in activities in the *About business* modules.
–   Ideas for further practice and extension activities.
–   A full answer key for the exercises in the Student's Book. (Answers and suggested answers for the module exercises are on a grey tint.)
–   Full recording scripts for all the listening activities.
–   Suggestions on how and when to use the *Internet research* tasks.
–   Tips for tailoring activities to suit lower- or higher-level classes.

Answer key for *Reviews* and *Grammar and practice*

The full answer key for the *Review* sections can be found after every two units.
The full answer key for *Grammar and practice* is at the end of the teaching notes for the Student's Book units on page 116.

Additional activities (photocopiable)

There is an additional, photocopiable speaking and listening activity for each of the eight units in the Student's Book which you can find after the *Grammar and practice* answer key. There are teacher's notes and answers for each photocopiable activity.

Tips for using this book

Answers

You may just want to use this Teacher's Book for the answers to the exercises in the Student's Book. The answers to all the module exercises are in a grey panel at the end of the teaching notes for each exercise.

Teaching notes

Words, sentences and questions in italics are items that can be read out to the class. Expected answers follow in brackets. For example:

'Get students to guess these words:
this means the same as buying (purchasing)
when you pay someone money for working, you give them this (salary)', etc.

Terminology

The following terms are used frequently and you may wish to remind students what they mean:

- Scan reading: to read a text for specific information. It is often done at speed and it is not necessary to understand every word of the text.
- Skim reading: to read a text in order to understand the overall meaning or 'gist'. As with scan reading, this type of reading is often done at speed and does not require readers to understand every word of the text.
- Listening for gist: to listen to something to get a general idea of what it's about without focusing on specific information or language that's used.
- Brainstorming: to generate a lot of ideas from students, by asking them to pool suggestions in groups, without stopping to evaluate the individual points.

Additional activities

The photocopiable reading activities can be used for revision, additional reading practice, or to fill out a lesson with a higher-level group.

The photocopiable speaking activities can be used for revision or to fill out a lesson with a higher-level group.

1 | Personal development

In the 20th century organization, people did not have to give too much attention to their own personal development. Line managers and job descriptions made tasks and responsibilities clear. If training was needed, the organization provided it. Career progression was simple: move up the ladder one step at a time, restricting yourself to organizations that were in the same field.

In the 21st century things are likely to be different (although of course we never know). People will be managed inside matrix organizations – that means having a variety of people to report to. Empowerment will replace control. People will not rely on organizations to provide them with job-specific training, instead they will take responsibility for their own learning and development (perhaps in areas that are quite unrelated to their present job but that improve their employability in the future). Career progression will be based more on merit, and people will move more freely between organizations and jobs. There will be more job insecurity, but people will see multiple career paths as being open to them – not just a straight, corporate ladder. Learning will be continuous.

The nature of managerial skills is also likely to change. Imagination and creativity will become more important. People skills (such as teamworking and influencing) will become much more necessary. The ability to cope with change and complexity will be important. Sensitivity to cultural differences and diversity will play a greater role.

All of this points in one direction: self-managed personal development and continuous learning. Of course, this approach has it problems. The day-to-day demands of a job can sabotage learning opportunities. Lack of support from line managers may impede progress. There are difficulties in measuring the effectiveness of the process, but nevertheless the trend towards lifelong self-development as a career management tool seems unstoppable.

Where does self-managed personal development start? It has to start with gaining a deeper understanding of your present context – the business environment, the market, the key challenges of your organization and the business plan. The next step is to consider your career path: how you got to where you are now, what your successes and disappointments have been, what you have learnt about yourself, and what your dream job would be if there were no constraints (family, geographical, qualifications, etc.). Then you need to identify any support mechanisms that are available to you: Is there someone who can act as your coach, helping you develop a particular skill? Is there someone who can act as your mentor, providing more general guidance and advice? Is there a role model who can inspire you at a distance? Is there a learning partner – someone like yourself who has similar development needs and who you can share ideas and experiences with? The fourth and final step is to look for day-to-day activities that provide opportunities for learning. These might include new projects, secondment to another part of the organization, computer-based learning, structured reading, attending conferences, work shadowing, job swaps, training courses and workshops, and deliberately placing yourself in new and challenging situations like giving a presentation or chairing a meeting.

All this will inevitably lead to a process of self-analysis and reflection. You will become aware of your strengths and weaknesses, your various roles at work, your skills, the things you enjoy, your achievements and what you learnt in achieving them, your future options. This process will involve checking with others (colleagues, family and friends) to get feedback on your reflections and to see what they themselves think about you. Their input will provide some similarities and some differences, and both will send a message.

You will finish with some kind of action plan that helps you to focus on what you want to achieve, how you will achieve it, who can help you in the process, any constraints you might meet, and a timeframe.

Useful websites

http://www.businesslink.gov.uk/bdotg/action/pdp
http://worldwork.biz/legacy/www/downloads/Personal_Development_Plan.pdf
http://www.businessballs.com

1.1 About business

Developing your career

This module focuses on how to get on at work and takes a humorous look at how to build a successful career.

Internet research

A search for *success at work* will return a selection of websites offering further suggestions for getting on at work. You may want to use these sites for sources of further classroom material or for homework assignments.

You could also give website addresses to pairs of students and ask them to find top tips to share with the class.

Discussion

1 Before doing the discussion activity, ask the class to write down the following quotes as you dictate them (once quickly, then twice slowly). Then ask students to compare spelling in pairs and to choose a favourite.

'The only place where success comes before work is a dictionary.' (Vidal Sassoon)

'I owe my success to having listened respectfully to the very best advice, and then going away and doing the exact opposite.' (G.K. Chesterton)

'Success consists of going from failure to failure without loss of enthusiasm.' (Winston Churchill)

Before starting the activities in this first part of the unit, it is important to find out whether your students are working, or about to start work. If they are already working, this would be a good opportunity for them to describe their job roles and responsibilities. If they have not yet started work, this would be a good opportunity for them to talk about their future work ambitions and study plans.

You may also want to consider whether the class is a new group, whether the students already know each other, and whether it is a continuous enrolment class or a closed group. If this is a new group, you can incorporate the topics in this first part of the unit into getting-to-know-you discussions. In a continuous enrolment context, the topics can provide an opportunity for new and established students to get to know each other.

For the discussion activity, write each of the topics on a separate piece of A4 paper. Then write the following question on the board:

What advice would you give to a new employee on how to make a good impression and 'get on' in their career?

Next, explain to the class that they are going to generate ideas in answer to this question. Tell students to work in pairs and give each pair a sheet of paper with a topic on it. Ask the pairs to note down as many ideas as they can about their topic. Set a time limit of up to a minute for this. Next, tell each pair to pass their sheet of paper to another pair, so that each pair now has a new topic. Again, ask them to note down as many ideas as they can. Repeat this process until each pair gets their original sheet back. Pairs then feed back the advice and suggestions to the class. The class then decides on the top five pieces of advice.

Note: If students have not yet started work they may have fewer ideas about business lunches, conferences or meetings. You could nudge them a little by mentioning liquid lunches and ideas adopted to limit time wasted in meetings such as holding meetings standing up.

2 Before getting students to read the article, elicit / pre-teach the meaning of *top tip* (best piece of advice), *drastic* (extreme, desperate) and *out to get you* (wanting to see you fail). You will also need to elicit / pre-teach the meaning of *to get on* (in this context meaning *to make progress*) and *stance* (an attitude towards a particular matter).

ANSWER:

The author describes life at work humorously, as a battle. It is described as ruthless and cutthroat, with people doing whatever they can to get to the top.

Words that indicate the author's humorous stance through comic exaggeration and the idea of battle are *minefield*, *kidnap* and *blackmail*.

Scan reading

3 Before going straight into this task, refer back to the advice that students brainstormed at the beginning of the lesson. You could now ask students to quickly scan the text to see whether any of their ideas are mentioned.

Elicit / pre-teach the meaning of *to steer clear of something* (an idiom meaning *to avoid*).

Give students a short time to scan the text and match the headings to the paragraphs. Allow them to compare answers before taking whole-class feedback.

ANSWERS:

a 4	b 1	c 8	d 9	e 3	f 7	g 2	h 6	i 5

Reading and discussion

4 An alternative way of doing this exercise, if you have a class of six or more students, is to cut the text into sections. Distribute a section to each student. Ask the students to read through their section of text and to highlight the key points and top tips. Monitor and help students with any language difficulties. Once all students have read their extracts and have highlighted the key points, get them to mingle and to tell each other what their text is about and the top tips the writer provides. Once the mingle activity is complete, ask students to work in pairs and to jot down all the advice they can remember. Elicit answers from the class. Finally, ask students to read through the whole text, highlighting the key points of each section and summarizing the advice given for each section. Monitor and clarify any language points as necessary. Finally, give students a short time to compare in pairs before taking whole-class feedback.

SUGGESTED ANSWERS:

1 **Get yourself noticed** = it's a good idea to show initiative / volunteer. This will provide you with plenty of work, which you should try to avoid doing.

2 **Ignore all emails** = if something is really important the person who sent the email will try to contact you again.

3 **There are good and bad bosses** = good bosses are interested in you, encourage you, give you interesting work to do, and leave you to work on your own initiative. Bad bosses give you work to do and then complain when you do what they ask.

4 **Dress up not down** = it's important to dress appropriately for the job.

5 **Share opinions at appraisals** = do not expect your boss to have the same opinion as you. When giving appraisals, give recognition as well as criticism.

6 **Learn to recycle reports.** Many reports say much the same thing, and using an old one as a model can be useful. However, double-check all your changes!

7 **PAs keep businesses organized** = they are the engines that keep a business running.

8 **Don't be scared to be lazy** = the more you do, the more can go wrong.

9 **Steer well clear of all meetings** = most meetings are pointless. The best meetings are those for which people have really prepared. They require a lot of work, but are usually very worthwhile.

Listening for gist

5 1.01–1.03 The listening texts have the following items of vocabulary that may cause some difficulty for your students, and that you may like to pre-teach before doing the listening: *to scratch a few backs* (to do favours for people in the hope they will be returned. This is derived from the saying *you scratch my back and I'll scratch yours*), *mind share* (the amount of time spent thinking about something), *opt for* (phrasal verb meaning *to choose*), *to give it your all* (to do the best you can).

Alternatively, draw students' attention to them after the listening and elicit the meanings from the context.

Another technique is to pause the CD a moment before the phrase and ask students to note down what is said next and to guess the meaning from context. Once students have noted down each of the phrases, you can elicit them and put them on the board, along with their meanings.

Before doing the listening, write the following table on the board and ask students to copy it:

promotion	relationships with your boss	work-life balance

Explain to students that they are going to listen to three people talking about getting on at work, and as they listen they should make notes under the headings. Play the recording through once. Then give students an opportunity to compare their notes in pairs. Play each extract through once more, pausing after each extract. Again, give students time to compare notes. Once all the extracts have been played through a second time, elicit students' notes and put them on the board under the relevant headings.

Finally, ask students to refer back to the article and to discuss how the advice given in the recording compares. Take whole-class feedback.

ANSWERS:

promotion	relationships with your boss	work-life balance
Speaker 2: Make sure your boss thinks of you first when promotion time comes. Keep yourself on his / her mind by sending regular updates even if you haven't done very much.	Speaker 1: Develop a friendship with your boss, try to talk to him / her about personal things, in a natural way.	Speaker 3: Set limits for the amount of overtime you do. Know your limitations and turn down assignments if necessary.

RECORDING SCRIPT

 1.01

I think the key to surviving at work is the same as it's always been. Bosses have huge egos, and you have to feed those egos if you want to be effective. You have to scratch a few backs, and laugh at your manager's jokes even if they're not funny. But seriously, though, there's a right and a wrong way to befriend your manager – think of him, or her, as a person rather than as a figure in authority. Remember, they want to get on with the people they work with as much as you do. Show them you're a good guy on a personal level, not just professionally. Managers promote people they know and like, so developing a friendship with yours is a smart career move. Bringing up office politics and client complaints will only remind them that they're your manager. But talk about more personal stuff, you know, like their favourite team or a holiday destination, and you're speaking to a friend. Direct the conversation to things that feel natural. After all, this is how friends interact.

1.02

When the time comes for a promotion in your office, your manager will be thinking about all the great times when his or her team worked together successfully. You need to get more of your manager's mind share, and occupy it more often. So, for example, sending regular updates – even if there's nothing much to say – keeps you on your manager's mind as somebody who is getting the work done.

If you've been part of successful projects, opt for others that you know you'll succeed in. This'll help build your manager's confidence in you, and that will help you become the person your boss will turn to when more important projects come up.

1.03

Whatever your job, the desire to give it your all and get to the top is incredibly strong and often results in other aspects of your life suffering.

Some jobs require open lines of communication via smart phones and so on, but try to turn them off when you're not at work. Being keen isn't a sign of determination, but a lack of focus on your personal affairs. If you really have to work at home, find a place where you can't be disturbed, and put a time limit on your work.

At times, workloads become unbearable, and however sympathetic your manager might be, he or she'll try to get you to do as much as is humanly possible. But the key word here is humanly. There are limits to how much we can accomplish. So sometimes, it is OK to say no and turn down assignments. It doesn't mean you've failed, but that you're in control and you know your limitations.

1.2 Grammar

Tense, aspect and voice

This module focuses on the grammatical features of tense, aspect and voice. It introduces and consolidates the concepts of aspect and reviews the active and passive voices.

Did you know?

The fact that English has no future tense may come as a surprise to many students, as *will* is traditionally taught as such. You may find it useful to explain to students that *will* is in fact a modal verb with a variety of meanings, including *assuming*, *threatening*, *promising*, *offering* and *deciding*. Remind students that the present continuous (for future arrangements), the present simple (for timetables) and *going to* are all possible when talking about the future, and that *going to* is perhaps the safest option, although should be avoided in very formal contexts. *Will / Shall be* + verb + *ing* (or *will* in the continuous aspect) is the most formal future structure.

Review of aspect

1 1.04 Explain to students that they are to read the dialogue and select the most suitable tense form based on the context. Allow a few minutes for this, and monitor. Give students enough time to compare their answers in pairs before moving on to the listening task. Before students begin, you may want to pre-teach the following vocabulary: *to be up to* (doing recently), *suit you down to the ground* (be perfectly suitable for you), *blew his reputation* (destroyed his reputation), *the drinks are on me* (I'll pay for the drinks).

Play the recording through once only to allow students to check their answers. Students compare their answers in pairs.

After the listening task you will need to provide feedback on the reasons for the correct answers. You might find it useful to put the dialogue onto an overhead projector (OHP) or an interactive whiteboard (IWB) in order to highlight tense features and to enable students to follow your exposition. Allow plenty of time for student questions.

ANSWERS:

1 *have you been up to* – we prefer the present perfect here because it indicates a state leading up to the present, and also because the present perfect is strongly associated with *since* as a preposition or in this case a subordinator.

2 *saw* – this indicates a specific event in the past, so we use the past simple; also the past simple is associated with the adverb *last* (= *the last time*).

3 *hasn't anyone told you* – normally you only need to tell someone something once, so the aspect is simple. If it is continuous, it means that the person is being told repeatedly. The use of the present perfect here indicates news.

4 *have decided* – the present perfect is more likely as the decision has strong current relevance. The past simple is also correct, and would be more typical of American English.

5 *would you be doing* – *would* shows that the situation is hypothetical, and given the context that the job interview is in the future, the continuous expresses what Jon would be doing if he gets the job. The perfect continuous expresses what Jon would have been doing if he had got the job. Clearly he has not been rejected for the job so this combination of aspects is not appropriate.

6 *cover* – there is no reason to use the present perfect; the present simple here refers to 'all times' – past, present and future. This is a permanent state of affairs.

7 *have always got* – the present perfect is used here to describe a recurrent habit up to the present time. *Always got* is more distant (or American English) and suggests that this characteristic is no longer true.

8 *is going* – the present continuous is more likely as the action is both currently in progress and incomplete.

9 *blew* – the past is correct as the event referred to is in the past (when the documents were lost) and there is a specific reference to this in the sentence, so it is quite definite.

10 *have you been doing* – the present perfect continuous emphasizes the current importance of the action (present), what has been completed so far (perfect), and the fact that the action is ongoing or in progress (continuous).

11 *will have worked out* – *will* + the perfect aspect is more likely than the progressive as Jon means that by the future date mentioned (the end of the week) the strategy will be completed and every question will be covered. The continuous would suggest that at the end of the week he would still be in the process of formulating his strategy and it would not be finished.

12 *Aren't you being* – the present continuous suggests that Ed thinks Jon is behaving over-confidently / arrogantly at the moment, but is not generally over-confident / arrogant.

Note: For numbers 9 and 10 in this exercise both answers are possible, but will have slightly different emphases:
9 he *has blown his reputation for competence* would be more likely to be used if Jon was conveying news to Ed, rather than simply stating a fact.
10 *what have you done?* would be preferred if Ed wants to emphasize what has been achieved so far, rather than what is in progress.

RECORDING SCRIPT

1.04

Ed: So, what have you been up to since I last saw you?

Jon: Oh, hasn't anyone told you? I have decided to go for promotion. You know, for the new area manager job.

Ed: Great! What exactly would you be doing in the new job?

Jon: Well, you need to be quite flexible as there's a lot of travel involved – in fact the responsibilities cover six different countries.

Ed: That'll suit you down to the ground – you have always got out and about a lot I seem to remember. By the way, you know Jacob is going for it as well?

Jon: No, but I'm not threatened – he blew his reputation for competence over that lost documents episode.

Ed: OK, but what have you been doing to make sure you actually get the job?

Jon: Well, by the end of the week I will have worked out my interview strategy and there's no question they can ask me I can't answer.

Ed: Aren't you being a bit over-confident, or should that be arrogant?

Jon: We'll see. Drinks are on me if I get it.

Ed: Deal.

Speaking

2 Tell students they are going to interview their partners. Give them a few minutes to note down some ideas before the interviews. Put the following on the board:

My career, education and training.
What I've done over the past five years.
What I've achieved over the past five years.
What I'll be doing in the near future.

Ask students to make notes about themselves. Then give them a few minutes two interview each other. Monitor and note any language points for correction.

Using the passive

3 Check students understand the differences between active and passive voices. You could provide a few samples of each and ask students to identify which are active and which passive (e.g., *They cut my pay. / My pay was cut.*).

You may also want to elicit / pre-teach the meanings of the following words from the text: *to target* (to choose or aim at), *to foster* (to encourage), *a scenario* (an imaginary situation). *Scenario* could also be drilled for pronunciation.

Ask students to quickly read through the handwritten note and find answers to the following questions:

How long ago was the initiative launched? (six months ago)
How well rated is it? (highly)
How do the workshops usually begin? (with a scenario)

Now ask students to read the notes again and to highlight or underline all the instances of passive and active verb forms. Then ask them to compare in pairs before taking whole-class feedback. You may find it useful to have the text on an OHT or IWB so you can highlight the verbs.

Explain to students that they are to re-write the notes into an official company document, beginning as in the example on page 8. Give students plenty of time to complete this exercise, but be sure to set a time limit. Monitor to provide help and guidance where needed, making a note of language points that cause particular difficulty.

When students have written their documents, have them compare their answers in pairs.

4 Put the list of reasons provided in exercise 4 on the board. Read through them with students and explain the task. Give students a few minutes to discuss their choices of active and passive. Monitor to check progress.

As a final stage, display the suggested solution below on an OHP or IWB for students to compare with their own answers. Ask students to look again to the list of reasons in exercise 4 and match them to the numbered items in the model text.

SUGGESTED ANSWERS:

The Personal Development Initiative (PDI) was launched six months ago, and was / is targeted at those employees perceived to be most in need of inter-personal skills training. The PDI has been rated highly. The PDI covers all the areas of confidence-building, fostering team spirit, strategies for dealing with difficult clients, and self-awareness. A typical workshop starts with a secret role or scenario written on a piece of paper, which has to be memorized and then thrown away. The first participant then acts out the scenario while the second person guesses what it is. Partners change and the exercise continues. Finally the participants have to relate the given scenario to a particular event in their recent working life.

We want to avoid mentioning who did the action = *perceived* (reduced form, auxiliary omitted)

It is unimportant, or unnecessary, to say who did the action = *was launched, was / is targeted, has been rated, has to be memorized, thrown away*

The subject of the sentence is extremely long, so the active sounds better because it puts the long material at the end = *covers*

There is no reason to use the passive, so the active is better = *acts out, guesses, change*

Tense, aspect and voice

5 Dictate the following sentence to the class and ask students to write it down.

In a hierarchy every employee tends to rise to his or her level of incompetence.

Get students to check in pairs and then elicit the sentence from the students, writing it on the board. Check spelling and drill pronunciation and stress of *hierarchy* and *hierarchical*. Get students to discuss the quote and its meaning and how true they think it is.

Finally, tell students this theory was formulated by Dr J. Peter and Raymond Hull in a humorous book called *The Peter Principle* (1968). In a nutshell, what this means is that people are promoted so long as they work competently, until they reach a position at which they are no longer competent. And there they stay.

Pre-teach or elicit the following words: *actuality* (reality), *flawed* (imperfect), *aptitude* (natural ability), *criteria* (standards to judge something by).

The gapped text may be set for homework or used as a consolidation of the previous exercise on tense, voice and aspect. If students do this task in class, set a time limit and give students time to compare their answers in pairs.

ANSWERS:

1 worked   2 was published   3 are   4 be considered
5 are clearly being made   6 are based   7 is
8 is not actually doing   9 is based   10 not only gain
11 remains   12 may be summarized
13 are required to carry them out   14 may then be placed
15 are best suited

Internet research

As well as searching for *the Peter Principle*, you might like to suggest to your students that they search for *the Dilbert Principle*, which refers to a 1990s satirical observation by Dilbert cartoonist Scott Adams, stating that companies tend to promote their most incompetent employees to management in an attempt to limit the amount of damage they are capable of doing. Adams expanded his study of the Dilbert Principle in a book of the same name, which sold more than a million copies and was on the *New York Times* best-seller list for more that 40 weeks. Students would undoubtedly enjoy reading about this on the Internet.

1.3 Vocabulary

Behavioural competencies and setting goals

This module focuses on the vocabulary of behavioural competency and provides opportunites for vocabulary building and using vocabulary in context.

Behavioural competencies

1 Ask students to discuss what the difficulties would be of managing a rock group on tour. Take whole-class feedback.

2 Copy the four headings from the table onto the board and ask students to copy the headings onto note paper. Tell students you are going to dictate a set of behavioural competencies and that they should write them into the appropriate column. Dictate the list of words. Once finished, let students compare their answers in pairs. Go through answers as a class.

ANSWERS:

Team working	Managing and developing yourself	Customer service	Problem solving
effective communication, holding people accountable, leadership	flexibility, networking, self-awareness, self-development, time management	client focus, intercultural competence, results orientation	analytical thinking, decision making, innovation, managing change

3 Ask students to read through the gapped sentences and to put the five words into the appropriate spaces, changing the form as necessary. Get students to check in pairs before going through the answers. Then ask them to think about which competencies these definitions match. You may like to point out that students can look for synonyms / repeated vocabulary to help them in this task, e.g. *analysis / analytical thinking* and *customers / client focus*.

ANSWERS:

1 analysis   2 communication   3 priority   4 unexpected
5 application
Matching competencies:
1 analytical thinking   2 effective communication
3 client focus   4 flexibility   5 self-development

EXTENSION ACTIVITY

Get students to write the adjective and noun forms of each of the five verbs into a table, e.g.

v	adj	n
analyze	analytical	analysis
apply	applicable	application
communicate	communicative	communication
expect	expected	expectation
prioritize	prioritized	priority

Once the answers have been checked, drill the words, paying particular attention to the varying stress patterns.

Listening

4 1.05 Pre-teach / elicit the following vocabulary: *to assert oneself* (to behave in a firm, confident way), *to get the upper hand* (idiom: to be in a controlling position), *to juggle* (to manage several different activities at the same time), *insight* (the ability to see the true nature of a situation). Refer students back to the list of behavioural competencies in exercise 2. Ask them to listen to the performance appraisal and note down which of the competencies the speakers discuss. Give students a moment to discuss their answers in pairs before checking.

ANSWER:

They discuss leadership and time management.

RECORDING SCRIPT

1.05

Jill: OK, Tony, let's move on. Have a look at the list of behavioural competencies. Which do think you've demonstrated over the last few months?

Tony: Well, this is the first time that I've had to co-ordinate a group of people. I've done a lot of work with my team over the last 6 months. This has all been quite new for me and it's been challenging but also really rewarding.

J: What aspects have you found particularly useful, or satisfying?

T: Well, organizing the promotional campaign for the European tour for the Bosnian group was a lot of fun. It was tough, but I felt we achieved a lot given that it was all quite last minute, and the musicians weren't easy, as you know.

J: Yes, OK. I think you had a lot of support from your colleagues on that, didn't you?

T: Yes, the team were great, working all hours, especially Hannah, who's so new to the job. I think she really rose to the challenge of dealing with the press.

J: That was good. She's doing well. How did you make sure she was given all the support she needed?

T: Well we had regular update meetings every week so that she could tell me about any problems or concerns she had. I also always made sure that I was available for her when she needed me; she found it really difficult in the beginning to assert herself and not let the journalists get the upper hand. She would often come to me and we would work together on what she was going to say to them.

J: Yes, that seems to have been a strategy that worked. Was there anything that you don't think you handled particularly well with regards to the Bosnian project?

T: In the beginning, as I said, it was all quite last minute – I was always so busy dealing with other stuff, you know, juggling all the other projects, that I found it really hard to plan ahead.

J: Can you think of a specific example?

T: Yes. The one that sticks in my mind the most was when I was trying to arrange the transport for the French leg of their tour. At one point I got so far behind that we almost had to rearrange a couple of their concert dates because I had forgotten to book their accommodation for the next town. Karla had to spend a lot of time on the phone calling hotels so that they had somewhere to stay. I dread to think where they might have ended up staying! It could have been really embarrassing.

J: Yes, I understand Tony. What do you think would help you in this ...?

5 Before playing the extract again, ask the pairs if they can remember any specific examples of leadership and time management that Tony mentions. Then play the extract again, asking them to note the examples given.

ANSWERS:

Leadership: He mentions organizing a promotional campaign for the European tour. He also mentions providing support for Hannah, a member of his team.
Time management: He talks about the time he was trying to arrange the transport for the French leg of a tour.

Setting goals

6 Before giving students the collocations exercise, ask them to read through the text and to guess what words might fit in the gaps. These do not have to be from the list of pairs, but can be students' own ideas. Elicit suggestions from the class. Next, ask students to match the pairs of collocations. Check their answers and check the meanings of the phrases. Now ask the students to fill the gapped text using the collocations.

ANSWERS:

1 clear guidelines   2 measurable objectives / targets
3 realistic targets / objectives   4 written record
5 valuable insight 6 performance appraisal

7 Pre-teach / elicit the following words: *astute* (showing good judgement), *up-front* (open and honest), *interim* (short-term). Next, ask students to read through the gapped text and to put the correct word form into each gap. With weaker groups this could be guided by asking students to decide which part of speech (adjective, noun, etc.) goes into each gap according to the context. It should then be a relatively easy matter for students to devise a correct form of the words. Note: the last item (non-committal) is challenging. You can help students by telling them it has a negative prefix, and also by writing the word on the board in phonemics.

ANSWERS:

1 successful   2 achievements   3 perception
4 evaluation   5 defensive   6 responsive   7 effectively
8 non-committal

8 In this exercise it is relatively straightforward for students to identify which objectives are 'specific', 'time-bound' and 'measurable', as there are clear definitions or quantities / periods of time. However, it is more difficult to tell which objectives are 'achievable' and 'realistic', so we have to assume that in Tony's context the objectives are indeed 'achievable' and 'realistic'.
Before doing the exercise, you might like to ask students to remind you of what SMART targets are.
Once students have identified the targets in the text, get them to check in pairs before taking whole-class feedback.

ANSWERS:

To finalize 80% (M) of promotional plans for artist publicity (S) eight weeks before any planned tour date begins (T).
To involve junior staff (S) in at least 50% (M, A) of arrangements.
To ensure publicity exposure (S) covers at least three different channels (print, radio, web, mail etc.) (M, R).
To update budgets (S) by the end of each quarter (T, R).

9 For this personalization activity, students are asked to make a list of three short-, medium- and long-term objectives. You could model the activity by telling students about your own short-, medium- and long-term objectives. You could put these on the board in the following way:

short-term   medium-term   long-term
1
2
3

Ask the class to ask you questions about your objectives and to tell you whether or not they think them realistic or idealistic. Outline, defend or alter your decisions accordingly. Now give the class a few minutes to note down their nine objectives. Then put them into groups of three to read, compare and discuss their lists.

Internet research

A web search will return a large number of websites with content on the topic of behavioural competencies, including authentic instances of the ways in which organizations apply the principles of behavioural competency in the workplace. You could ask your students to locate some specific examples of the ways in which companies apply these principles and to report back to the class.

1.4 Management skills

Self-awareness and communication

This module focuses on adjectives to describe personality and promotes psychological self-awareness.

Discussion

1 In small groups, students brainstorm ways they can obtain feedback on their behaviour. You can probably start the ball rolling here by talking about the various methods used to give teachers feedback: peer-observation, Director of Studies' observation, end-of-course questionnaires, references, etc. Other prompts you could use to encourage discussion include interpreting people's reactions, getting feedback from supervisors, customer feedback forms, coaching, mentoring, appraisal interviews, reports, references, friends reporting what other people say, training sessions, recording yourself on video, personality tests and quizzes, asking people directly for their opinions.

2 Most of the adjectives here will probably be known to the students but a few are false friends so highlight these: *sensible* (not *sensitive*), *sympathetic* (not *easy to get on with*), *sentimental* (usually negative in English). Also, some could be drilled for pronunciation, e.g. *bold, proud, ingenious, knowledgeable*. Finally, some cause spelling problems. Ask students to cover their books and dictate the following words: *independent, ingenious, knowledgeable, self-conscious, spontaneous, religious*. Students compare their answers in pairs before checking.

Some students may be reluctant to choose adjectives for their partners, especially if they are relatively unknown to each other but, if the atmosphere is kept light-hearted and there is an understanding that first impressions can be misleading, a lot of fun can be derived from the activity. You can demonstrate the activity by choosing a student you know quite well and encouraging him / her to choose six adjectives to describe you. You can then select your own set of adjectives which you feel describe you.

3 Draw the Johari window on the board. Demonstrate the three stages of this part of the activity with the adjectives previously elicited from the student you chose in exercise 2. Make clear that the students must write their adjectives in the spaces in the Johari boxes, not next to the numbers, as these spaces will be used in the listening activity. Students may like to copy the boxes onto a separate sheet of paper to allow more room for all the relevant adjectives.

Listening

4 🔊 1.06 You might like to pre-teach *pane* and *traits* before beginning this exercise. Play the recording through once. Allow students to compare their answers in pairs before re-playing the recording and eliciting the correct answers.

ANSWERS:

1 you   2 you   3 others   4 others   5 Arena   6 Façade
7 Blind Spot   8 Unknown

RECORDING SCRIPT

🔊 1.06

The Johari window is so called because it was created by Joe and Harry – Joseph Luft and Harry Ingham, back in 1955 in the United States. It's a useful tool for helping people to reach a better understanding of their interpersonal communication and relationships. The window has two columns and two lines: the column on the left contains information which you know, and the column on the right, information which you don't know. Similarly, the top line contains information which other people know, and, as I'm sure you've already guessed, the bottom line has things which others don't know. Has everybody got that? Good.

So, that means that the window has four panes, which each tell us something about ourselves. The pane on the top left is called the Arena. It tells us things about ourselves which are public knowledge; things that you know and that other people know. The pane on the bottom left contains things that you know, but that others don't know. It's called the Façade, because other people's perceptions of you are incomplete if you choose not to share certain information about yourself.

Now you can probably work the last two out for yourselves. The last two panes are called the Blind Spot and the Unknown. The Blind Spot, as its name suggests, covers the things which other people see but we ourselves are blind to. Asking other people for feedback can help us reduce our Blind Spot. The Unknown, obviously, covers the things nobody knows, your hidden talents and undiscovered potential. The remaining adjectives that neither you nor your partner chose in the previous exercise either do not describe your personality, or perhaps describe traits of your character which nobody has discovered yet.

Discussion

5 Students should be encouraged to use the phrases provided when discussing the accuracy of the Johari windows, perhaps with a different partner.

6 Elicit from the class what each of the largest panes in the window is called and therefore what psychological implications this might have if it was larger than the others. They can discuss this in pairs as you monitor and offer prompts as necessary. They then say which manager would be the best to work for. Students can go on to discuss their experiences of good or poor management. If all or the majority of your class have yet to start work, they can discuss the best or worst teachers they have had.

SUGGESTED ANSWERS:

1 A large Blind Spot suggests a manager who does not listen to other people's ideas or feedback. He / She may be perceived as arrogant or authoritarian.
2 A large Façade suggests a manager who is reluctant to disclose his / her own ideas and feelings. He / She may be perceived as defensive and indecisive.
3 A large Unknown suggests a manager who does not communicate his / her own ideas nor shows interest in those of others. He / She may be perceived as unimaginative and bureaucratic.
4 A large Arena suggests a manager who shares his / her own ideas and feelings and listens carefully to those of others. He / She may be perceived as open and objective.

Listening

7 1.07–1.11 Students listen to two people playing the Truth game and try to decide which questions they are discussing. You could elicit the meaning of *megabucks* (huge sums of money) in the last part of the recording. Play the recording all the way through the first time, then play it again section by section and elicit answers from the class.

ANSWERS:

1 How do you react under pressure?
2 How do you cope with failure?
3 How motivating is money for you?
4 What would you like to change about yourself?
5 What do you see yourself doing in ten years' time?

RECORDING SCRIPT

1.07–1.11

1
A: OK, Shall I have a go at this?
B: Be my guest.
A: Well, I have to confess that I sometimes tend to panic, you know, if it all becomes too much. I get very stressed out.
B: You're kidding! You always seem so cool, calm and collected!

2
A: Would you like to take this one?
B: Sure. But, frankly, I'm more used to success. Hmm. How do I cope? I've never really thought it about it that much; let me see …

3
A: How motivating is it? I haven't the slightest idea! I've never had enough to tell!
B: Mm. Personally, if I'm totally honest with myself, I'd have to say, very.
A: It can't buy you love!
B: No, it can't. But it does make the world go round, doesn't it?

4
A: OK, your turn.
B: I'll pass on this one, if you don't mind.
A: No, of course not. Hm. What don't I like about myself? That's not easy to answer.
B: Let's leave that one, shall we?
A: Yeah, good idea.

5
A: Wow, that's a long way in the future! I honestly haven't got a clue! How about you?
B: I'm not sure. If you really pushed me, I suppose I'd say I hope I'll be working for a large company, a multinational, perhaps somewhere abroad …
A: … and earning megabucks!
B: Am I really so transparent?

8 Students order the jumbled sentences, compare in pairs, then listen a final time before checking their answers as a whole class. Elicit the correct answers and put them on the board.

ANSWERS:

1 Shall I have a go at this?
2 I have to confess that …
3 Would you like to take this one?
4 I've never really thought about it that much.
5 I haven't the slightest idea!
6 If I'm totally honest with myself, I'd have to say …
7 I'll pass on this one, if you don't mind.
8 Let's leave that one, shall we?
9 I honestly haven't got a clue!
10 If you really pushed me, I suppose I'd say …

9 Students match the expressions to their various functions.

ANSWERS:

a) 1, 3   b) 2, 6   c) 4, 10   d) 5, 9   e) 7, 8

Truth game

10 Students change partners and play the Truth game in pairs. Assign a different colour to each pair, going clockwise around the board. The pairs discuss each question and then the question in the middle of the board.

Encourage students to speak as much as possible and to ask follow-up questions to draw out as much information from their partner as possible. At this stage you could discreetly monitor and provide on-the-spot extra help or correction. Alternatively, you could save any corrections for post-discussion remedial work.

11 With their new partners, students repeat the Johari activity and see if, since playing the Truth game, there have been any significant changes in their windows

Internet research

An Internet search using the keywords *Nohari window* will provide an interesting, if somewhat negative, variation on the concept of the Johari window. Obviously, there are a lot of risks involved with encouraging the students to do this much more negative version of the activity. However, the negative adjectives associated with this version of the window will probably be less familiar than the positive ones, so this provides an excellent vocabulary-building opportunity. Also, as student interest will undoubtedly be high, meanings can be clarified and students can at least discuss with a partner which faults they would ascribe to themselves.

1.5 Writing

Job descriptions

This module provides practice in using the appropriate grammar and vocabulary for writing job descriptions.

Discussion

1 Ask students to read through the rubric and highlight the name of the company, the company's business sector and the job they are recruiting for. Elicit the answers.
Write the following on the board:
Design Team Leader
  qualifications:
  experience:
  competencies:
Give students a few minutes to jot down their ideas and to compare in pairs. Elicit suggestions and put them on the board. At this stage you could turn students' attention to the list of competencies, qualifications and experience from the person specification, exercise 5, page 15 of the Student's Book. Tip: a Google search for *Design Team Leader + essential qualifications* is an excellent source of suggested qualifications required for this type of role.

Reading

2 Draw students' attention to the job description and headings. You may need to explain that *Standards* refers to *Standards or criteria of work*. Ask them to match the headings to the relevant sections labelled A–G. Students check in pairs. Elicit answers and put them on the board.

ANSWERS:

A Job Title B Job Type C Salary D Line manager
E Job Aims F Duty / (ies) G Standard(s)

EXTENSION ACTIVITY

As a brief extension at this point, you could ask students a few questions about the job description, e.g. *Who does the Team Leader report to?* (Deepak Mehta, Creative Director); *What size budget will he / she manage?* (€200,000); *What proportion of his / her duties involve training and conferences?* (10%).

Prepositional phrases

3 Write the prepositions on the board and draw students' attention to the gaps a–g in the job description. Give students a couple of minutes to complete the gapped phrases and check their answers in pairs. Elicit answers and put them on the board.

ANSWERS:

(a) on (b) to (c) in (d) in (e) by (f) in (g) within

EXTENSION ACTIVITY

As a very quick extension activity, write the phrases on the board, erase the prepositions and spot-test students. Alternatively, students can test each other in pairs.

---

4 An alternative way of doing this matching exercise is to put the phrases onto pairs of cards, e.g.

as set out in	in accordance with

Students then work in pairs to match the items. Elicit answers and put them on the board.

ANSWERS:

1 f 2 e 3 b 4 a 5 c 6 g 7 d

EXTENSION ACTIVITY

As a quick extension activity, students can test each other in pairs. For example:
A: *Which phrase means **as set out in**?*
B: *In accordance with.*

---

5 Check students understand the meaning of *desirable* (useful but not essential) in relation to person specifications. Draw the class's attention to the list of competencies, qualifications and experience and ask them to note which characteristics they think are essential, desirable and not necessary. Then ask them to match each person specification with the corresponding duty or standard on the job description. In order to do this they will need to look back at the job description on the previous page.

SUGGESTED ANSWERS:

E = essential, D = desirable
Financial management skills: E; 5
Customer service orientation: E; 1, 2, 4, 5, 6
Leading a team: E; 4, 6,
Achievement: E; 1, 2, 3, 4, 5
Analytical thinking: D;1, 2, 4
Flexibility: D; 1, 2, 4
Self-awareness: E; 1, 2, 4, 6
Degree or equivalent in Graphic design: E; 1, 2, 4
Knowledge of English, French and one non-European language: D; 1, 6
Two years' previous experience in a design department: E; 1, 2, 4

Analysis

6 You could display the box of guidelines using an OHP or an IWB in order to clarify the task and as a useful way of conducting feedback. Ask students to read the job description again and to check which guidelines are true and which false. Ask them to pick out further examples from the text in support of their answers.

ANSWERS:

1 True
2 False: the present tense and infinitive are usually used
3 True
4 False: unless needed, omit articles
5 True
6 True

Writing

7 Ask students to quickly read through the rubric and the text. Put the following questions on the board:
What type of company is Himalayan Heights Inc.? (A travel / tour company)
What are the three main duties of the job? (arranging flights; managing finances; training and supervising staff)
Ask students to answer the questions as orientation to the text. Now explain that students should rewrite the job description using the language guidelines and model job description. Set a time limit for this. Monitor, helping students with the task instructions and language points. You might find it helpful to give students a skeleton job description to fill in, e.g.

Himalayan Heights Inc. Job description / Person specification			
Job title:	Bookings clerk	Department:	Flight department
Duties:		Standards:	

Students' written work can be collected and used for post-correction and feedback.

SUGGESTED ANSWER:

Duty: 1 (60%) To arrange, book and confirm clients' transport (flights, transfers) both on the phone, over the Internet and in person.
Standard: All flight requests are dealt with within 24 hrs (Internet), or immediately (phone, in person). Clients are provided with all details in writing, and tickets / vouchers where appropriate.
Duty: 2 To manage all financial transactions. Analysis of financial data, ensuring efficient use of resources. Performing projections relating to business travel trends.
Standard: Fully informing the accounts department to keep them up to date. Correctly submitting the accounts and reconciling them on a monthly basis.
Duty 3: Training and supervising part time staff. Hiring, delegating and determining workloads. Evaluation of staff performance.
Standard: Part time staff give positive feedback and continue to work for HH Inc. in subsequent peak periods. Feedback they receive from clients is 80% positive.

Internet research

There is a large number of websites offering advice on how to write an effective job description. Two tasks that students could be asked to do are to read some websites on the topic and:
1 make a list of DOs and DON'Ts for writing job descriptions;
2 collate the essential elements to include in job descriptions.

1.6 Case study
The glass ceiling

This module raises awareness of the issue of sexual discrimination in the workplace and provides opportunities for extensive oral fluency practice on this topic.

Discussion

1 Direct students' attention to the visual and try to elicit the phrase *the glass ceiling* and its meaning (an invisible barrier that prevents women, racial minorities, gay people and the disabled getting to the top). Hillary Clinton said in her speech to endorse Barak Obama for president: 'And although we weren't able to shatter that highest, hardest glass ceiling this time, thanks to you, it's got about 18 million cracks in it.'

Reading

2 Before reading, point out the visual of Gemma and elicit speculation about her character. Then explain that the class will read information about this employee from the company's personnel file. You could also highlight the difference in meaning and pronunciation between *personnel* and *personal* here. You could read the text aloud to the class in an appropriately formal style. Draw a large blank Johari window on the board and ask students to copy it so that it fills a sheet of A4. Then have students answer the questions and compare their answers in pairs, before taking whole-class feedback.

ANSWERS:

1 strengths: a valuable and dependable member of her team, efficiency, outgoing, strong communication skills, keen to take the initiative, ambitious
weaknesses: tendency to overreach her authority and to favour unconventional methods, lack of maturity
2 she lacks a formal marketing and management background
3 she is aware of the difficulties of reconciling the care of her four-year-old daughter with an inevitably heavy travel schedule, she does not appear to realize that that SEVS has never employed a woman as a Marketing Manager
4 See Johari window below. Note: two of the points from her personnel file go into the Blind Spot box. The others from this first reading go into her Arena box. This should be agreed by the whole class before continuing.

	Gemma knows	Gemma doesn't know
others know	**Arena** • valuable and dependable team member • efficient, outgoing, strong communication skills, keen to take initiative, ambitious • tendency to overreach her authority and to favour unconventional methods • lacks a formal marketing and management background • disappointed about not getting the job	**Blind Spot** • lack of maturity • SEVS has never employed a woman as a Marketing Manager
others don't know	Façade	Unknown

Listening

3 💿 **1.12** Play the first recording through once and get students to note down the key points, compare with a partner and build up the Johari window. Note: *take the initiative* in the recording is paraphrased as *she's a self-starter*. Play the recording through a second time to give students an opportunity to add to or modify their answers.

ANSWERS:

	Gemma knows	Gemma doesn't know
others know	Arena • valuable and dependable team member • efficient, outgoing, strong communication skills, keen to take the initiative, ambitious • tendency to overreach her authority and to favour unconventional methods • lacks a formal marketing and management background • disappointed about not getting the job	Blind Spot • lack of maturity • SEVS has never employed a woman as a Marketing Manager • if she was a man, they'd be begging her to take the job • the boss will never agree • doing an MBA won't make any difference at SEVS • she tends to rush into things • she's not always very patient • very intuitive but not always very logical
others don't know	Façade	Unknown • is she really ready? • has she got what it takes to fight the system? • does she really want her career badly enough?

RECORDING SCRIPT

💿 **1.12**

Ruben: So how is Gemma taking it?

Steve: Well, not great. She's pretty angry, to be perfectly honest. I mean, let's face it, what else does she have to do to get the job? If she was a man, we'd be on our knees begging her to take it!

R: Steve, you know as well as I do that the boss will never agree to a woman Marketing Manager. You can sing Gemma's praises as much as you like, but you're not going to change his mind.

S: So even if she does the MBA, you reckon it won't make any difference?

R: 'Fraid not; not here, anyway. But between you and me, I wonder if she's really ready.

S: Why not? You said yourself it would give her the marketing know-how she needs.

R: Yeah, it's not that. I just feel she lacks maturity – you know, the way she tends to rush into things. I know you Americans are obsessed with efficiency, but there are limits!

S: That's a little below the belt, isn't it Ruben? Anyway, she's half Spanish, as you well know! OK, I agree, she's a self-starter, and she's not always very patient. But she's very intuitive: when she knows she's found the right solution, she just goes for it!

R: Intuitive, yes ... but not always very logical. I'm not sure how well she really thinks things through. You've got to be able to argue your case on an MBA – it'd certainly take her out of her comfort zone. But at the end of the day, I'm not convinced she has what it takes to fight the system here

in Spain. Does she really want her career badly enough to do an MBA? It's going to be tough. I just feel she might be happier if she accepted the situation and made her family her priority, rather than banging her head against a brick wall.

S: Well, I don't know, and I'm not sure she does – although she certainly seems to have plenty of self-belief ... There's only one way to find out, and I for one will be backing her to do the MBA. I think she could surprise us all.

R: Well, I certainly wouldn't stand in her way. If that's what she wants to do, she deserves her chance – even though it may mean we lose her sooner rather than later. But I still think at the end of the day, she'll back down.

S: Hmm.

Reading

4 Students read through the email and add further notes to the Johari window. Monitor and check. Give students time to compare their notes in pairs before building up the Johari window on the board.

ANSWERS:

	Gemma knows	Gemma doesn't know
others know	Arena • valuable and dependable team member • efficient, outgoing, strong communication skills, keen to take the initiative, ambitious • tendency to overreach her authority and to favour unconventional methods • lacks a formal marketing and management background • disappointed about not getting the job	Blind Spot • lack of maturity • SEVS has never employed a woman as a Marketing Manager • if she was a man, they'd be begging her to take the job • the boss will never agree • doing an MBA won't make any difference at SEVS • she tends to rush into things • she's not always very patient • very intuitive but not always very logical
others don't know	Façade • having doubts about whether she's good enough to do the MBA • not as ambitious as others think • tense and irritable at the moment • not the most organized person in the world • has been headhunted for job in Sweden • misses her parents	Unknown • is she really ready? • has she got what it takes to fight the system? • does she really want her career badly enough?

Discussion

5 Students make a note of Gemma's career options at this point. You could help by suggesting she has four options.

Option	Pros	Cons
1 stay in present job and keep trying to get promotion	her work is appreciated; she could take time to gain maturity	little or no chance of promotion
2 do the MBA	an MBA would enhance her prospects	Still little chance of promotion at SEVS. Hard work, and she might fail and look stupid.
3 move to Sweden	good job and better prospects	husband would be unhappy
4 work part-time	husband would be happy	she would have to leave SEVS and give up hopes of getting into management

Listening

6 🔊 1.13 Play the recording through once or twice.

ANSWERS:

1 Gemma is very disappointed about not getting the job. She's not always very patient, and is tense and irritable at the moment. She has been head hunted for a job in Sweden.
2 See Johari window below.

	Gemma knows	Gemma doesn't know
others know	Arena • valuable and dependable team member • efficient, outgoing, strong communication skills, keen to take the initiative, ambitious • tendency to overreach her authority and to favour unconventional methods • lacks a formal marketing and management background • disappointed about not getting the job	Blind Spot • lack of maturity • SEVS has never employed a woman as a Marketing Manager • if she was a man, they'd be begging her to take the job • the boss will never agree • doing an MBA won't make any difference at SEVS • she tends to rush into things • she's not always very patient • very intuitive but not always very logical
others don't know	Façade • having doubts about whether she's good enough to do the MBA • not as ambitious as others think • tense and irritable at the moment • not the most organized person in the world • has been headhunted for job in Sweden • misses her parents • she has always wanted a real career • she's thinking about accepting the job in Sweden	Unknown • is she really ready? • has she got what it takes to fight the system? • does she really want her career badly enough?

3

Option	Pros	Cons
stop work and have a baby, move out into the country	husband would be happy	give up any ideas of a 'real' career

RECORDING SCRIPT

🔊 1.13

Xabi: Hi Gem! What's for dinner?

Gemma: Yes, I did have a good day at work, thank you, what about you?

X: Come on, Gemma, let's not go there, I'm starving, that's all – I didn't have time for lunch.

G: Well, I didn't have time to think about dinner. I've only just finished putting Nina to bed.

X: Well, is there something I can do to help?

G: You can make something if you want. I'm not hungry.

X: You're still upset about not making Marketing Manager, aren't you? Look, if the people at SEVS don't appreciate your talents, why not go somewhere else? I'm making good money now, you could go part-time, maybe do an MBA, or even stop work for a few years. We could move out into the country, you could spend more quality time with Nina.

G: Spend more quality time in the kitchen, you mean!

X: Gemma, you know that's not what I mean. Look – Nina's four already. Don't you think it's time we started thinking about giving her a little brother or sister?

G: Listen, Xabi, if you think I'm just going to stay at home and cook, clean and make babies, then you'd better think again! I've always wanted a real career, and I'm determined to have one!

X: Yes, but if SEVS won't promote you …

G: Then I'll go elsewhere! In fact I've already had an extremely good offer I'm thinking about accepting.

X: You've had another job offer? Well, that's great – but why didn't you tell me?

G: Because I knew you wouldn't like it.

X: Come on Gemma, I admit I'd rather you spent more time at home, but if you've had a good offer, you know I'd never stand in the way of your career.

G: Really?

X: Really. So what is it?

G: It's Svenska Glastek: they've offered me a job as Marketing Manager in their automobile division; I could really go places with the Swedes, I mean, they practically invented equal opportunities!

X: Svenska Glastek? I didn't know they were in Spain.

G: They aren't. The job's in Stockholm.

X: Stockholm? Now, hold on, Gemma, I can't possibly move to Stockholm …

G: See, I told you you wouldn't like it!

X: But my home's here in Seville – there's my career to think about, and my family, and my friends …

G: Well, I've had it up to here with your career, your family and your friends! What about *my* career? You men are all the same! When are you going to start taking women seriously?

Discussion

7 Get students into groups of five, assign a role card to each and ask them to discuss the advice they should give to Gemma. Finally, hold an open-class discussion.

Internet research

Advise students that if they search using the terms "glass ceiling" + "statistics" they will get many interesting statistics and articles speculating on the reasons for the gender disparity at the highest levels.

2 | Corporate image

Subject background

This unit is about corporate image, and also about corporate social responsibility.

When we think of corporate image we immediately think about branding and visuals, but it is important to remember that other factors contribute to a company's image. These include the experiences that customers have when they interact with the company, its ability to provide need-satisfying products or services, and its reputation.

So a reasonable definition of corporate image might be: 'the impression that various audiences have of a company, formed as a result of all the conscious and subconscious messages they receive, both intentional and unintentional, good and bad'. Marketing experts try to actively suggest a mental image to the public, and to do this they use all forms of promotion such as advertising and public relations. Of course there are other factors that affect the company image that are outside the control of marketers, such as the behaviour of customer service staff and the contribution of stories in the news media.

The closely related term *corporate identity* is wider and less marketing-orientated. It can be defined as: 'the sum total of a company's history, beliefs, environment and visual appearance that has been shaped by the nature of its technology, its ownership, its people, its ethical and cultural values and its strategies'. When a company is new, its identity emerges spontaneously as a direct extension of the founder's personality. But as an organization grows and becomes more complex, the corporate personality can easily become uncoordinated and confusing. Certainly the easiest way to manage corporate identity is to focus on the visuals: logo, advertising, website, brochures, stationery, architecture, uniforms, signage, etc. All these have to be aligned, to present one image to the outside world. Other aspects of corporate identity / corporate image are much harder to plan and control, and the area that is furthest from the reach of a company's marketing department is its reputation, and in particular its ethical values.

Over recent years many businesses have found themselves under attack for unethical behaviour; for failure to take into account the impact of their business activities on society and the environment. This has had a direct impact on their image and on their profits. Because of this there is now a well-developed movement in the business world for corporate social responsibility (CSR). This movement says that companies should go beyond their statutory obligation to comply with legislation and voluntarily take further steps to improve the quality of life for employees, the local community and society at large.

The practice of CSR is subject to much debate. Critics argue from a range of perspectives: economic liberals say that CSR distracts from the fundamental economic role of business (it is for governments and civil society to pursue social and environmental aims, not companies), while social liberals say that the profit motive will always lead companies to disregard the wider society, and so CSR is nothing more than hypocrisy and superficial window-dressing, designed to 'put lipstick on a pig'.

Nevertheless, CSR is playing a bigger and bigger role in conventional business life. It has found a home within risk management (reputations that take decades to build up can be ruined in hours through incidents such as corruption scandals or environmental accidents); it has become a part of HR strategy (as an aid to recruitment and retention, particularly within the competitive graduate market); and it has become a part of brand differentiation (playing a role in building customer loyalty by projecting distinctive ethical values). The concept of 'social accounting' or 'social auditing' – to go alongside financial accounting in the annual report – is now well established for large companies.

Useful websites

For corporate image and corporate identity:
http://www.identityworks.com
http://www.answers.com/topic/corporate-image
And for corporate social responsibility:
http://www.csr.gov.uk
http://www.csreurope.org
http://www.ethicalcorp.com
http://www.corporate-responsibility.org

2.1 About business

Corporate image

This module focuses on the way a large corporation has changed its image to move with the times.

Discussion

1 Write the name *McDonald's* on the board (if possible, also bring in a copy of the company logo). Give students a minute to work in pairs and to brainstorm as many words associated with McDonald's as they can. Take whole-class feedback and put relevant answers on the board.

Now draw students' attention to the discussion questions and table, and draw a copy of the table on the board. Ask students to complete the task. Give students a short time to compare their tables in pairs before eliciting answers and putting them on the board.

ANSWERS:

Company founded in: Des Plaines, a suburb of Chicago in the state Illinois, USA

Logo: Yellow, M sign

Products / menu: as a takeaway, fast-food restaurant, its main products are different types of burgers and French fries

Core market: fast-food consumers – children and young people, low-income groups due to relative cheapness of the food

Company founded by: Ray Croc and Dick and Mac McDonald in 1955

Mascot: Ronald McDonald, a clown figure

Appearance of restaurants: plastic seats, strip lighting, bright colours

Image of the company: the quintessential fast-food restaurant – McDonald's presents itself as offering good value for money, producing convenience food and being child friendly

---

EXTENSION ACTIVITY

As an interesting extension activity, direct students to the McDonald's website to do a short research activity into the history of the company. The history pages are divided into periods. Students could be asked to research a period each and to report back to the class.

Reading for gist

2 Ask students to read the text quickly once and check, change or add information to the table. Elicit answers from the class. Students can then scan the text to find out why McDonald's became unpopular at the end of the 1990s. You can speed up this stage by asking students to find the phrase *At the end of the 1990s* (paragraph 3). Elicit answers and put them on the board. Finally, students read through the text again to find examples of the way McDonald's has changed. If necessary, guide students to the appropriate sections of the text.

ANSWERS:

1 See table above.
2 (Suggested answer:) McDonald's came to represent obesity, dead-end jobs and health scares related to meat consumption.
3 a) They have been re-styled. The new look is described as 'sleek', 'green' and as 'colourful retro modernism'.
   b) The menu is healthier. McDonald's now offers a range of salads and fresh fruits. The products are labelled as organic and free-range, and are sourced ethically, e.g. the coffee is certified by the Rainforest Alliance.
   c) McDonald's clearly wants to give the message that environmental concerns and healthy eating are now core corporate values.

Reading for detail

3 Direct students' attention to the text and ask them to highlight or underline the eight phrases listed. (A variation on this is to read each phrase aloud for students to find in the text.) Once all the phrases have been highlighted or underlined, ask students to work in pairs to discuss what they think the expressions mean and to make a note of their answers.

If the task is too difficult for the class, you could read out the answers below in random order and ask students to match them to the expressions. Elicit and check through the answers.

ANSWERS:

1 the yellow *M* sign that is the McDonald's logo
2 a low-paid, low-status job with no career potential
3 Bovine Spongiform Encephalopathy (BSE) is a disease which affects cattle but which can also cause disease in humans who eat infected meat. When it was discovered that the causes of BSE are related to commonly practised intensive farming methods of raising cattle, this caused many people to become reluctant to eat meat
4 an embarrassing mistake which would have a negative effect on the company's image
5 McDonald's new approach to the design of the restaurants, which appears to be one of simplification and minimalism in design, i.e. clean lines, muted colours and more open space.
6 a deceptive, dishonest scheme a company uses for making money
7 in a bold, defiant or aggressive manner
8 similar to Starbucks, the coffee house chain, which prides itself on the quality of its coffee and has a sophisticated, urban image

4 Students will need to read the relevant sections of text in closer detail in order to work out who or what the names refer to. This process can be guided or supported by using prompt questioning, e.g.
The text mentions Jacobsen's 'modernist classic'. What does 'modernist classic' refer to?

ANSWERS:

1 a furniture designer
2 Hemel Hempstead, a town in the south-east of the UK
3 the Prince of Wales who has spoken publicly about the dangers to health of fast food
4 Watford Football Club
5 chief executive of McDonald's UK since April 2006
6 a well-known chef in the UK who appears on television and has campaigned to raise awareness of healthy eating and animal welfare in the food industry

EXTENSION ACTIVITY

The text contains a large number of other such cultural references (e.g. Rainforest Alliance, Tottenham, Newsnight). This relies heavily on students having the required schematic knowledge. You could exploit this feature of the text by giving your students one or two of these references each and asking them to do a web search to find some information about each.

5 Students might find it difficult to identify the writer's stance (attitude to the subject). If so, you could draw students' attention to the language points identified in the answer below. You could also ask students to identify whether the writer has a positive or negative attitude to the subject.

SUGGESTED ANSWER:

The writer's stance could be described as sceptical. His choice of vocabulary to describe the traditional McDonald's suggests distaste for the original style of the chain – 'the garish red signs, the strip lighting, the tacky plastic seats and sinister clowning Ronald'.

His use of quotation marks when describing certain aspects of McDonald's activity places an ironic distance between himself and his own views and what he is reporting, e.g. 'what McDonald's calls the "less is more" treatment'.

His choice of extravagant and rhetorical language to describe certain events also suggests scepticism and ironic distance, e.g. 'Under its golden arches, and under our very eyes, McDonald's has been transforming itself', 'emblematic of all that was rotten in capitalism', 'disdain for the dead-end McJob.'

The final sentence of the article, 'It still makes you fat, doesn't it?' is placed in such a way that it effectively undermines the idea that the new-generation McDonald's should be associated with healthy eating and concern for the environment.

Listening and discussion

6 1.14 Before starting the listening, pre-teach *greenwash* (a play on the expression *whitewash*, meaning to cover up wrongdoing, fault or error). Students may ask about the meaning of *crotchety* (bad-tempered) but you may decide not to teach them this unless they specifically ask.

To focus students' attention on the listening questions, dictate the questions and ask students to write them out on paper. Get them to check the questions in pairs and then to discuss what they think the answers could be before listening to check. Elicit suggestions from the class.

Play the recording once through. Get students to compare answers in pairs. Elicit answers from the class. Then play the extract again.

ANSWERS:

1   It may be difficult for McDonald's to maintain its commitment to green policies since energy, water and food prices are all rising. Meat in particular is going to become more and more expensive to produce. It could be particularly challenging for McDonald's to keep its prices down and retain its profile as a low-budget restaurant chain.

2   People are less embarrassed and defensive about eating fast food. People are aware of the dangers of excessive consumption of fast food due to these issues having had a lot of exposure in the media. However, they do not see McDonald's as being worse than any other fast-food chain and they are prepared to make the informed choice to eat fast food when they want to.

RECORDING SCRIPT

🔊 1.14

Cynics might assume its environmental moves are mere greenwash but 'they are more than cosmetic,' according to Tim Lang, professor of food policy at City University. 'I was sceptical when McDonald's started altering its menus and playing around with greener options. I thought it was a temporary blip, but they've hardwired it into their system. There is another problem, however – will they be able to maintain this commitment to more sustainable foods? And will they be able to maintain their prices? The fundamentals of the food supply chain are going in an awesome direction – energy, oil, water and food commodity prices are all rising. McDonald's is no longer in denial mode. They are more engaged, but will they be able to engage with these fundamentals? They will not be alone. All big food companies are facing these changes. But as a meat purveyor, McDonald's is going to be very exposed.' What seems to have changed, and what is most noticeable among the customers I meet, is an absence of embarrassment or defensiveness about dining under the golden arches. There is an acute awareness of the health perils of junk food and a healthy cynicism about the corporate food industry, but it no longer seems to affect McDonald's sales. Giles Gibbons, managing director of Good Business, the 'corporate responsibility consultancy' created by Steve Hilton (the man who rebranded the Conservatives), believes that customers are still not completely convinced by its revamp. McDonald's comes bottom of Good Business's 'concerned consumer index', which suggests that people remain suspicious of its brand. 'The business has regenerated itself but the brand is lagging behind. It's a very long road. You can't win people's trust back overnight. You've got to continue to take leadership decisions that people are delighted and surprised by, and over time that will lead to people feeling more trusting and happy to associate themselves with you.'

Why McDonald's is thriving despite this enduring cynicism is because people have realized that their concerns about obesity, industrial food production and environmental degradation cannot be the fault of one brand, argues Gibbons. Or, to put it a different way, if all global food corporations are as bad as each other, why worry unduly about McDonald's? 'Companies have responded, but people also understand the issue of obesity better,' says Gibbons. (It's only Prince Charles who makes crotchety statements about banning McDonald's these days.) 'The debate is more grown-up at the same time as McDonald's has evolved. The combination of these two factors means that people are less embarrassed to be associated with it.'

Internet research

Naseem Javed in his web article entitled *It's a good thing … corporate image is only a house of cards …* says that 'Corporate image is like a house of cards, delicate and fragile, like a crystal palace, it can't have stones thrown at it.' He refers to some of the companies whose corporate image has been damaged or destroyed by scandal. As an added dimension to the topic, you could ask your students to research the corporate scandals of Enron, Worldcom, Adelphia, Parmalat and Tyco.

2.2 Grammar

The future, tentative and speculative language

This module is a review of forms used for the future, including modal verbs and structures that express degrees of likelihood. Students are given the opportunity to practise selecting the most appropriate of these, in the context of an extract from a trade magazine and minutes from a meeting.

Did you know?

Reassure students that the variety of different options for expressing the future actually means that there are therefore many more chances of getting it right! Also, remind them that *going to* to express the future is usually acceptable (except in formal contexts).

Recognizing longer future forms

1 There are quite a few words that may be new to the students in these sentences, so clear up any vocabulary questions first. Encourage students to attempt to guess meaning from context and highlight the pronunciation of *mortgage* /'mɔː(r)gɪdʒ/, *grossly* /'grəʊsli/, *rival* /'raɪv(ə)l/ and *appalling* /ə'pɔːlɪŋ/ by drilling and putting the phonemics on the board. You may also like to mention the very different pronunciation of *data* in American and British English. Students should underline the future expressions in pairs and decide on the degree of probability for each example. Take whole-class feedback.

ANSWERS:

1 C   2 P (in the negative sense)   3 T / P   4 C / P   5 P
6 C / P (depending on how one interprets expect)
7 C / P (in the negative sense)   8 P   9 P   10 P / T
11 C   12 P / T

2 Students, working individually, should now be able to complete this table quite quickly. Some of the expressions could be checked for accuracy of pronunciation, e.g. *on the verge of*, *poised to*, *are bound to*.

ANSWERS:

Certain: be poised to, be on the verge of, be on the brink of, be set to, be bound to, be certain to
Probable: will, probably, should
Tentative: may, could

3 Students replace their underlined expressions in the sentences in exercise 1 with possible alternatives from the table. Many answers are possible here.

Speaking

4 Model this activity yourself by first of all summarizing a current news story and then speculating on how the events will develop in the near future. You may find it useful to make some notes in advance. Ask your students to make some notes about a news story they know about. Monitor and help as required and then ask students to discuss their stories in pairs.

5 Ask students to close their books. Read the gapped text to the class in the style of a news bulletin, so that students can comprehend its gist before gaining a more detailed understanding. Remind students that they do not need to understand every word in such texts and should always try to deduce unknown words from context. Lexis causing difficulty here might include *to have plans afoot* (to be in the process of being carried out), *to woo back* (to encourage to return), *revamped* (improved, renovated) and *pods* (a capsule / long narrow container). Again there are many possible alternative correct suggestions for alternative expressions.

SUGGESTED ANSWERS:

1 is set to unveil / is poised to unveil / is about to unveil / is on the verge of unveiling
2 is certain / bound to shake up
3 may / might / could respond
4 are likely to / should / will probably focus on
5 may / might / could just work
6 should / could / might close

Tentative language

6 Students work individually to make these sentences more tentative. As they do so, circulate and provide as much help as necessary.

SUGGESTED ANSWERS:

1 There is little doubt that in today's modern business world far too much emphasis is placed on corporate image.
2 I can't believe you appear to be trivializing such a serious matter!
3 The marketing department tend to blame us for poor sales; they're the ones who are responsible for our corporate image.
4 Given our image, it is going to prove challenging to break into the American market.
5 It appears likely that our consumers are going to demand more information about carbon footprint.
6 The board have expressed concern / are concerned about your abilities to lead the department.
7 It might / would be a good idea to rewrite this report on our CSR projects.
I would suggest rewriting / you rewrite this report on our CSR projects.

Listening

7 🔊 1.15 Direct students' attention to the illustration suggesting problems with cleanliness in hospitals. Inform or elicit from the class facts about the widespread problems with MRSA and other superbugs in NHS hospitals in the UK. Some discussion of healthcare provision, as regards the public / private sector balance, in the students' countries might be interesting here. Pre-teach *to foot the bill* (to pay the bill) and *to cover our backs* (to protect oneself) then play the recording once through for gist. Then replay the recording, encouraging students to note down more information. Note that students will need to recognize the speakers from the initials given in the Student's Book. Students compare in pairs, then take whole-class feedback.

7   How to handle an incident that could have a damaging effect on Bug-O-Cide's corporate image.

RECORDING SCRIPT

🔊 1.15

Dave: ... OK, so what do you think, Manu?

Manu: Cheers Dave. As far as I can see it's just not *Bug-O-Cide's* problem, we're not to blame. There's no way we're going to foot the bill for the clean-up costs, the hospital haven't even paid us for ages. If anyone should pay it's them!

D: Manu, you're absolutely right about the hospital not paying us but we can't expect them to pay for our mistake. We could offer to split the costs of the clean up. Our image is certainly more important than whatever services we offer and we need to remember that. If we are seen to be doing something to help this crisis it's got to be good for us.

Elena: *Bug-O-Cide* has got to concentrate solely on our new soft-focus literature and stop worrying so much about bad publicity. The average person on the street doesn't know who we are and what we do. We've got to get our name known out there, that's far more important than bad publicity!

M: Stuff the soft-focus literature Elena! You know, *Bug-O-Cide's* owners are bound to blame us all personally if people find out about this – they've got absolutely nothing to lose and they never take responsibility. As Dave says, image is everything, we need to preserve it at all costs.

D: I just know we're going to fail this health and safety inspection right across the board because of this. What we've got to do is find a way to cover our backs.

E: Responsibility comes from inside. You have to feel it.

M: Well I don't feel any, and if you ask me I say it's the Director who's really responsible. Why isn't he here at the meeting anyway? He's never around when you need him and what's more ...

8   Students use their notes from the recording and the phrases from exercise 5 to complete the minutes using tentative language. If students have difficulty with this you could write the answers up on the board in random order and students could then match them to the gaps.

SUGGESTED ANSWERS:

1   thought / said / suggested
2   said that he
3   it might be a / it would be a
4   expressed concern / was concerned
5   would be / prove challenging / difficult / impossible
6   would have

Internet research

Andy Gillett has a very good exercise at his site at the University of Hertfordshire. If students choose the *Hedging* link at the top of the page they can read his introduction, his language examples and do the exercise at the bottom.

2.3 Vocabulary

Corporate social responsibility

This module develops and extends vocabulary related to Corporate Social Responsibility, with opportunities for students to practise using the vocabulary in discussion and presentation.

Discussion

1   As an optional lead-in, do an Internet search for *images* and *corporate social responsibility*. Print some of the images and bring them to class to generate initial discussion around the topic.

Pre-teach *to prevail* (meaning *to predominate*: to be larger in number, quantity, power, status or importance). Dictate the following words and ask students to write them down: *brand, environment, hypocrisy, profits, responsibility*. Get students to compare their answers in pairs, then elicit and put the words on the board. Check / drill pronunciation and stress. Students complete the gapped quotations with the words and then check in pairs. Elicit answers.

ANSWERS:

1 responsibility   2 hypocrisy   3 environment
4 brand   5 profits

2   Ask students to discuss what they understand the quotes to mean: which are for and which are against CSR, and which they agree with and which they disagree with. Finally, open this up to whole-class discussion.

Listening

3   🔊 1.16–1.21   Dictate the CSR activity types (*eco-efficiency, corporate philanthropy*, etc.) to the class and ask them to write them down. Get students to check in pairs, elicit spelling and write the terms on the board. Drill for pronunciation and word stress. Next, draw students' attention to the definitions in exercise 4.

You may need to check / pre-teach the meaning of the following lexis: *coined by* (to devise a new word or phrase), *enhancing* (making greater, as in value, beauty, or effectiveness; or improving), *explicit* (fully and clearly expressed or defined) and *vicinity* (a nearby, surrounding or adjoining region; a neighbourhood).

Now ask students to complete the definitions in their own words. Get students to compare their answers in pairs and elicit answers from the class before playing the recording for the first time.

4   Explain to the class that they will now hear the definitions in full, and should note down as much information as they can for each. Play the whole extract through once. Then give students an opportunity to compare in pairs. Monitor to check progress. Then play the extract again, but this time pause after each definition and give students a few moments to complete their answers and to check in pairs / small groups. Now ask individual students to come to the board to write up the definitions. Ask the class to feed the answers to the student at the board. Finally, check through with the class, paying attention to spelling. You could also exploit this opportunity to drill selected items for pronunciation.

ANSWERS:

1   Eco-efficiency was a phrase coined by the Business Council for Sustainable Development to describe the need for companies to improve their ecological as well as economic performance.
2   Corporate philanthropy – donating to charities is a simple and reputation-enhancing way for a company to put a numerical value on its CSR 'commitment'.
3   Cause-related marketing is a partnership between a charity and a company where the charity's logo is used in a marketing campaign or brand promotion.
    The charity gains money and profile and the company benefits by associating itself with a good cause as well as increasing product sales.
4   Sponsoring awards. Through award schemes, companies position themselves as experts on an issue and leaders of CSR simply by making a large donation.
5   Codes of conduct. Corporate codes of conduct are explicit statements of a company's values and standards of corporate behaviour.
6   Community investment. Many companies develop community projects in the vicinity of their sites, to offset negative impacts or give back to the community and local workforce. Community investment covers a whole range of initiatives including running health programmes, sponsoring schools, playgrounds or community centres, employee volunteering schemes or signing a memorandum of understanding with communities affected by a company's impacts.

5 Before listening to the recording again, ask students to answer the questions in this section from what they remember. Students compare in pairs, then listen one last time to check and modify or add information.

ANSWERS:

1   An oil company installing solar panels on the roofs of its petrol stations and reducing the carbon emissions of its operations whilst remaining committed to a continual increase in oil and gas production.
2   McDonald's network of Ronald McDonald Houses to 'improve the health and wellbeing of children' and BP's sponsorship of the National Portrait Award. Easy and very PR-friendly – corporate giving is more easily dismissed as a PR exercise than other forms of CSR, companies are shifting to making larger donations to a smaller number of charity partners and combining giving with other activities.
3   Tesco's computers for schools promotion. Companies choose charities which will attract target consumers.
4   The Reebok Human Rights Awards, Nestlé's Social Commitment Prize and the Alcan Prize for Sustainability.
5   Ernst & Young or PricewaterhouseCoopers are mentioned but as external verifiers of corporate codes of conduct rather than in connection with their own corporate conduct code. Codes vary in content and quality from company to company, and cover some or all of the following issues: the treatment of workers, consumer reliability, supply chain management, community impact, environmental impact, human rights commitments, health and safety, transparency and dealings with suppliers, and other issues.
6   GlaxoSmith–Kline supports a wide variety of health and education programmes in areas where it operates, ranging from training midwives in Vietnam to AIDS awareness outreach for Brazilian teenagers.

RECORDING SCRIPT

 1.16–1.21

Eco-efficiency was a phrase coined by the Business Council for Sustainable Development to describe the need for companies to improve their ecological as well as economic performance. Minimizing the company's environmental impact, particularly around highly visible aspects of its operations or in areas where it makes financial savings, is a particularly popular tactic amongst companies whose products are inherently destructive to the environment. For example, an oil company installing solar panels on the roofs of its petrol stations and reducing the carbon emissions of its operations whilst remaining committed to a continual increase in oil and gas production.

Donating to charities is a simple and reputation-enhancing way for a company to put a numerical value on its CSR commitment. McDonald's network of Ronald McDonald Houses to 'improve the health and wellbeing of children', and BP's sponsorship of the National Portrait Award are two high-profile examples. Because it is easy and very PR-friendly, corporate giving is more easily dismissed as a PR exercise than other forms of CSR. In an effort to respond to this criticism companies are shifting to making larger donations to a smaller number of charity partners and combining giving with other activities.

Cause-related marketing, such as Tesco's highly successful computers for schools promotion, is a partnership between a company and a charity, where the charity's logo is used in a marketing campaign or brand promotion. Companies choose charities which will attract target consumers. The charity gains money and profile, and the company benefits by associating itself with a good cause as well as increasing product sales.

The Reebok Human Rights Awards, Nestlé's Social Commitment Prize and the Alcan Prize for Sustainability are high-profile examples of corporate sponsored award schemes. Through award schemes, companies position themselves as experts on an issue and leaders of CSR simply by making a large donation.

Corporate codes of conduct are explicit statements of a company's values and standards of corporate behaviour. Codes vary in content and quality from company to company, and cover some or all of the following issues: the treatment of workers, consumer reliability, supply chain management, community impact, environmental impact, human rights commitments, health and safety, transparency and dealings with suppliers, and other issues. Some codes are monitored by external verifiers. In many cases these are large accounting firms such as Ernst & Young or PricewaterhouseCoopers. This has led to the criticism that monitors will place the aims of the company, and not the environment or society, at the forefront when carrying out their assessment.

Many companies develop community projects in the vicinity of their sites, to offset negative impacts or give back to the community and local workforce. Community investment covers a whole range of initiatives including: running health programmes, sponsoring schools, playgrounds or community centres, employee volunteering schemes, or signing a memorandum of understanding with communities affected by a company's impacts. GlaxoSmith-Kline, the pharmaceutical multinational, for example, supports a wide variety of health and education programmes in areas where it operates, ranging from training midwives in Vietnam to AIDS awareness outreach for Brazilian teenagers.

Reading

6 Before starting this exercise, prepare cards with the target vocabulary and definitions on them. For example:

run the risk	to be in a situation where something bad could happen
smokescreen	something you do or say as a way of hiding your real feelings, intentions or activities

Prepare one set of cards for each pair of students. Set the following comprehension questions:
Does the text convey a positive or negative view of CSR? (it conveys the negative aspects)
What does the writer say about off-shoring? (that it makes economic sense, but might not be ethical).
Ask students to read through the text to answer the questions. Then give out the vocabulary cards and ask students in pairs to match the words to definitions. Go through the answers with the group. Next, get students to test each other on the meanings, e.g.
A: *Which phrase means 'to avoid something difficult or unpleasant'?*
B: *to sidestep*
To consolidate, allow students to do the matching in their coursebooks. As an additional activity, the definitions can easily be incorporated into a vocabulary test at the end of the week.

ANSWERS:

1 e 2 b 3 a 4 f 5 d 6 c

Discussion and presentation

7 You may want to incorporate some additional materials on how to give effective presentations before setting this task. For this activity, students will need to use the information cards on pages 110, 112 and 115 of the Student's Book. Divide the class into small groups or pairs. Explain that they are going to prepare and deliver short (five-minute) presentations to the class on an aspect of CSR. Provide students with the following presentation structure (based on the questions provided in the task):

1 **Introduction**
   introduce yourselves and the CSR initiative you are presenting
2 **The effectiveness of the initiative**
   benefits to the company
   benefits to society
   strengths and weaknesses of the initiative
3 **Areas for improvement / points to consider**
   how the company can avoid charges of 'tokenism'
   suggestions to improve / extend the initiative
   benefits those changes would bring

Ask students to prepare their presentations using the information sheets and addressing each of the points according to the structure above.
Give students plenty of time to prepare and rehearse their presentations. As the students give their presentations, make notes on language points that arise (pronunciation, grammar, vocabulary, etc.) for post-correction. Finally, get the class to vote on the best existing CSR initiative.

Internet research

Searching Google for *CSR policy* will return lots of company Corporate Social Responsibility statements. Ask your students to do this search and to make a note of the policy statements of a selection of companies. Then ask them to compare these in class. Students could also vote for the best companies according to the strength of their CSR policy statements.

2.4 Management skills
Time management

This module deals with the management of time in order to gain maximum benefit from it. It also deals with the skill of effective delegation. Please note that in this module the **Internet research** is a necessary prelude to activity 5. However, if you do not have time or resources for the Internet activity, you can omit activity 5.

Discussion

1 Begin by asking the class to discuss in pairs / threes which is their favourite day of the week, and why. Take whole-class feedback, then direct their attention to the cartoon showing how moods and feelings are different during the week. Students work with a partner and put into words the message of the cartoon, and say if they agree or not.

SUGGESTED ANSWER:

People are more aggressive and demanding at the beginning of the week, and more open to suggestion towards the end of the week. It is therefore important to choose the best time for strategically important tasks.

2 Check understanding or pre-teach *aptitude* (natural ability) and *making redundancies* (firing people). With the same partner, students speculate which day might be best for each of the different tasks listed in the bullet points.

SUGGESTED ANSWERS:

asking for a rise: Thursday / Friday
brainstorming: Wednesday
getting important jobs done: Tuesday / Wednesday
setting goals: Monday
holding meetings: Tuesday
doing sport: Friday
finding a new job: Tuesday
making redundancies: Friday

3 This is a very brief jigsaw reading activity. In pairs, student A reads about Monday, Tuesday and Wednesday whilst student B reads about the other days of the week. They then exchange the information that they have just obtained from their reading. For the activity to work well, if you have an odd number of students, it is probably best for you to pair up with the student without a partner. You will need to pre-teach and drill for pronunciation the following lexis: *to curb* (v) (to reduce), *hardball* (idiom) (aggressive attitude / activity), *grievance* (n) (cause for complaint), *succumb* (v) (to submit / lose the battle). Encourage students to provide supporting evidence from their own experience to back up their (dis)agreement with what they have just read / heard.

Prioritizing and delegating

4 Give students plenty of time to write their lists of activities which they could do on that day. If you are teaching learners who are already working it might be better for them to imagine a busy day at work in their country (without classes). Those who have yet to begin work can think about assignments and study tasks (reading and projects).

Internet research

In Paired Comparison Analysis, a range of options are compared and the results are scored to find an overall winner. First of all, a range of plausible options is listed. Each option is then compared against each of the other options, to determine the preferred option in each case. The option with the highest score is the preferred option. There are a number of websites that provide very clear examples and instructions of Paired Comparison Analysis. Ask your students to find one such website and to note down the instructions and examples given. Students can then use their findings in the next task.

5 Students use the Paired Comparison Analysis from their Internet research to prioritize their urgent and important tasks.

Discussion

6 If you are teaching a class of students who have yet to begin work, it might not be appropriate to discuss the first four questions on the list here with reference to their own personal tasks. However, students who are already working will probably enjoy answering all of these questions and comparing which items on their lists they would be reluctant to delegate or otherwise, and why. All classes however should be able to do this activity by simply thinking about tasks in terms of the table: which are urgent and important **A**, urgent but not important **B**, etc. Questions 5 and 6 should be answered after brainstorming the advantages and disadvantages of delegation. You can then put this list of pros and cons on the board.

SUGGESTED ANSWERS:

1   probably the As – urgent and important tasks which need to be done now
2   probably the Cs – important but not urgent tasks which someone else can do well
3   probably the Bs – urgent but not very important tasks, and perhaps the Ds – not urgent and not important tasks where new team members could acquire experience without risk
4   probably the Ds - not urgent and not important tasks; but they may become more important or more urgent later
5   delegation gives managers time to manage, think, be creative, do important jobs, motivates and develops team members, gives flexibility, cuts costs, allows managers to evaluate team members' performance
6   insecurity, lack of trust, lack of time, need for control, ignorance, fear of other people's reactions, enjoying being busy or doing simple tasks

Listening

7 **1.22–1.26** Students read through the guidelines for effective delegation then listen to Margaret delegating to Robin and match each extract to guidelines 3–7. Play the recording, stopping after each section, and elicit answers from the class.

SUGGESTED ANSWERS:

3:1 4:5 5:4 6:2 7:3

8 Play the recording all the way through and allow students to compare their answers in pairs. Then take whole-class feedback. Check the meaning (*to compose*) and conjugation (*draw, drew, drawn*) of the irregular phrasal verb *draw up*.

ANSWERS:

1 to look into
2 prepared to take on
3 let me know
4 give me an update
5 let / know / handling
6 treat this as
7 get / to take over / How / sound
8 get back to me / run past
9 go ahead / draw up
10 comfortable with

9 This is preparation (a kind of controlled practice) for the forthcoming roleplay and serves to encourage students to use the semi-fixed expressions that they have just been listening to. It may be an idea therefore to display the suggested answers on the OHP or board if you have a weaker class.

SUGGESTED ANSWERS:

1 I'd like you to … Is that something you'd be prepared to take on?
2 The reason I'm asking you to do it is that …
3 I suggest you give me an update every …
4 No, I'd appreciate it if you could treat this as confidential.
5 Yes, I thought I'd get … to take over some of your …
6 Think about how much time you'll need, and let me know what you decide.
7 As a first step, could you get back to me with proposals we can run past …
8 I'll let … know you're handling …

RECORDING SCRIPT

 1.22–1.26

1

Margherita: Have a seat, Robin.

Robin: Thanks.

M: I know you're busy, so I'll get straight to the point. We're expecting budget cuts, so I'd like you to look into ways of reducing our travel costs. The reason I'm asking you to do it is that you're the person who has to make the most business trips, so you know more about it than anyone else.

R: Well, that's probably true.

M: So, is that something you'd be prepared to take on?

2

R: When do you need my report?

M: Well, the absolute deadline would be the end of the year. But I'd like to move as quickly as possible, really. Think about how much time you'll need, and let me know what you decide. In any case, I suggest you give me an update every two weeks or so, OK?

3

M: That's great, Robin. So, I'll let Kim know you're handling the project, and I'll send out a memo to all the reps, asking them to make time to talk to you.

R: Thanks Margaret. What about the travel bureau, should we tell them?

M: No, I think we should leave them in the dark for the moment, don't you?

4

M: I'd appreciate it if you could treat this as confidential, at least for the time being.

R: Of course. No problem. But, erm, I'm just a little bit concerned about the workload. I'm still trying to clear the backlog from my trip to Brazil!

M: Yes, I realize that, and I certainly don't want to overload you. I thought I'd get Estelle to take over some of your paperwork for a few weeks. How does that sound?

5

M: As a first step, could you get back to me with proposals we can run past Human Resources? If they're happy, you can go ahead and draw up new procedures. Overall, we need to cut the travel budget by at least 15%. Are you comfortable with that?

R: Sure.

Roleplay

10 Students act out the delegating roleplay, if possible with real work-based tasks from exercise 4. If this is not possible, students can use fictional tasks: working on a cost-cutting project, organizing a relocation, budgeting for the coming financial year, etc. The student who is observing should be reminded to comment on effective delegation as well as to offer constructive criticism.

2.5 Writing

Press releases

This module focuses on the language of press releases and gives students practice in writing this specialized business genre.

Internet research

As an alternative lead-in to the lesson, ask students to search the Internet using the keywords *press release* and *company name*, e.g. *press release Adidas* or *press release Tesco*. This will provide you and your students with an excellent selection of authentic press releases. Allocate a company to each of your students and ask them to find a press release and to summarize it using the following points:

Company:
Date of press release:
Topic of press release:
Two or three main points mentioned:

Once students have gathered their information, ask them to mingle to ask each other questions and tell each other about the news they have read.

Reading

1 Make a copy of the headline and subheading of each press release to display on the board (using an IWB or OHP). First, display the headlines and subheadings and ask students to work in pairs. Ask students to discuss what strategy each company is using to promote its products and why they are doing this. Elicit answers from the class and discuss points arising. You may find it useful to check comprehension by asking students what a makeover is (a great new look) and who or what Lang Lang is (a world-renowned pianist).

SUGGESTED ANSWERS:

Text A: strategy: a makeover, to improve the appearance or packaging of the product. The reason the company is doing this could be to make the product appear more modern and to boost sales. Maybe also to more effectively target a specific consumer group.

Text B: strategy: a celebrity brand endorsement, using a famous person to promote the brand. The reason the company is doing this may be to give the impression that Sony is a patron of the arts and to increase the appeal of the brand amongst fans of Lang Lang.

2 You may prefer to prepare photocopies of the two texts for this exercise, so that you can give one text to each student in each pair. Ask each student in each pair to quickly read their text to check the points raised in exercise 1. Next, ask students to highlight the key points made in each paragraph of their text. Students work in pairs to tell their partner about the text they have read, summarizing the key points. Next, elicit the key points of each press release in open class and clarify/extend any points arising. If you have not already done so, you can now draw students' attention to both texts on page 26 of the Student's Book.

SUGGESTED ANSWERS:

(the following are the key points students should identify and summarize)

Text A: Paragraph 1 – new packaging, flavours, ingredients. Paragraph 2 – makeover is result of consumer research: clearer brand design; healthier, low-fat, natural ingredients. Paragraph 3 – Brand Manager says company responds to consumer comments. Paragraph 4 – Skinny Cow, producer of low-fat ice cream, loved around the world.

Text B: Paragraph 1 – three-year sponsorship deal, pianist to appear in events and campaigns, will use Sony products, particular focus on China. Para 2 – Lang Lang popular worldwide, very talented, popular with traditional and younger audiences, Sony welcomes him as 'brand ambassador', especially loved in China. Paragraph 3 – Lang Lang thrilled to represent Sony, loves using Sony products, will share his love with his fans. Paragraph 4 – Sony, producer of professional and consumer audio, video, IT and game technology products; well-placed to become world leader in entertainment and electronics.

Analysis

3 Write the paragraph labels (*back-up paragraph*, *contact information*, etc.) on the board. Ask students to label the paragraphs of the texts. Let students check in pairs before eliciting the answers.

ANSWERS:

headline
subhead
lead – a summary of the story
back-up paragraph
information about the company
contact information

Language / Style

4 Dictate (once quickly, once slowly, once quickly) the two headlines to the class and ask students to write them down. Get students to compare what they have written in pairs or threes. Either elicit the headlines and put them on the board or ask two members of the class to write them up, with other students feeding the words to the students at the board. Ask students to comment on the main features of the headlines. Elicit comments and provide input as needed.

SUGGESTED ANSWERS:

Points to note are the use of capitals for main content words (not prepositions), no full-stops or commas, little or no use of articles, use of the present simple and *to* + infinitive verb forms, and the dominant use of nouns.

5 Students practise writing headlines from the extracts provided. Rather than all students working through all extracts, you may prefer to allocate one or two extracts per pair of students. Monitor to check and provide help or clarification during the task. Once students have finished writing the headlines, ask them to read them out to the group. If students have not written out all of the headlines, ask them to finish this for homework.

SUGGESTED ANSWERS:

1 Superways Captures Four Times More Online Orders than Closest Competitor
2 Mr Fix-it to Focus on Growth and Long-term Plans
3 Jenkins and Health-Ex Form Worldwide Collaboration for Novel Medication
4 Reykjavik on Ice / Reykjavik to Offer Cool Tourism
5 RSNO Holds Music Workshops for Elderly and those with Special Needs

6 Elicit from the class the usual verb forms that are used in press releases. Refer students back to exercise 2 if necessary. Students read through the press release and decide on a suitable verb form for each gap. Monitor to check which items cause greatest difficulty. Get students to compare in pairs before checking through the answers. Provide guided feedback using concept questions to guide students to the correct answers.

ANSWERS:

1 has announced   2 will reduce   3 marks
4 represents   5 will enable / enables   6 is
7 to be gained   8 is expected

7 Ask students to highlight or underline examples of inappropriate style in the text. You could highlight the first yourself as an example (*Because they want*). Monitor while students do this and offer help as needed. Next, elicit the inappropriate language and put it on the board. Now ask students in pairs to rewrite the phrases in an appropriate formal style. Elicit suggestions to the board and clarify as necessary.

7 (SUGGESTED ANSWER)

1 Because they want – Aiming
2 how we get on – our relationship
3 said – remarked
4 meet – conform to
5 said – commented
6 biggest - greatest / main / most significant
New engines make easyJet 25% cleaner
Aiming to be one of the world's most environmentally efficient airlines in the industry, easyJet has announced that their new engines will reduce NOx (mono-nitrogen oxides) emissions by 25%.
'Today marks a new chapter in our relationship with the airline,' remarked Jean Dubois, president of the engineering firm. 'Our engine represents the best of available technologies for the environment and will enable easyJet to conform to future regulations with significant margins.'
'Climate change is a real and pressing danger,' commented Andy Harrison, CEO of easyJet. 'Furthermore, the greatest benefits are to be gained from environmentally sensitive companies developing technology to enable our industry to achieve the green growth that is expected of us.'

Writing

8 Draw students' attention back to the headlines in exercise 5 and explain that they are to write a press release for one of the items. Ask students to work in pairs and to choose one of the headlines to write about. Next, ask students to create some extra information, such as quotations and statistics, to add to the press releases. Next, with the whole class, read through the tips 1–5 in exercise 8 and ask students in their pairs to generate some additional content using the tips to help them. Finally, ask students to work alone to write their press releases. Set a time limit of 20 to 25 minutes for this. If time is short, set the task for homework.

2.6 Case Study

Pixkel Inc.

In this module students give a presentation of their ideas for improving a start-up business's corporate image. They also practise fielding questions after their pitch has been delivered.

Internet research

The Hire was a series of short films for BMW, delivered via the company's website. These video clips were very popular and, even though BMW removed them from its website, have continued to spread via websites such as YouTube (where they can still be viewed). Reference is made to them in the recording, so you could ask students to search for one or two of the movies to watch for homework prior to the lesson.

Discussion

1 Begin a discussion about the last time students bought an electronic device. Individually, they rank the criteria that affected their selection. They then explain their ranking to a partner.

Reading

2 Introduce the email by directing students' attention to the visual of Caitlin and explaining that she is the new Director of Corporate Communications for a start-up (a new business) which designs chipsets (a group of chips designed to work as a unit to perform a function) for digital cameras. Elicit the meaning of the following expressions in the email: *wizard* (someone who is very good at something), *hands-off* (allowing other people to make their own decisions), *to hit the ground running* (to be successful from the start of an activity), *to bounce some ideas off someone* (present ideas and get further input), *lab* (abbreviation of *laboratory*). Ask students to compare their answers in pairs then take whole-class feedback.

SUGGESTED ANSWERS:

1. A company which is not managing its growth, with urgent problems of leadership, profitability, delivery, cash-flow and public relations.
2. She needs to get results quickly; she can't expect help from Bill, and it is difficult to meet other managers.
3. She would like to have someone to help her brainstorm and evaluate possible solutions.

Listening

3 🔊 1:27 Students look at the photographs of the management team. Check that everyone is clear about the roles and names of the team members. Students listen for the first time and make notes about what is said about each of the ten issues listed.

SUGGESTED ANSWERS:

1. there's no team spirit, they need to work together better
2. people keep leaving the company
3. the working environment is incompatible with a high-tech image
4. recruitment is difficult because working conditions are poor
5. the company has a reputation for late payment and discounting
6. the market is really tough, with more and more competition from India and China
7. they need money to take the brand upmarket
8. finance keeps cutting budgets
9. the product has no visibility for the end user
10. develop medium- and long-term objectives

4 Students listen again and, in pairs, match the statements to the team members who attended the meeting. They then deduce the meaning of the idioms from the context.

SUGGESTED ANSWERS:

1. Ben Rainey, Marketing. Pixkel's reputation with customers and suppliers is not very good, and it will be very expensive to strengthen the brand.
2. Carla Buenaventura, HR. There is no team spirit, and people do not take responsibility. Getting people to work together is almost impossible.
3. Jerry Woo, Supply Chain. Pixkel has an excellent product, but sales and marketing are incompetent or lazy.
4. Alex O'Driscoll, Finance. There is no mission statement or business plan, so nobody knows what their long-term objectives are.
5. Lena Zimmer, Sales. The market is very difficult with a lot of competition – final customers do not know or care whether the camera they buy uses a Pixkel chipset.

RECORDING SCRIPT

🔊 1.27

Caitlin: I think everybody knows that Bill wants me to develop a strategy to improve our corporate image, so the main reason I called this meeting was just to try to get a handle on what's happening, and what you feel needs to change, OK? Unfortunately Bill can't make it – he's busy in the lab.

Ben: Ha! The invisible man strikes again!

Carla: Let's try to be constructive, OK? Maybe I can start. This is Carla, by the way. Don't get me wrong, Caitlin, I think a coherent image strategy is very valuable, but surely our first priority has to be getting everybody pulling in the same direction!

Ben: Ah, come on Carla, get real! We're talking cash-flow and supply chain here, not one of your touchy-feely, HR team-building programs!

Caitlin: (interrupts) Sorry, hang on, is that Ben?

Ben: Yep.

Caitlin: Look, Ben, can we come to you next? Let's just let Carla have her say, all right?

Ben: OK, OK. Just trying to keep the meeting on track.

Caitlin: Carla?

Carla: Thank you, Caitlin. I was just saying you can't have an effective image strategy when everybody is pursuing their own agenda. Right now there's just no team spirit; problems are always someone else's fault. I'm telling you, we can't seem to agree on anything! It's no surprise we can't keep our people – I already had three developers quit this year!

Lena: It might help if conditions were more in line with a high-tech image. Those labs are like prison cells!

Carla: Lena's absolutely right there, unfortunately – and it doesn't make hiring any easier, I can tell you!

Caitlin: OK. Thanks, Carla. Ben, let's hear what you have to say now.

Ben: Well, like I said, our cash-flow problems really damaged our profile in the marketplace! We're not paying our suppliers, so they ain't too happy, and our customers know we're cash-starved, so they're literally squeezing us dry!

Lena: Yeah – and with the Chinese and the Indians slashing prices, it's no picnic! We're still increasing our volumes, but we're being forced to discount more and more.

Caitlin: This is Lena, right?

Lena: Yeah, sorry Caitlin.

Caitlin: That's OK – Ben?

Ben: Yeah, Lena's team's having a hard time. I'm trying to take us upmarket, but to do that we need some serious money, and finance just keeps cutting our budget!

Alex: Now hold on a minute, Ben, that's not fair! Costs have to be kept under control!

Ben: Under control? My marketing budget is down 15% this year! You people in Palo Alto have *no idea* how difficult …

Caitlin: Hang on, Ben, and um …

Alex: Alex.

Caitlin: Alex. Sorry. Look, we're all in the same boat – let's just focus on the problems, OK?

Carla: You see what I mean?

Jerry: Can I come in here, Caitlin? Jerry Woo.

Caitlin: Sure, go ahead Jerry. You're over in Taiwan right now, is that right?

Jerry: Yeah, I'm with our subcontractors here. I don't know how much you know about our chipsets? Our digital pixel technology provides far better resolution, contrast and colour than standard CCD cameras, so you'd think they'd be easy to sell, right? Unfortunately Lena's people don't seem to be able to get their act together.

Lena: Jerry, it's not as simple as that.

Jerry: Just hear me out, OK? It's the same problem with marketing – lots of talk about added value, but in the end we're still discounting! So, I'm working day and night to supply enough product, and taking the blame when we can't deliver, but we're not making any profit! From where I stand, the answer is pretty obvious!

Ben: I can't believe I'm hearing this!

Lena: Caitlin, it's Lena again, can I just say something here?

Caitlin: Just a second. OK, Jerry, I hear what you're saying. Thanks for that.

Jerry: Sure. Just my two cents.

Caitlin: Now, Lena?

Lena: Well it's always easy to blame sales! OK, we have a good product, but it's completely invisible! The final customer doesn't have any idea what the chipset does, or who made it – so it's really tough to persuade manufacturers they're getting added value from using *our* technology rather than one of the big names. I'd like a lot more support from marketing – not just on things like the logo, the slogan, colour coding or the website, although they all could use serious updating – no, I'm talking about educating customers to demand high-quality chipsets in their digital cameras. That would really make our lives a heck of a lot easier!

Caitlin: Yes, I see what you mean, Lena. All right, can I bring Alex in? We haven't heard much from you yet, Alex, what's your take on all this?

Alex: If you set the cash-flow problem aside for a moment, the figures aren't actually that bad. As long as we keep costs under control, which I've more or less managed to do up to now, we have excellent growth and we're still in the black. The real problem is just a general lack of direction. Nobody really knows what our medium- or long-term strategy is supposed to be. I mean, we haven't even got a corporate mission statement, let alone a business plan!

Caitlin: OK, thanks for that, what I think we need to do is …

Discussion

5 Put the students into small groups to categorize the major issues Caitlin is faced with, and which should be prioritized. These can be elicited and put on the board.

Listening

6 and **7** 🔊 1.28–1.35 Students listen and make notes on the suggestions for improving Pixkel's corporate image. Elicit students' answers and put them on the board. Then tell students to work in pairs and discuss the pros and cons of each one.

SUGGESTED ANSWERS:

- develop a clear mission statement and commitment to CSR
- produce a catchy or memorable slogan
- our sales team needs a better image and communication skills
- include our company name in all our product titles
- develop a good logo, a good slogan and use celebrities to advertise our products
- get our CEO to do some publicity stunts
- produce a range of associated products bearing our company name
- make some short promotional movies to release onto the web

RECORDING SCRIPT

🔊 1.28–1.35

Alex O'Driscoll: The obvious place to start is with a clear mission statement and a commitment to social responsibility; you know, some high-profile community project to show we can be trusted.

Lena Zimmer: Remember 'Intel inside'? Nobody had ever heard of Intel, but look at them now! That was a stroke of genius!

Carla Buenaventura: We need to work on the sales teams' image and communication skills – customers' judgements are based 72% on appearance, 20% on how you communicate and only 8% on the actual words you use!

Ben Rainey: We should take a leaf out of Microsoft's book: they never refer to 'Word' or 'Excel' – it's always 'Microsoft Word' and 'Microsoft Excel.'

Jerry Woo: We should develop a neat logo, a great slogan, and use celebrity endorsements: look what they did for Nike. 'Just do it', the swoosh, the world-class performers – that's a winning combination!

Alex O'Driscoll: Why not make Bill the next Richard Branson? Everybody knows Virgin because of his publicity stunts, like the hot-air balloon, and they don't cost an arm and a leg either!

Lena Zimmer: T-shirts, baseball caps, polo shirts, staff uniforms … and maybe change our name? Make Pixkel visible and cool!

Ben Rainey: How about a viral movie to build our brand? Did you ever see that series of short films BMW did with Clive Owen? That was awesome!

Discussion

8 Put students into groups of three to draw up an action plan for Pixkel as preparation for the forthcoming presentation. Make sure that you mix the ability levels within each group. Give them a clear time allocation, e.g. ten minutes, and remind them that all three should talk during the presentation. Monitor students at this stage to provide help and correction. If groups finish early, encourage them to expand certain sections, work on intonation and to think about paralinguistic features such as gesture and eye contact.

Presentation

9 If possible these presentations should be audio- or video-recorded to encourage students to aim for a high standard. Encourage those listening to make notes so that follow-up questions are well informed. As a class, conduct a vote to see which group came up with the best suggestions and delivered the most convincing presentation. You also can make notes on linguistic points for follow-up remedial work in later classes.

Review 1 and 2 answers

Review 1

(page 30 in the Student's Book)

1 Personal development

1

1 c
2 g
3 b
4 e
5 h
6 d
7 a
8 f

2

1 have clearly been conducting
2 is
3 prepared carefully
4 was properly thought through / was thought through properly
5 are often asked
6 have not thought about
7 come away
8 actually is / was
9 To keep
10 should be held

3

1e 2c 3a 4f 5d 6b

4

1 analyse, analytically, analyses, analytical
2 communicative, communications
3 innovatively, innovative, innovate

5

■■■

analyst
analyse
innovate

■■■■

analyses
innovative

■■■■

innovative

■■■■■

innovatively

■■■■■

communicative

■■■■■

analytical
analytically

■■■■■

communications

6

-able   adaptable, dependable, knowledgeable
-ible   responsible, sensible
-ive   assertive, reflective, responsive, sensitive
-ful   careful, cheerful, helpful, powerful
-ant   observant
-ent   confident
-worthy   trustworthy
-ic   energetic, idealistic, sympathetic

7

1 frustrated
2 reputation

Review 2

(page 31 in the Student's Book)

2 Corporate image

1

1 b
2 e
3 d
4 a
5 c
6 j
7 f
8 i
9 h
10 g

2

6, 2, 3, 5, 4, 1

3

1 is sure to
2 is likely to
3 is poised to
4 might possibly
5 probably won't
6 is expected to

4

1 run
2 pay
3 expose
4 sidestepping
5 coin
6 set
7 offer
8 facing

5

1 build a new image
2 bouncing some ideas off
3 it's a jungle out there
4 the bottom line
5 reluctant to delegate
6 hands-off approach
7 flavour of the month
8 hit the ground running

3 | Supply chain

Subject background

This unit is about supply chain management, and also about logistics.

A supply chain is the system involved in moving a product from supplier to manufacturer to final customer. At the beginning of the chain – the upstream end – the process may begin with the extraction of raw materials and then move on to the making of small parts and components. These are put together into sub-assemblies, which in turn are connected together to make the finished product. At the other end of the chain – the downstream end – the finished product is distributed, perhaps via wholesalers, to the retail outlet and the final customer. Along the whole chain, many companies are likely to be involved and there will be storage and transportation issues at every step. Supply chain management (SCM) is the management of this complex process.

The related term *logistics* is sometimes used in a similar way to SCM. However it usually has a more restricted scope, referring to activities within one company and to distribution of the finished product alone (i.e. the downstream end). SCM includes the upstream end of the chain and work-in-process inventory inside the factory as well, and it also includes the major area of procurement (finding and choosing suppliers, and then purchasing from them). SCM involves multiple companies – suppliers, manufacturers and retailers – working together to get a product to market.

A key role in both logistics and SCM is provided by 3PL firms – third-party logistics providers. These are specialized transportation firms who in an international context also deal with customs clearance, etc.

SCM relies on an IT system that is very well integrated between the different channel partners. Parts, components, work-in-process soon to be completed, finished goods at the factory gate, and finished goods on their way to the retailer (at a wholesaler or distribution centre) all need to be tracked. They may be in storage or in transit. Bottlenecks in the system need to be foreseen and avoided: Just-In-Time (JIT) processes mean that items should arrive at the next point in the channel only as they are needed, pulled by customer orders. A build-up of stock at any point in the channel is costly – not just in terms of storage costs, but also in terms of the working capital that is tied up in the dead stock sitting on a shelf. Items have to be in the right place at the right time in the right quantity all the way through the supply chain.

Coordinating information between multiple suppliers, the manufacturer, various 3PL firms and multiple retailers is an IT nightmare. There are also strategic and security issues – how much information should be shared with these outside companies? To what extent are they partners, or do their own profit maximization objectives conflict with those of the manufacturer? How easy is it to switch to a new supplier for cost or quality reasons when the original supplier has such a tight integration with business processes? When things go wrong at a supplier – perhaps a quality issue – should the manufacturer have the right to appear on site and monitor how the issue is resolved? Where JIT breaks down, and there is a build-up of inventory at some point in the channel, who pays for the storage costs? Should a truck wait until it is full before leaving, or leave half-full so that the items can get to the next stage in the chain?

The complexity of SCM is likely to grow in line with globalization. In the old days, a manufacturer of cars, white goods, consumer electronics or sports shoes might have done most of the production itself. These days the company with the brand name on the product is likely to be just an assembler and marketer, with the parts coming from a huge number of other companies. These outsourcing companies who supply the parts may be spread all over the world, and several outsourcers in different countries may make the same part – so that the brand-name assembler can play one supplier against another, switching production in an instant according to demand, local costs, etc.

Useful websites

http://logistics.about.com/cs/a.htm
http://www.logisticsit.com/supplychain
http://www.supplymanagement.com
http://www.bettermanagement.com/siteindex.aspx (then look under Industries\Manufacturing\Supply Chain Management)

3.1 About business

Outsourcing

This module introduces the topic of outsourcing through a range of engaging listening, reading and discussion activities to provide opportunities for students to practise using new language in context.

Internet research

A search of the Internet for the advantages and disadvantages of outsourcing provides a lot of useful background information on the topic. For example, www.bizhelp24.com has a useful summary of the key pros and cons of outsourcing:

Advantages
- allows a business to focus on core activities
- streamlines a business's operations
- gives you access to professional capabilities
- shares the risk
- peace of mind that the process is in good hands (reliability)
- do not have to worry about continually introducing new technologies
- improves service quality
- frees up human resources
- frees up cash flow
- increases the control of your business
- makes the business more flexible to change (i.e. demand)

Disadvantages
- the fear of the service provider ceasing to trade (bankruptcy, etc.)
- you may lose control of the process
- creates potential redundancies
- other companies may also be using the service provider. Therefore in some cases, the best interests of the service provider may be diluted by other users
- you may lose focus of the customer and concentrate on the product (the outsourced process)
- the loss of talent generated internally
- employees may react badly to outsourcing and consequently their quality of work may suffer

Discussion

1 Before starting this discussion, get students to brainstorm the pros and cons of outsourcing. Use the points above for your own reference. Now turn to the particular scenario presented in the Student's Book. Ask students to work in groups of three and to make notes about the points they raise as they discuss the situation. Monitor and provide prompts as needed. Once the discussion is complete, elicit students' ideas and put them on the board.

SUGGESTED ANSWERS:

better: because Manpower is a respectable and reliable employer, your job will not depend on your relationship with the owner, you will have better opportunities for training and more interesting work, you are sure to be paid legally and efficiently, you may have better insurance cover

worse: because Manpower may expect you to work harder and may be less flexible, your relationship with your employer is impersonal, you may be asked to work in other places, you may lose your job more easily, your net pay may be lower than before

Listening

2 1.36 First, ask students to listen to the recording and make notes. You could ask them to make notes about the following:
Motorola
Accenture
BC Hydro
BT
HR
Next, ask students to compare their notes in pairs. Elicit ideas and put them on the board. Ask students to read through the questions and to answer as many as they can from memory. Then play the recording through a second time for students to check and add to their answers.

ANSWERS:

1 By suggesting no more than 50% of the audience will still be employed by the same company in five years. This grabs the audience's attention and shocks them into changing their attitudes towards outsourcing.
2 When the outsourcing service provider hires the people who used to be employed by the client to do the same work.
3 a) over 650   b) 1,500   c) 1,100
4 Workload increases: outsourcing assumes greater efficiency.
5 Working for several different clients means work is more interesting, and specialist firms provide enhanced career opportunities.
6 The knowledge drain: when employees refuse lift-out and leave the company altogether. This can be avoided by giving regular updates on the outsourcing process, explaining the benefits for the employee and for the company, and having an open-door policy.

RECORDING SCRIPT

1.36

Good morning, ladies and gentlemen.
Let me start by asking you a question. In five years' time, how many of you will still be employed by the same company as today? Well, probably not more than half of you. If that idea shocks you, get used to it, and get used to it quickly. Outsourcing is already with us, and it's here to stay. One day you're working for a Global 2000 corporation, the next day – Poof! – you're working for an outsourcing service provider. You're sitting at the same desk, doing similar work, with the same colleagues – but now you're a consultant. That's 'lift-out'! All right; this morning I'm going to give you a brief idea of how lift-out works, and what the future holds for those who move out. After that we'll open up for questions and discussion. Let's look first at some examples: at technology company Motorola Inc. more than 650 HR employees moved over to service provider ACS. BC Hydro, a British Columbia-based utility, not only outsourced its HR services to Accenture, but also its customer services and IT. And they didn't stop there: they also handed over financial systems, purchasing, and building and office services. In total, some 1,500 BC Hydro employees were lifted out to the new service provider. Accenture also cut an outsourcing deal with BT, the giant London-based telecommunications company. Eleven hundred BT employees became employees of Accenture HR Services. At one time BT had an HR staff of some 14,500 employees. Today, only about 500 are left.
So, what happens to staff after lift-out? Well, first of all, the bad news is, their workload usually increases! Outsourcing works on the assumption that functions can be performed more efficiently than they were by the corporation, so when you increase efficiency, clearly, you increase the workload. On the other hand, I'm glad to say that there are compensations! The good news is that the job becomes more interesting. As you can see on this next slide, most people are

very attracted by the idea of working for several different clients instead of a single corporation; we find that between 50% and 60% of employees who are outsourced are happier as a result.

Another very significant benefit of lift-out, and a second reason for that statistic, is career opportunities. Working for an outsourcing company in IT or HR actually provides more and much better career opportunities. For example, if you're working in HR in a large industrial corporation, your career choices are pretty limited; HR is seen as a cost, and it's very difficult to change to another department. But if you are outsourced to a specialist firm like Accenture, where HR is a source of revenue rather than a cost, even if your background is in HR, it's perfectly possible to move to marketing, or sales or even high-level management.

So this is something that I really want to stress: when you prepare people for lift-out, it's very important to emphasize these positive aspects and to help staff to accept change. Because of course with lift-out, there is always the risk of the knowledge drain – that's when too many employees refuse the lift-out and prefer to leave the company altogether. When they leave, they take with them a great deal of valuable knowledge and experience. So, as my next slide shows, there are a number of ways you can minimize the risk of the knowledge drain. You should provide regular updates on the outsourcing process, by email or in meetings; you should take every opportunity to explain the benefits for the employee and for the company; and of course you should have an open-door policy to give advice to anyone who needs it.

All right then, are there any questions so far?

Reading

3 **Alternative activity:** As an alternative approach to the task, cut the text into sections and distribute one section to each student in the class (with classes of more than eight students, subdivide the class into groups). Ask students to read their section and to summarize it in a single sentence. Also, ask them to highlight and check the meaning of any unknown vocabulary in the section. Monitor and help with this stage. Once all students have written a summary sentence, ask each one to dictate their summary to the class and ask the class to write it down. Each student will now have eight student-generated summary sentences. Now ask them to read the whole text and match their summaries to the paragraphs. Finally, ask students to quickly read through the summaries in the Student's Book and to match them to the paragraphs. You may need to elicit / pre-teach the meaning of *bits* (the most basic unit of information that can be stored in a computer) in paragraph 2, as this is key to finding the answer. Check through the answers, paying close attention to the parts of each paragraph that indicate the answers.

ANSWERS:

1 b   2 g   3 f   4 h   5 e   6 d   7 c   8 a

4 Give students a few minutes to locate the corresponding words and phrases. Get students to check in pairs before going through the answers. You may need to explain that a *cubicle farm* is a place where large numbers of office workers work in cubicles, such as in call centres.

ANSWERS:

is about to	The Melanie Griffith phase **is coming ...**
miracle technologies	breakthrough app
online service jobs	financial analysis, research, design, graphics, cubicle farm
inexpensive	the equivalent of your latte budget
knowledge workers	smart, educated, English-speaking people
never became intelligent	the superbrain that never arrived *in silico*
incredibly fast	the speed at which the Indian tech industry is learning new skills is breathtaking
relaxed	diminished / détente
monster	silicon invasion
repetitive jobs	bookkeepers, secretaries, typesetters
the overall result	the net effect
is reassuring	There is some solace in history
products to data	atoms to bits
adding up numbers	data crunching
printing documents	the typing pool
handling phone calls	the switchboard

5 Ask students to locate the five sentences in the article (i.e. paragraphs 1, 3, 4, 7 and 8). Alternatively, read the sentences aloud and ask students to scan for them. Ask students to discuss their interpretations in pairs before taking whole-class feedback.

SUGGESTED ANSWERS:

1 Like textile mills, which were abandoned when the textile industry was relocated, American call centres (cubicle farms) will also be abandoned.

2 There is no distinction between manufacturing and management jobs: only Indians appear to have any job security.

3 Thirty years ago, people feared that there was no limit to the jobs that computers could replace. Now, people have the same fears about offshoring.

4 We are still in the phase when we see India as a threat rather than an opportunity.

5 A future American economy based on innovation and creativity.

Discussion

6 Give students a few minutes to read through the questions and to consider their own opinions. They can make notes if they wish. Next, put students into groups of three to discuss the questions. Elicit opinions from each group in open-class discussion. Monitor the discussions and note any language points for post-correction.

3.2 Grammar
Noun phrases

This module deals with the formation of complex noun phrases. They are presented in the context of the transportation of coffee from producer through to consumer. Students are then given the opportunity to use the phrases in a short sales pitch.

Did you know?

The nominalization explored here is a pronounced feature of technical and academic writing and can make texts dense and difficult to read, for native and non-native speaker alike. However, it is a way of packing information into text, and is a useful way to increase the level of formality in students' writing. Aside from the study of relative clauses, this area of grammar may be relatively unexplored by the students, as most ELT materials concentrate instead on verb grammar.

Noun phrases

1 Introduce the topic by asking the class to discuss with their partner if they prefer tea or coffee, how many cups a day they drink, whether they have a favourite brand or coffee shop and which country they believe produces the best coffee. Pre-teach or elicit the meaning of *modes* (particular ways of doing something), *harvesters* (machines or people that harvest crops), *overseeing* (watching something in order to check that it works or happens in the way that it should) and *bewildering* (confusing and difficult to understand). Students then work individually to match the phrases in the two columns. Ask them to compare their answers in pairs before taking whole-class feedback.

ANSWERS:

1 b	2 e	3 d	4 a	5 c	6 h	7 j	8 i	9 g	10 f

2 Ask students to look at the title and check that they understand the distinction between *free trade* and *fair trade*. Free trade can be defined as a system of international trade in which companies do not have to pay high taxes on the goods bought from or sold in other countries. Fair trade can be defined as the principle of charging a price for goods that does not put producers in developing countries at a disadvantage.

Students work individually or in pairs to put the noun phrases into the gaps in the text. You may like to highlight the *Caveat emptor!* phrase at the end. Its usage here is unusual, in that it refers to the repercussions of purchasing goods without considering their origins (rather than the more usual injunction to check that goods are not in any way faulty before purchasing).

ANSWERS:

1:7j	2:1b	3:10f	4:2e	5:3d	6:4a	7:8i	8:9g
9:5c	10:6h						

Defining relative clauses

3 Point out that students must use the information from the text above to write their defining relative clauses. You might like to reassure your students that the omission of the relative pronoun is not really an issue here. In these sentences, the noun in question is invariably the subject, not the object of the relative clause.

SUGGESTED ANSWERS:

1 A complex supply chain is a process that / which involves different modes of transport across continents and oceans. Or: A process that involves different modes of transport across continents and oceans is termed a complex supply chain.
2 A distribution centre is a place where products are sorted and redirected before being transported on. Or: The place where products are sorted and redirected before being transported on is called a distribution centre.
3 Smallholder producers are farmers who operate on farms of less than 25 acres. Or: Farmers who operate on farms of less than 25 acres are known as smallholder producers.
4 The fair trade policy is a system that / which requires minimum standards of personal and environmental welfare.

Internet research

Divide your class into two groups. Ask one to search for *coffee supply chain* and the other for *fair trade coffee supply chain* and to make notes. Pair students from each group to compare their notes and to discuss the distinction between coffee that is fair trade (and its supply chain) and that which is not.

Building noun phrases

4 Check the pronunciation and meaning of *depot* (a large building where things can be stored until they are needed) and *autonomously* (independently). Focus students' attention on the example given and remark upon the way it packs information into one sentence and avoids the use of many short sentences. You may like to provide another example for students on the board:
That order was from Pixkel. That order was profitable. That order was nearing completion. You processed that order this morning. That order failed to go through because you did it badly.
That profitable order nearing completion, which failed to go through because you processed it badly this morning, was from Pixkel.
Students then work with a partner to combine the short sentences into one sentence using modifiers and reduced relative clauses as in the above example.

SUGGESTED ANSWERS:

1 You will love our ethically sourced coffee, which is of the highest quality.
2 Our smart, flexible approach ensures the right solution for you every time.
3 Our strong and trusted brand is recognized worldwide.
4 Our huge range of specialized medical equipment is hard to beat.
5 Fast-expanding and with thousands of flights per day, Heathrow is a global airport hub.
6 Originally a military term, logistics offers integrated transport solutions at the right price.

Describing products and systems

5 Discuss the visuals with the class, eliciting descriptions from the students as to what each portrays. If your students are already working, they may be able to compare the mission statements of their organizations or to bring in promotional literature which describes the nature of the businesses they work for. If your students are not yet working, they can search online for the mission statements of their favourite companies (or political or religious organizations) and compare them in the following class. Next, ask students to work in pairs to prepare a short sales pitch to make to the rest of the group, using the pictures as input. Monitor and offer guidance where appropriate. The main aim is for students to express the ideas conveyed by the pictures, using their own words but paying close attention to the use of noun phrases and clauses. As the students make their sales pitches, make a note of language points arising for post correction and feedback.

SUGGESTED ANSWER:

Our mission statement is that we provide 'total supply chain management solutions'. This is reflected in the very high customer satisfaction we've achieved as a result of our consistent rates of on-time delivery. Our new fleet of trucks, all clearly bearing the RDC Solutions company logo, and our state-of-the-art distribution facility, which has recently been refurbished with the most up-to-date technologies and the latest sorting and delivery systems, ensure that all goods are efficiently sorted and delivered on time. Our well-qualified, experienced and committed staff will work round the clock to ensure we provide a first-class total supply chain solution to all our customers.

3.3 Vocabulary

Logistics

This module focuses on vocabulary development in the field of logistics, with opportunities to use the vocabulary through controlled practice and discussion.

Internet research

A keyword search for *Just in Time* will return a lot of websites discussing and outlining this aspect of supply management. Divide your class into two groups. Ask group A to search for the advantages of Just in Time, and group B for the disadvantages. Then pair students from each group to discuss the pros and cons of Just in Time.

Discussion

1 The quiz can be done orally. Simply read the questions and multiple-choice options and ask students to note their answers down on paper. This can be done in pairs to promote discussion. At the feedback stage, points can be awarded for correct answers. The answers reveal that logistics is a costly, time-consuming and labour-intensive process.

2 Draw students' attention to the pictures of a cow and yoghurt. Ask students to devise a flow chart outlining the main stages in the processing of milk to yoghurt, and its distribution. Elicit student suggestions and put them on the board.
Before doing the matching task, you may need to pre-teach / elicit the following vocabulary: *to audit* (to examine something carefully, especially to decide on its effectiveness), *to evaluate* (to think carefully about something before making a judgement about its value, importance, or quality), *to source* (to get a product or basic material from somewhere).
For the matching task, prepare the questions and decisions on cut-up cards and give one set to each pair of students. Monitor to check progress. After checking the answers, give students an opportunity to test each other:
A: *Which plant will make the new yoghurt?*
B: *Define production location.*
Finally, let students complete the exercise in the Student's Book as a record.

ANSWERS:

1 c   2 a   3 g   4 b   5 d   6 e   7 i   8 f   9 h

Listening

3 and **4** 🔊 1.37 Explain to students that they are going to listen to an extract of a presentation on reverse logistics. Ask them to note down what the speaker says about each of the three scenarios.
You may need to elicit / pre-teach the meaning of *salvage* (the action of saving property or possessions from being destroyed in a fire, flood, etc.).
Provide extra guidance for exercise 4 by asking students to identify the part of speech (verb, noun, adjective) of each word given. Also, ask students to decide which parts of speech fit into the gaps according to the words before and after the gaps. Allow students a few minutes to do the task. Monitor to check progress and give students an opportunity to compare in pairs. Play the extract once through for the whole class to check and confirm their answers.

RECORDING SCRIPT

 1:37

In simple, forward logistics, goods, information and financial transactions move from one end of the supply chain to the other. As you can see in the top half of the slide, traditionally, raw materials are moved to the manufacturer, where they are transformed into finished goods. These then move forward via warehouses and distribution centres to retail outlets, and then on to the consumer.

The goal of reverse logistics is to maximize the value of all goods which, for one reason or another, are removed from the primary distribution channel. This is achieved by moving them beyond the expected end point of the supply chain. So in the bottom half of the slide, you can see that goods can be moved back from the consumer toward the manufacturer. Products can be repositioned and sold to customers in a different geographical location or in a different retail organization; they can be returned to distribution for salvage or, for example, for donation to charity, or they can go back to the manufacturer to be destroyed or recycled.

Discussion

5 Ask students to work in threes for this task. Ask the groups to select a product they are familiar with or would like to produce. You could provide some options for your students to choose from (e.g. cars, technology products, foods, clothing). Refer students back to the strategic decision stages a)-i) in exercise 2 and explain that they are to devise a supply and reverse logistics chain for their chosen products and will then present their ideas to the class. You might find it useful to model this activity for your class and the following is a suggestion:

- *product:* high-quality olive oil.
- *source raw materials:* visit olive groves in the South of France, Spain and Tuscany to see where we can get a regular supply of high quality produce.
- *validate vendor quality:* employ an independent expert to audit the olive growers and production centres.
- *define production location:* from our visits and audit, identify the best plant to produce and bottle the oil.
- *define product quality:* we will provide only high-quality expensive oils to the hotel and restaurant trade.
- *source transportation channels:* use lorries and cross-channel ferries to transport goods to warehouses.
- *consider using JIT:* use JIT for 50% of the product, and warehouse storage for the remainder.
- *decide inventory levels:* keep warehousing to a minimum by holding minimal amount of surplus stock and no bulk packaging.
- *decide location of distribution centres:* main warehouse (central UK), four small regional depots (one in each region: north, south, east, west).
- *choose logistics provider:* Granville Freight and Haulage Ltd.
- *Role of reverse logistics:* reposition stock between UK centres (when needed); return out-of-date or returned stock to the producer.

Present this model to your class. Then use the logistics and reverse logistics flow chart to illustrate your project. Ensure students fully understand the task. Give groups plenty of time to plan their presentations. Provide as much help and support as needed. With large classes, remix the groups and ask students to present their group's ideas to each other; with small classes ask each group to present their projects to the class.

Listening

6 1.38 You may need to elicit / pre-teach *cradle-to-grave* (through your whole life), *scan-based-trading* (where retailers pay suppliers for a product when consumers purchase it, rather than at the time it is delivered to the store), *proactively* (taking action and making changes before they need to be made, rather than waiting until problems develop) and *to mitigate* (to reduce the harmful effects of something). In this exercise students will need to listen to the seven key value propositions listed. If necessary, you can make this task easier by dictating the seven value propositions in random order and asking the class to write them down. Get students to check what they have written in pairs, then elicit answers and put them on the board. Play the recording through once and ask students to put the propositions in order. Elicit back to the board. Next, play the extract again and ask students to make a note of what the speaker says about each proposition, e.g.
Use technology: to provide cradle-to-grave control over the supply chain
Let students compare notes in pairs before eliciting answers and putting them on the board. Finally, ask students to look through the list of propositions and benefits to match the halves using their notes.

RECORDING SCRIPT

1.38

So how do USF Processors provide added value using reverse logistics? First of all, by using technology, especially Scan-based trading, to provide cradle-to-grave control over the supply chain. For instance, by repositioning product between different stores we can minimize and often eliminate Stockouts. Another example is date codes: by managing date codes proactively, we can minimize Stales; obviously this is particularly important in the grocery business. Also, by managing in-store inventory we can predict Unsaleables in sufficient time to be able to reposition them in secondary channels, for example in Thrift Stores.

Another very real issue in today's world is the threat of bio-terrorism. In the event that a product recall becomes necessary, USF Processors can manage the recall process quickly and efficiently in order to mitigate the manufacturer's liability. Similarly, where product is unsold, efficient handling of Returns allows us to minimize cost exposure. And because we capture and utilize accurate, meaningful and objective data on all these processes, manufacturers and retailers can improve their business relationships and achieve dramatic improvements in contracting.

7 This fun anagram activity can be done in pairs. Give students a short time to solve the anagrams. Then check with the class. Next, ask students to match the words to the paraphrases in exercise 6.

Discussion

8 One way to approach this task is to get students to discuss each problem in turn. First of all, write these three questions on the board: *What is the category of problem? How would you use reverse logistics to deal with it? How could you avoid such a problem in the future?*
Ask students to work in groups of three. Read the first problem out to the class and ask the groups to discuss it with reference to each question on the board. Elicit a suggestion from each group before moving to the next problem. Repeat this process for each problem. Alternatively, assign a different problem to each group and ask them to discuss it in relation to the questions and then to feed back to the whole class.

SUGGESTED ANSWERS:

1 Returns – return the phone to the logistics centre or manufacturer for reconditioning or salvage – in future use better packaging and / or a more specialized forwarder
2 Returns – recall the product for testing and destruction or repositioning – use tamper-proof packaging
3 Unsaleables – reposition stock in a different, less fashion-conscious location – manufacture and supply product on demand to avoid surpluses
4 Stales – return stock to manufacturer for recycling – use scan-based trading to identify potential stales before it is too late
5 Returns – recall all products to manufacturer for salvage or recycling – use better quality suppliers and safety controls
6 Unsaleables – reposition stock in a different location or retail organization, or perhaps Thrift Stores – supply product on demand to avoid surpluses

---

EXTENSION ACTIVITY

Research the Internet for information on 'The Beer Game'. This is a production–distribution game, in which participants discover the important interrelationships between different elements in the supply chain. You may like to recommend your students research 'The Beer Game' for homework.

This module introduces students to JM Fisher's *Process of Transition*. They write a mission statement, define a goal and draw a force field analysis chart for it. They are also provided with listening practice in the form of an interview with a Change Management consultant, and practise recognizing and constructing cleft sentences for emphasis.

Internet research

By reading about and taking note of the diagrams which illustrate JM Fisher's *Process of Transition*, students reflect upon the psychological stages that any individual undergoes when he / she experiences major changes in his / her life or work. Before students find the diagrams, you could dictate the stages in random order and ask them to work in pairs and order them. They can then check their answers with the diagram. Students who are already working can probably talk about major changes at work quite easily, and those who have yet to begin work can think about other personal examples (e.g. choosing a university course, moving home, getting married).

Discussion

1 In small groups, students must decide upon major changes they would like to introduce to an imperfect system operating within their country. Whether you are teaching abroad or in a multinational class, healthcare, tax or transport systems are invariably recognized as imperfect and in need of change, so this should provoke a lot of fruitful discussion.

2 Students should apply the SMART model to formulate a mission statement. Working students are probably already familiar with the concept of mission statements, and those who have not yet started work can easily find examples on the Internet. The student task force should think about their purpose and values, who their primary clients are, what their responsibilities are towards these clients and how they intend to accomplish their mission. An extract from Oxfam's mission statement could act as an example:

Oxfam works with others in fighting poverty and injustice around the world, through effective, appropriate and enduring solutions. We aim to tackle the root causes of poverty and develop lasting solutions to poverty, hunger, and social injustice.

Listening for gist

3 🔊 1.39 Play the recording once through and elicit the answer from the class. You may like to pre-teach/elicit the meaning and pronunciation of *inventory* /ˈɪnvəntəri/ (a list giving details of all the things in a place), *inertia* /ɪˈnɜː(r)ʃə/ (a situation in which something does not change for a long time) and *resilient* /rɪˈzɪliənt/ (able to recover easily).

ANSWER:

Goran Radman helps retail companies to meet customer needs and demand by setting up an on-demand supply chain, using CPFR.

Listing for detail

4 Elicit the meaning of *Holy Grail* (an ultimate goal or ambition that is hard to obtain) before replaying the recording. Then explain *the whole is greater than the sum of its parts* (synergy) and *ROI* (return on investment). Students compare answers in pairs. Take whole-class feedback.

ANSWERS:

1 on-demand supply chain
2 customer needs and demand
3 waste, unnecessary overhead or logistics
4 collaborative planning, forecasting and replenishment
5 greater than the sum of its parts
6 strengthen the driving forces, and weaken the restraining forces
7 consumer power
8 better results
9 inertia
10 giving away secrets
11 buying the wrong technology
12 not acheiving ROI

RECORDING SCRIPT

 1.39

Interviewer: Goran, you specialize in helping companies to manage change; more specifically, in helping retailers move towards an on-demand supply chain. First of all, remind us exactly what an on-demand supply chain is, will you?

Goran: Sure. The on-demand supply chain is the Holy Grail of retailing: a way of adjusting all a company's business processes, in real time, to meet customer needs and demand, literally day by day, and even hour by hour.

I: So you provide exactly what your customers want; no less, and no more? No waste, no unnecessary overhead or logistics, no stockouts, no returns: is that really possible?

G: Like I said, it's the Holy Grail! But the on-demand model can be created today if businesses are prepared to share the right information at the right time. It's all about collaboration – what we call CPFR.

I: Which stands for ...?

G: Collaborative planning, forecasting and replenishment. If retailers, manufacturers, logistics partners and so on all sit down together and define clear processes which transcend their organizational boundaries, then the whole is definitely greater than the sum of its parts.

I: Yes, I can see that. But it seems that the change involved in setting up an on-demand supply chain can be difficult to accept – which is where you come in?

G: That's right. One of the first things we do in helping a retailer change to CPFR is to look at a force field analysis. We identify two types of forces: *driving* forces, which are the forces pushing the company towards change, and *restraining* forces, which are the factors pushing in the opposite direction, resisting change and trying to maintain the status quo. Very often there's an equilibrium between the driving forces and the restraining forces – so nothing happens. My job is to try to strengthen the driving forces, and weaken the restraining forces.

I: Can you give us some examples of these forces?

G: Well, increasing consumer power is a very strong driving force. If retail companies can't adapt to the global market place, they simply won't survive. It's probably the most powerful force for change. Then there's the prospect of significantly better results thanks to faster turnaround, reduced inventory, increased sales, fewer out-of-stocks and better sell-through of products. Better results may not be the strongest driving force, but obviously they are very significant.

I: So what about the restraining forces, what are they, things like inertia?

G: Well, inertia is certainly one of them. It's easier to do nothing than to change! But that's a relatively weak factor. There are much more powerful restraining factors like the fear of giving away secrets.

I: Really?

G: Oh, yes. Many retailers fear that sharing key competitive information with supply chain partners puts them at risk. In fact, experience has proved that the reverse is the case. The more manufacturers know about a retailer's plans and sales, the more willing they are to be variable, resilient and responsive.

I: I see. And what other restraining factors are there?

G: Well, other issues are not quite as strong as secrecy, but fear of buying the wrong technology, or not achieving return on investment are quite common.

Discussion

5 In small groups, students discuss the restraining and driving forces for the listed possible changes. Be prepared to define *Just in Time (JIT) manufacturing* (a process by which companies do not keep lots of excess inventory; instead, they manufacture a product as an order comes in).

SUGGESTED ANSWERS:

changes	driving forces	restraining forces
upgrading computer software	increasing efficiency, reducing errors, ensuring continued support	fear of choosing the wrong technology, unwillingness of staff to retrain
outsourcing business processes like HR and IT	increasing productivity, more specialist skills, reduced exposure if business decreases	fear of giving away secrets, fear of losing control
adopting JIT (Just in Time)	reducing waste, increasing productivity and ROI	fear of creating bottlenecks, fear of depending on suppliers
offshoring production	reducing cost of goods, more flexible legislation	fear of stakeholder dissatisfaction, fear of quality issues

6 Students now draw a force field analysis chart for their original goal in exercise 1 and score the forces from weak to strong. They then discuss how they could *strengthen* /ˈstreŋθ(ə)n/ (a difficult consonant cluster so drill for pronunciation) the driving forces and weaken the restraining ones.

Listening

7 1.40–1.47 Students now listen to extracts from Goran's conversation and match each to Kotter's key steps. Pre-teach the phrasal verbs *to buy into* (to accept something) and *let up* (slow down or stop).

ANSWERS:

1 d   2 g   3 a   4 e   5 b   6 h   7 f   8 c

Cleft sentences

8 Focus students' attention on the example sentences given (perhaps write them on the board) and elicit that the original sentences are split into two clauses to add emphasis. Students then listen again to recognize when they are used in the extracts.

Take on board (accept) and *roll out* (introduce) can be pre-taught. Be prepared to explain *bury one's head in the sand* (refuse to accept reality) as you go through the answers. *Unfreeze-Change-Refreeze* comes from an early model of change by Kurt Lewin. *Unfreezing* means to change the existing mindset, *refreezing* is when the new mindset is crystallizing and one's comfort level is returning to previous levels.

> **SUGGESTED ANSWERS:**
>
> *The reason why I want you to hold a brainstorming session is to encourage people to stop burying their heads in the sand.*
> *It's them that need to be empowered to make change work.*
> *What's essential now is to refreeze things*
> *What they don't realize is that if we don't unfreeze the situation fast, your supply chain is going to start falling apart!*
> *It's them that should take ownership of the project …*
> *Another thing you have to bear in mind is that if you let up, people can very easily slip back into old habits.*
> *What's really critical at this early stage is to engage the hearts and minds of the team who are going to guide the project to success.*
> *What would be really good would be to get everyone together every Friday …*
> *… what's important is that it's short term.*

RECORDING SCRIPT

 1.40–1.47

a) OK Maria. The reason why I want you to hold a brainstorming session is to encourage people to stop burying their heads in the sand. We all need to step back so we can see the big picture and develop a really clear vision of where we want this company to go.

b) At this stage, you should encourage staff to tackle problems themselves. It's them that need to be empowered to make change work. Give them autonomy, and then make sure you catch them doing something right, and congratulate them!

c) Well, Maria, you've done a great job. What's essential now is to refreeze things, to consolidate the changes so they really stick. We don't want people to dismiss CPFR as just the flavour of the month, do we?!

d) Now, the thing that people need to take on board is that this is really urgent. What they don't realize is that if we don't unfreeze the situation fast, your supply chain is going to start falling apart!

e) As the next step, Maria, what you should do is get all the staff on board. It's them that should take ownership of the project, so you need to communicate so well that they really buy into making this thing work.

f) Another thing you have to bear in mind is that if you let up, people can very easily slip back into old habits. So let's build momentum by rolling out the changes in waves, OK?

g) I suggest we hold a team-building day. What's really critical at this early stage is to engage the hearts and minds of the team who are going to guide the project to success.

h) Right now it's getting into the habit of winning that counts most. What would be really good would be to get everyone together every Friday to celebrate each week's progress. Or every two weeks if you want, but what's important is that it's short term.

9 Students reformulate the sentences as cleft sentences to give greater emphasis. Monitor and allow students to compare their sentences in pairs, then review the suggested answers.

> **SUGGESTED ANSWERS:**
>
> 1 What we all need to do is to stop burying our heads in the sand and step back so we can see the big picture.
> 2 What you should do is encourage staff to tackle problems themselves.
> 3 The thing you have to do is to catch them doing something right.
> 4 What some people will do is to dismiss CPFR as just the flavour of the month
> 5 What's really important is that they buy into making this thing work.
> 6 The reason we should roll out the changes in waves is to build momentum.
> 7 It's their hearts and minds that we need to engage.
> 8 It's getting into the habit of winning that counts most.

10 You may find it useful to prepare an action plan of your own in advance of the lesson and present this in class in order to provide a model for your students. Refer students back to the objectives they identified in exercise 1 in order to offer a better service to customers. Now ask students in their groups to prepare an action plan using force field analysis and Kotter's eight steps to define and describe each stage of the action plan. Monitor and help as required.

Presentation

11 Students present their action plans to the rest of the class, using cleft sentences for emphasis where appropriate.

3.5 Writing

Corporate guidelines

This module focuses on the textual features of corporate guideline documents and provides practice opportunities in writing a set of guidelines.

Internet research

Ask students to consider buying and selling a range of goods / services (e.g. PCs, houses, cars). Ask them to do an Internet search for *purchasing / selling + tips / advice + name of the goods / service*. Get students in pairs to combine and evaluate the advice for buying and selling.

Discussion

1 Draw students' attention to the photo. Explain that this is the roof of the hotel and point out the fact that it has solar panels. Ask them to discuss what they think is unique about a hotel of this sort (i.e. it aims to be environmentally friendly). Ask students to brainstorm what purchasing considerations the management of such a hotel would have. To help students generate ideas, use the following prompts:
goods
services
construction
facilities
sources
suppliers, producers and manufacturers
trading agreements
transportation

Analysis

2 Photocopy the text, but do not include the option words. Give a copy of the text to each student and ask them to read through the extract quickly to see if any of their ideas from exercise 1 are included in the text. Now ask students to think of a suitable word for each gap from their understanding of the text. Get students to compare in pairs and then elicit their suggestions and put them on the board.
Elicit / pre-teach *acquired* (purchased / bought / obtained), *adhere to* (to obey a rule, law, agreement, etc.), *ensure* (to make sure that something happens or is done) and *sustain* (to provide the conditions in which something can happen or exist). These can be dictated to the class first and then elicited back and put on the board for explanation and drilling for pronunciation.
Direct students to the exercise in their books and give them a few minutes to fill the gaps with the options. Again, tell students to check in pairs and then take whole-class feedback. Tip: this text minus the options can be incorporated into a weekly progress test.

ANSWERS:

1 ensure	2 processes	3 do	4 encourage	5 sustain
6 acquired	7 adhere	8 creating		

3 Copy the sentence halves onto cards for each pair of students. Give students a minute or so to match the halves together. Elicit answers from the class.

EXTENSION ACTIVITY

Draw students' attention to the key phrases:
This policy has been compiled in accordance with ...
Only products / services / goods which / that can be demonstrated / shown as + verb +ing / to + verb may / can ...
Suppliers should provide ...
In order to conform to current requirements / legislation / regulations ...
Ask students to work in pairs and come up with alternative endings for the phrases for Hilltop's policies. If students are already working, they can write sentences appropriate to the companies they work for. Monitor and help as necessary. When pairs have constructed a few sentences, elicit suggestions from each.

ANSWERS:

1 e   2 d   3 b   4 c   5 a

Listening

4 1.48 The listening exercise covers Hilltop's policy on the sourcing of food and links with the extension activity in the previous exercise. Write the six headings on the board and ask students to copy them into their notebooks, ensuring they leave plenty of room to take down notes.
Explain to the class that they are going to hear a discussion about Hilltop's restaurant supplies and that as they listen they should take notes under the headings supplied.
Play the recording through once and give students a few moments to check their answers in pairs. Elicit answers and put them on the board. Play the recording a second time to allow students to add to or modify their notes. Again, let them compare their notes in pairs before eliciting answers and putting them on the board.

SUGGESTED ANSWERS:

1 only fresh food, and only when it's in season
2 banned, and minimal packet food
3 use glass, not plastic
4 where possible, but suppliers must be checked
5 more nutritious; in demand by tourists, source locally but may take some time
6 some seafood may not be caught during certain times of the year

RECORDING SCRIPT

1.48

Marcy: OK. Then let's move on to the food and drink supply situation. This is particularly important with the new sustainable, locally managed hotel and leisure complex opening in Cancun. And that's why we have José here. *Muchas gracias* and thanks for coming along, José!

José: *De nada*, not at all. My pleasure, Marcy.

M: Well, as you'll appreciate, we need to ensure our sustainable food supply policy aligns with that of the other hotels to date.

J: Of course. I really like what I've seen so far.

Damon: And of course, we hope we can implement one or two new ideas.

M: The first point is about fresh produce – you both have a copy of the company's ethical sourcing policy?

J: Yes, I have it here, man it's impressive but complex.

M: And, Damon, if you can note down any amendments?

D: Of course.

M: OK, so point one. I think this stays the same – with buying fresh and seasonal produce as far as possible. Obviously this means we have to change menus from one season to the next, but there is always plenty of variety to offer. OK, José?

J: Yes. Um – it says no fruit which comes from cans. Is this strict?

M: Yes, unless you can suggest a sustainable and recoverable canning operation, José? But along with minimal packet-food where fresh supplies are not available; I really don't think it's an issue with all our wonderful fruit and veg.

J: No, of course! We're very proud of it.

M: What's perhaps more difficult is the packaging. In all our hotels in Florida we're using products from glass rather than plastic bottles, where we can choose, that is. This often entails sourcing from smaller cottage industries. We take the bottles back and they recycle them. It's far better than using plastic – there aren't any recycling facilities locally for that.

J: Well, that could be more difficult ...

D: In one or two areas it was a bit of a struggle at first, but in the end we found we were sourcing more local produce and thus servicing the area much better. It takes a bit of research, that's all.

M: Which leads us on to point three. This is about organic produce. It's no good buying organically unless we know the farmers. You know, a lot of the labelling these days is false. So it's a question of checking out suppliers to be sure.

J: And this is to do with better tasting food?

M: Well, yes, but largely to encourage farmers to use alternatives to pesticides, and leave out those nasty chemicals. It's due to a mixture of current subsidy regimes, laziness and convenience, but ultimately its potentially very harmful.

J: I see.

M: And ... Damon, what else was there we wanted to add?

D: A couple of things. Going back to organics. With the influx of North American and North European tourists, we feel there is an increased demand for wholegrain foods. I mean, they're far more nutritious, we all know that. And there's clearly no difficulty in sourcing them – it's a case of getting to the producer before foods are over-processed. Not that hotels in the area aren't already doing this, but within the guidelines we've already talked about, we're wanting to source these locally. That's likely to take a little longer to implement in Yucatan and Quintana Roo. José, what's your feeling on this?

J: Well, I can see the benefits. But I'd be reluctant to sign up to this immediately. Perhaps I can ask my staff to work on it, and then we can include it in year two. How would that be?

D: Marcy?

M: Uh-huh. Well, if you think it's a viable project in the short term?

J: Yes, I do. But before I say yes to this – you said there was something else?

D: Yes. But this one isn't difficult. It's about routine! We very much want to preserve the marine life stocks, so we have a ban on sourcing certain seafoods – conch and lobster for example – during specific periods. It's something we're proud of, and state on our menus. Our guests to date have been only too happy to order another exciting dish off the menu, in the knowledge they are not depleting vital stocks!

J: OK. No problem!

Language / Style

5 Prepare the six sentences on separate strips of card for each pair of students. Write two headings on the board: *informal* and *formal*. Ask students to arrange the cards into two groups according to whether the sentences are formal or informal. Elicit answers from the class.

Next ask students to discuss which features of each sentence enabled them to decide which sentences were formal and which informal. Elicit students' comments and add them to the columns on the board.

SUGGESTED ANSWERS

1 noun phrase; use of passive
2 noun phrase; use of passive; avoidance of pronouns
3 noun phrase; use of passive; avoidance of pronouns

6 In this controlled practice exercise, students are required to write a set of guidelines for Hilltop's food policy. Ask students to look back at the notes they made during the listening exercise and to review the statements they wrote in the extension activity for exercise 3. Ask students to combine this information to write a set of guidelines on Hilltop's food policy in a suitable formal style, as exemplified in exercise 5. Set a time limit for this.

Monitor students' work and offer help as required. Give students an opportunity to compare in pairs before taking whole-class feedback.

7 Provide the following prompts relating to Hilltop's policy on water: *waste, rainwater, cleaning, bathing, swimming pools*. Ask students to work in pairs or groups of three to brainstorm ideas about what Hilltop's policy would be in this area. Elicit ideas and put them on the board. Ask the class to use the collated ideas to write a corporate guideline document on Hilltop's water policy using the ideas generated and adding any extra ideas they feel appropriate. Set a time limit for this (20-25 minutes). Collect the students' work for correction and evaluation.

3.6 Case Study

WEF Audio

In this module, students roleplay a meeting called to decide what strategy to adopt to restore profitability to a family business. They discuss Just in Time, outsourcing and relocating as various options to improve the situation.

Internet research

There are a large number of websites that have articles discussing the pros and cons of being in business with family members. You can divide the class and assign the task of researching the advantages to one half of the class and the disadvantages to the other half. They then pair up and compare their research findings. This could be done as homework before or after this class. Or, if done in a computer room during class time, a time limit should be set to ensure that students scan the articles quickly to extract the relevant information. Note that the formal word *siblings* is used in the instructions.

Discussion

1 Focus students' attention on the humorous quotation at the top of the page. Tell students to work in small groups and discuss which sectors favour family businesses (in the UK, traditionally retail, agriculture, etc.) and in which cultures they are common (Arabic, Chinese, Mediterranean). Groups then go on to brainstorm their advantages and disadvantages. Take whole-class feedback. If your students are struggling, you may like to use the following prompts:
Pros: family work harder for less reward, more solidarity, drive, pride, customers like buying from a family business that represents traditional, less commercial values
Cons: established hierarchies or factions, business decisions affected by personal relationships, more resistance to criticism and change

Reading and discussion

2 Using the visuals in the Student's Book, introduce the family members who run WEF Audio and the product the business produces to the class. Be prepared to explain *audiophile* (a person dedicated to high fidelity in the playback of music), *physicist* /ˈfɪzɪsɪst/ (someone who studies physics, especially as their job) and *to diversify a product portfolio* (to introduce novelty into your product range).

SUGGESTED ANSWERS:

1 high-quality, traditional, reliable, perfectionist but also high-tech – perhaps an inherent conflict in these values?
2 recently – 'is now applying ...' after almost 50 years of producing a single product
3 in response to customer demand, to create growth, as insurance against a declining core market, to spread risk by moving downmarket away from a labour-intensive, upmarket product

3 Put students in pairs to interpret the figures in WEF's business scorecard. Drill pronunciation and draw students' attention to the spelling of *deteriorate* /dɪˈtɪəriəreɪt/.

SUGGESTED ANSWERS:

1 Non-productive functions like sales and innovation have improved. Operations processes like efficiency and inventory have deteriorated, with a resulting rise in salaries and cost of sales and a worrying decrease in profitability. Customer and employee indicators have deteriorated: quality, delivery times, customer satisfaction, employee satisfaction and turnover.
2 The company has focused on developing new products which have increased the workload and the cost of sales, resulting in low profitability. Customers have been disappointed by falling quality standards and slower delivery times. Despite efforts to retain employees with better salaries, staff turnover has continued to increase. The change from a traditional high-margin product to a new mass-market product appears to have been handled poorly.
3 Cutting costs, restoring profitability and improving customer and employee satisfaction

Listening

4 🔊 1.49 Students listen a first time and compare their answer to the gist question in pairs, before checking with you. There are a few idioms used in the listening text whose meaning you may wish to clarify or elicit from the class, e.g. *the writing's on the wall* (the future is clear, used negatively), *a vicious circle* (a process in which the existence of a problem causes other problems, and this makes the original problem worse), *to go ballistic* (to become extremely angry), the products are *his baby* (his personal project) and a marriage being *on the rocks* (having serious difficulties and likely to fail soon). Make sure students also understand the business expressions *stagnant* (not growing or developing), *streamline* (to improve a business, organization, process, etc. by making it more modern or simple), *high-end* (more expensive and advanced) and *premises* (the buildings and land that a business or organization uses).

ANSWERS:

a) introduce Just in Time
b) outsource production of the new product range, focus on high-end products
c) relocate production of new products and her husband Karl to North Africa

5 Replay the recording and allow students time to complete the table and to compare their answers again. Take whole-class feedback. Be ready to explain *boost revenue* (increase income).

ANSWERS:

1 new products are boosting revenue
2 products are becoming more sophisticated = need to stock more components
3 increased sales mean increased workloads
4 productivity
5 (increased) inventory
6 much more cheaply
7 handle
8 too
9 damage our reputation
10 build a factory
11 unions
12 relocate Karl

RECORDING SCRIPT

 1.49

Bettina: Hi George. This seat free?

George: Uh huh.

B: Thanks. Good Schnitzel?

G: Mm. Excellent. The food's really improved here recently.

B: Yeah – Eva's latest strategy to reduce staff turnover. Doesn't seem to be working, though.

G: No. People here just don't like change, even when it's for the better.

B: Have you seen the latest scorecard?

G: Yes. Not great, is it? Too much competition from China and Hong Kong.

B: Well I'm not sure that's really the problem. OK, the Chinese are a lot more efficient than we are, but sales are pretty good, and still rising.

G: Hm – for the moment, but I reckon the writing's on the wall. Our core business is stagnant. It's the new products that are boosting revenue; they already account for nearly 40% of turnover. The thing is, they only contribute 10% or 12% of profits. With our traditional methods, we're just not competitive. Our margins are just too small.

B: I'd agree that we've been too focused on product development for the last two years, when we should have been worrying about profitability.

G: That's exactly what I'm saying. Look at inventory – the products are becoming more and more sophisticated, so we're tying up more and more cash in stocking components. Not to mention returns. We've never had that problem with the 'Emotion' speakers. And we need to hire more and more workers, but we can't even keep our skilled people happy because of the extra workload from increased sales! It's a vicious circle!

B: Hm. More water?

G: Please.

B: So what are you saying? We should drop the new products?

G: No, we have to think of the future. But we need to introduce Just in Time. Streamline the process, cut production costs, increase productivity and cut delivery times. Today's market wants product on demand. I know Karl would like to try it.

B: Maybe he would, but the old man would never agree to it! Quality is everything for Franz, you'd never persuade him we'd maintain quality levels with Just in Time. And what you mustn't forget is that if you don't hold inventory, then your suppliers have to increase theirs, so that's likely to push costs up.

G: Mm. Can you pass the bread, please?

B: There you go. What I say is we should outsource all the new products, and just focus on the high-end speakers. Offshore contractors can produce much more cheaply than we can. They'd handle returns too, and we could forget all the staffing headaches.

G: You think Franz would trust them? And what about Karl? The new products are his baby – I can't see him telling a Chinese sub-contractor all his secrets! No, it's too risky, it could very quickly damage our reputation. And apart from anything else, we've already invested a lot in production here in Austria.

B: Hm. I'm not sure that would count for much. You going to eat that dessert?

G: Be my guest, I'm supposed to be on a diet.

B: Waste not, want not, I always say. Mm! So, have you heard the latest rumours about Eva and Karl?

G: What do you mean?

B: Well, you know, their marriage has been on the rocks for a while now, even though Franz is keen to keep them together. I've heard that Eva wants to relocate the new products to North Africa. OK, she'd have to find premises, but apparently you can build a factory really cheaply over there – and of course the salaries are far lower than they are here!

G: Well, it might cut costs – but the logistics would be complicated, and the unions would go ballistic! But what's it got to do with Karl and Eva's marriage?

B: Can't you see? Eva doesn't just want to relocate *production* to North Africa – she wants to relocate Karl!

G: Hm!

Simulation

6 Divide the class into four groups to prepare what they are going to say at the meeting. Pre-teach *irrespective of* (despite a particular fact, situation or quality), *status quo* (the present situation, or the way that things usually are) and *to jeopardize* (to risk damaging or destroying something important).

7 The students regroup to hold their meetings. Allow at least 15 minutes for the meeting. This is a good opportunity to discreetly monitor and make notes of any language errors for remedial work in later classes. Ensure that *A.O.B.* (any other business) is understood by all.

4 | Managing conflict

Who is in the conflict?

There are various types of conflict:

Conflict between colleagues. There may be a clash of personalities, strong differences of opinion over work, or overspill from personal issues outside work.

Conflict within teams. Conflict arises when there is rivalry between colleagues, when there are disagreements over a team's goals, or when there is resentment that someone is not doing enough work.

Conflict between an employee and his / her manager. The employee may feel that his / her boss is too authoritarian or too weak, or that the boss favours other work colleagues when assigning tasks.

What are the signs of conflict?

Some signs of conflict are very visible. For example, a heated exchange between colleagues or a meeting that develops into an argument. However, not all forms of conflict are so obvious. Some individuals hide their feelings as a way of coping with a problem, while a team might react to pressure by cutting itself off from the rest of the organization. Symptoms of conflict include:

Motivation drops – fewer people volunteer to take on new tasks and there is little employee input at team meetings or briefings.

Behaviour changes – people start to make derogatory remarks towards each other and there are fewer social events organized.

Productivity falls – there will be more time spent on queries and complaints from customers if staff are not cooperating with each other.

Absence increases – unhappiness may lead to depression or stress.

What is causing the conflict?

Some of the issues that can cause conflict at work include:

poor management	poor communication
unfair treatment	poor work environment
unclear job roles	increased workload
inadequate training	lack of equal opportunities
a clash of personalities	bullying and harassment

How do you manage conflict?

1 Do not avoid the conflict, hoping it will go away. It won't.
2 Do not meet separately with people in conflict. If you allow each individual to tell their story to you, you risk polarizing their positions. You put yourself in the position of judge and jury.
3 Do not believe the only people who are affected by the conflict are the participants. Everyone in your office is affected by the stress.
4 Meet with the individuals together. Let each briefly summarize their point of view, without interruption. There can then be a short discussion so that all parties are clear about the disagreement. Intervene if either employee attacks the other employee. This is not acceptable.
5 Ask each participant to describe specific actions they'd like the other party to take so that the conflict can be resolved, e.g. 'I would like to have responsibility for all of the business development and follow-up with that client. The way the work is divided now means that Andy and I never know what the other person is doing.'
6 Ask all participants to commit to making the changes that are necessary. Let them know that you will not choose sides, and that it is impossible for a person external to the conflict to know the truth of the matter.

Mediating a conflict is challenging, but it is a part of the job of a manager.

Useful websites

http://www.cipd.co.uk/guides
http://www.innovativeteambuilding.co.uk/pages/articles/conflicts.htm
The first site above has a range of downloadable guides on many HR-related issues. Search the site for the guide called 'Managing conflict at work: a guide for line managers'.

4.1 About business

Management style

In this module, students read about various management styles, listen to a professor presenting different models for management and discuss which kind of manager they are or would be.

Internet research

An Internet search for the keywords *management style questionnaire / quiz* will return lots of free online quizzes on the topic of management styles. Students can work in small groups and try the same or different quizzes, then compare results. This would work equally well as a prelude or a follow-up to this lesson.

Discussion

1 A lot of good vocabulary should come out of this discussion, as students brainstorm personal qualities and rank them in order of importance. Most words students come up with will probably be adjectives, so help to turn these into nouns and pay close attention to pronunciation. Elicit spellings and put them on the board.

Reading

2 Be ready to explain *abrasive* (behaving in a way that seems rude to other people, because you say what you think even if it is not nice) and the cultural reference *Dr Jekylls and Mr Hydes* (people with split personalities). Ask students to discuss questions 1–3 in pairs, then conduct open-class discussion. Next, ask students to compare their own ideas to those mentioned in the article.

SUGGESTED ANSWERS:

1 Most bosses think they do a pretty good job of keeping their subordinates happy.
  Many bosses who are brusque have genuine feelings for their subordinates, so they are surprised when they learn that others see them as cold and insensitive.
  Few managers, even those with hard-driving styles, see themselves as abrasive.
2 Not usually: 'Career advisers say that unless you modify your behavior, it is unlikely that top management will continue to reward you.'
3 Field marshals are control freaks who tend to intimidate others.
  Street fighters, like Mr Bibeault, are extremely competitive, with every interaction producing a clear winner and loser. They typically insist on having the last word and always think they are right.
  Rebels like being the exception to the rule.
  Dr Jekylls and Mr Hydes have good interpersonal skills in one part of an organization, but have trouble with everyone else.

3 Other lexis you may like to clarify for your students includes: *subordinates, demeanor, brusque* /bruːsk/, *bottom line, flaws* /flɔːz/, *a Napoleon, to bark out, to belittle, traits* /treɪts/ and *peers*.

ANSWERS

1 To try to make something seem less unpleasant than it is.
2 Mr Bibeault's directness and no-nonsense style suited David Corcoran in general, but there were sometimes difficulties.
3 They only see what they believe to be the essentials, to the exclusion of anything else.
4 Someone who wants to control every aspect of a situation and will not allow other people to share in making decisions.
5 Being constantly ready to fight to get what you want produces levels of stress which can often cause a heart attack.
6 Sometimes managers can be loved by their subordinates but have trouble with their bosses.

Listening

4 🔊 1.50 You may like to pre-teach or elicit the meaning of: *cajole* /kəˈdʒəʊl/, *cutting edge, to plot a position, perish, autocratic, impoverished, recruit* (n.) /rɪˈkruːt/, *quadrants*, and *procrastinate*. Students listen first time for gist and match the charts with the people who devised them.

ANSWERS:

1 c   2 a   3 e   4 b   5 d

5 Play the recording again. Students label the charts and compare their answers in pairs. Take whole-class feedback.

ANSWERS

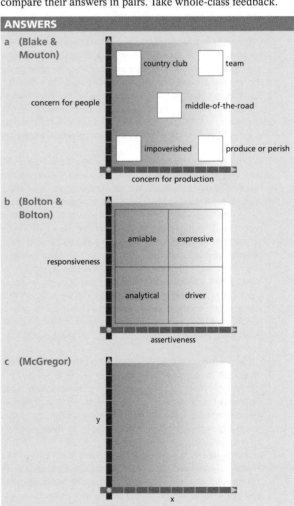

d (Kilmann)

e (Hersey &
Blanchard)

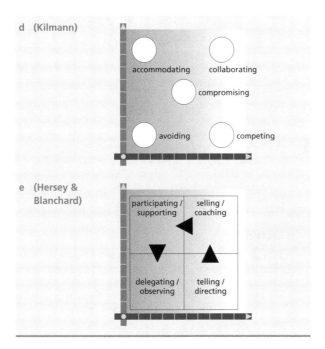

RECORDING SCRIPT

🔊 1.50

As you are probably aware, there are a great many models for describing management style and conflict management, but they are all based, more or less, on McGregor's theory x and theory y. Like the horizontal and vertical axes on a graph, they confront opposing views of human motivation. The theory x manager assumes that people are lazy; they need to be cajoled, threatened or even punished in order to get the work done. The theory y manager, on the other hand, believes that workers can be creative, self-motivated, and autonomous; the role of the theory y manager is to help people obtain satisfaction from a job well done. Type x and type y workplaces are sometimes referred to as 'hard' and 'soft'.

Building on McGregor's work in the early 1960s, Robert Blake and Jane Mouton devised a managerial chart which defines five leadership styles, as illustrated by the five squares on the chart. Although it's hardly cutting-edge, this model is still considered to be very useful today, and forms the basis of several more recent conflict style inventories. This time the x axis is expressed as 'concern for production', and the y axis as 'concern for people'. Each axis has a scale of nine points, from low to high. The results of a questionnaire on attitudes and opinions are used to plot a manager's position on the grid. For example, a person who scores 'nine, one' – that's to say nine on the x axis and one on the y axis, is defined as having a 'produce or perish' style. This type of manager is obsessed with achieving goals whatever the human cost, and may seem autocratic and abrasive.

Other positions on the grid are the 'country club' style, with a 'one, nine' score, where the manager values the security and comfort of employees at the expense of productivity; and the 'impoverished' style with a 'one, one' score, where managers are interested in neither production nor people, but only in doing the minimum necessary to hang onto their jobs for as long as possible.

In the middle of the grid, a score of 'five, five' represents the 'middle-of-the-road' style. This type of manager tries to find a compromise where they can keep people reasonably happy and at the same time achieve reasonable results. Finally, a score of 'nine, nine' is called the 'team' style: by encouraging teamwork and using coaching skills, managers provide high job satisfaction and meet production targets.

Now then, more recently, Hersey and Blanchard observed that, as an employee gains experience and skills, a manager needs to change styles and adapt to the employee's development stage,

hence the arrows on the chart. They redefined 'nine, one' as 'telling' or 'directing'. This would be an appropriate style, for example, to manage a new recruit, who needs to be told exactly what to do, and to be carefully directed. 'Nine, nine' becomes 'selling' or 'coaching'; 'one, nine' is now 'participating' or 'supporting'. Finally, very experienced and autonomous members of staff who can take on complete projects with very little help from their manager will react best to a 'delegating' or 'observing' style of management.

All right, let's move on now to conflict management. Take a look at another model which was devised by Robert and Dorothy Bolton. Here the x axis measures assertiveness, and the y axis shows responsiveness. Assertive people are considered to be forceful and demanding, whereas responsiveness is a measure of how much awareness of emotions and feelings a person shows. As you can see, the grid is divided into four quadrants: going anti-clockwise from 'nine, one' to 'one, one', they are: the 'drivers', who are very interested in getting what they want, and not very interested in how anyone else feels about it; the 'expressives', who are prepared to be assertive about telling people how they feel; the 'amiables', who are prepared to be unassertive in order to keep everyone happy; and finally, the 'analyticals', who are quiet, shy and let everyone else get what they want.

Now, the last model I want to mention briefly is a conflict management model by Thomas Kilmann. This considers different behaviours in situations of conflict. Starting with the circle at 'nine, one,' and going anti-clockwise as before, first we have 'competing', the behaviour of someone who is prepared to do whatever is needed to win. Then we have 'collaborating', where a person will work hard to try to find a solution which satisfies everyone. Next we come to 'accommodating'; this is where someone will prefer to sacrifice their own needs or goals in order to satisfy someone else. The circle in the bottom left corner represents 'avoiding' – as the name suggests, this describes simply avoiding dealing with the problem by procrastinating or side-stepping; and finally, in the middle of the grid, we have 'compromising', where a person will look for concessions which will lead to an acceptable deal.

OK. I'm sorry if I've covered quite a lot of ground rather quickly today – are there any questions?

Discussion

6 Students discuss in small groups. Then open up the discussion to the whole class. Ensure you elicit or pre-teach the meaning and pronunciation of *phony* /ˈfəʊni/ and *trainee* /ˌtreɪˈniː/.

4.2 Grammar

Conjunctions

This module gives practice in using 'linkers' in gapped sentences. Students select the best linkers to use, in the context of a conversation. They then construct a longer text about a conflict situation at work by employing these cohesive devices. The module also includes a follow-up discussion and letter-writing activities.

Did you know?

Remind students that conjunctions join two parts of a sentence, coordinators join clauses of the same quality and type and subordinators join clauses which add supporting detail to the main clause. You may like to add that other parts of speech (e.g. *after* and other prepositions of time) may act as conjunctions in a sentence.

Subordinators and coordinators

1 Before students begin the gap-fill, elicit or pre-teach the meaning of *to take the initiative* /ɪˈnɪʃətɪv/, (to start something independently), and *to kill two birds with one stone* (to achieve two results with a single action). You could also elicit the meanings of some of the linkers and put them on the board before they begin: *unless* (only if not), *provided* (only if), *whereas* /weərˈæz/ (used for comparing two things but showing that there is an important difference between them), *supposing* (if, imagine) and *while* (when/but/though, depending on context). Tell students to be careful with *in case* as it only means to take precautionary action in English, it cannot also mean *in the event of* as in many other European languages. Although different answers may fit in each gap, there is only one set of answers possible so that every one is correct.

ANSWERS:

1 Though	2 and	3 while	4 unless	5 provided
6 As	7 whereas, as if	8 but	9 so	10 in case	11 or
12 Supposing

Expressing meanings through subordinators

2 Elicit or pre-teach the meaning of the following lexis before the students begin the activity: *to be on someone's case* (idiom, to criticize someone all the time), *to turn the tables on someone* (idiom, to succeed in gaining an advantage over someone who until now had an advantage over you), *to be on solid ground* (idiom, to be confident that something is likely to be correct or accepted) and *to track someone down* (phrasal verb, to locate someone). Students compare in pairs before whole-class feedback. You may like to ask students to practise the conversation in pairs, paying particular attention to stress and intonation (provide a model first with a strong student). When doing this, they should use the first of their choices in each sentence.

ANSWERS:

1 so that, in order that   2 since, because
3 once, as soon as   4 provided, as long as
5 as though, as if   6 whereas, while
7 as soon as, the minute   8 Whenever, When
9 because, since   10 Just as, Like

3 Vocabulary that you might like to clarify before students begin includes: *a brief* (official instructions to do a job, saying how it should be done) *to organically grow* (to increase in a natural and continuous process), *prohibitively expensive* (collocation, too much to afford), *to find common ground* (to find shared interests) and *to come to a head* (to reach a crisis point). Depending on your class size and how much time you have available, students could be organized in different ways to accomplish this task. They could work on a section each in pairs before coming together to read out their suggestions to build up the complete text, or they could divide up the sections between them in small groups.

SUGGESTED ANSWERS:

Section 1
Two employees, Lee and Jasmine, are chosen to work on a special project and they are given their brief: two weeks to come up with a business plan for their new target market. Although they are from different departments and do not know each other, they are expected to quickly work together.
Section 2
When the boss is in the room they seem to get on well, but / although in private they appear suspicious of each other. While / Whereas / Although Jasmine is an outgoing person, Lee seems to be a rather private person. Jasmine's key idea is to focus on a persuasive 'hearts and minds' strategy to organically grow sales, and / but / while / whereas Lee's plan involves an 'in your face' TV-led campaign aimed at growing sales fast, which Jasmine argues would be prohibitively expensive and too unsubtle.
Section 3
Halfway through the first week, communication has apparently broken down as / because / since the two employees cannot find any common ground to move forward. Jasmine insists on discussing their differences, while / whereas / although / but Lee is more concerned with the deadline. He wants to quickly get on with the task itself, so they agree to work independently on separate plans.
Section 4
Things come to a head in the middle of the second week when / as Jasmine argues that Lee is being too secretive and not sharing his ideas, but Lee responds by accusing Jasmine of trying to control him all the time.
Section 5
Lee, meanwhile, argues that Jasmine's plans will not work because to build brand recognition organically through local initiatives would take too long, so her plans probably wouldn't work. Eventually Lee persuades Jasmine to go with his plan.
Section 6
When / As the day of the deadline comes Lee realizes their plan is actually quite weak. The television network is too fragmented and the advertisements would not easily reach the target consumers, but / although it is too late to change anything.
Section 7
The marketing director arrives and when she takes one look at the plan she realizes it is nowhere near ready. She blames both participants.
Section 8
As soon as / Once / When / The minute the marketing director leaves the room, the participants launch into a heated argument over who is to blame. The marketing director returns to collect her papers and witnesses the employees shouting at each other, so she gives them each a written warning.

Discussion

4 Students discuss in small groups responsibility for the conflict, how it could have been avoided and how best it might be resolved. Take whole-class feedback.

Writing

5 This would work well as a follow-up homework exercise. Remind students of letter-writing conventions (perhaps providing them with a model) and explain they must write in character, as either Lee or Jasmine.

Internet research

Ask students to work in pairs or threes and to brainstorm what they think are the five most common causes of communication breakdown at work. Elicit ideas from the class. Next, ask students to search for the keywords *causes of communication breakdown at work*. Ask students to read three or four sites on the topic and to list the five most commonly cited causes. Once students have done this, ask them to work in small groups to compare their findings.

4.3 Vocabulary

Managing conflict

This module provides vocabulary development on the topic of conflict in the workplace, with opportunities for controlled and freer practice.

Internet research

As the box suggests, an Internet search for *workplace harassment* returns lots of pages on this topic. Divide your class into three groups. Give each group one sub-topic: *What does / does not constitute harassment? How can companies eliminate harassment / bullying? What should you do if you are harassed / bullied?* Then mix up the students and get them to pool their findings.

Discussion

1 For this task students have to unscramble five anagrams of words that collocate with *conflict*. The scrambled words can be written on the board and the activity can be done as a race in pairs, with points given for the pair to get each solution first.

Once the anagrams are solved, get students to rank the collocations from most to least desirable. This can be done as a pyramid discussion: first they rank the collocations in pairs, then they form groups of four with another pair and mutually decide a new ranking, and so on until finally you have full-class agreement on the best ranking.

ANSWERS:

resolve – the most constructive, suggesting that solutions are found which satisfy everyone

defuse – desirable, but less so than resolving as defusing may not result in a long-term solution

avoid – stifling conflict may sometimes be a worse option than allowing it to run its course

spark – not usually very desirable, but sometimes conflict is necessary and productive

escalate – least desirable; if conflict is inevitable, escalating it is unconstructive

Listening

2 1.51–1.58 Before looking through the list of eight problems, ask students to listen to the eight extracts and to note down in their own words what the problem is in each case. Ask students to compare their notes in pairs and then elicit ideas and put them on the board. This will give you a good indication of how much they have understood.

You may need to elicit / pre-teach *to get someone's back up* (to annoy someone), *to get off on the wrong foot with someone* (to immediately establish a good relationship with someone when you first meet them or first start working for them) and *to fly off the handle* (to lose one's temper, to become angry).

Ask the class to read through the eight statements and to answer as much as they can from memory. Then play the recording through a second time for students to check and add to their answers.

ANSWERS:

a buyer is not going to put up with a supplier's mistakes: 5
a management trainer got someone's back up: 8
an intern got off on the wrong foot with his supervisor: 6
an assistant is fed up with her boss: 3
an employee who gets on her manager's nerves: 4
someone flew off the handle with a customer: 2
someone is fed up with an auditor: 7
two colleagues don't get on: 1

3 Students will probably have noticed the idiomatic expressions while doing the previous listening task, so they should not have much difficulty completing the task from memory. Give the class a few minutes to fill in the gaps, then get them to confer in pairs. Students may want to use dictionaries at this stage and this is at your discretion whether or not to allow this.

To check the answers, play the extracts again. Ask students if they can work out the meaning of each idiom from the context. Use prompt questions, e.g. *Why did Pavel go ballistic?*

Be prepared to provide accurate definitions yourself though. You may need to explain *to be at the end of one's tether* (to feel very upset because you are no longer able to deal with a difficult situation), *to rub someone up the wrong way* (to do or say things that annoy someone), *to be blinkered* (to have opinions that are very limited, conservative and often old-fashioned), *to be like chalk and cheese* (to be completely different) and *the last straw* (the last in a series of irritations or annoyances).

ANSWERS:

1 ballistic – Pavel
2 tether – Ed
3 way – Dave
4 straw – Jo
5 fussy – Nisha
6 voice – Dave
7 word – Katrina
8 cheese – Lin and Nisha
9 blinkered – Mr Jarlberg
10 sink – Jo

EXTENSION ACTIVITY

Personalization. Form some personalized questions incorporating the new idioms and collocations (or get your students to form the questions), e.g.
Have you ever had to resolve a conflict? Tell me about it.
Have you ever got off on the wrong foot with someone? When? With whom?
Do you know anyone who likes the sound of their own voice? Who?
You could also ask students to test each other in pairs using meanings and definitions, e.g.
A: *Which expression means to lose one's temper?*
B: *Go ballistic.*
Finally, get students to discuss the questions in the Student's Book.

RECORDING SCRIPT

 1.51–1.58

1
Ed: Things are a bit tense between Lin and Nisha, aren't they?
Jo: Yeah – I heard them having words again this morning.
Ed: They should never have been put in the same office, they're like chalk and cheese, those two.
Jo: Hm. They certainly don't seem to have much in common.

2
Dave: D'you hear about Pavel?
Jo: No, what?
Dave: Apparently he's in trouble again; he lost it with a customer.
Jo: Really?
Dave: Yeah, he'd just spent all morning installing a milling machine for Custom Labs and then the production manager told him it was in the wrong place – he went ballistic!
Jo: I'm not surprised – they're a right pain at that company!

3
Lin: I've had it up to here with Mr Jarlberg!
Dave: Why, what's he done?
Lin: Well, I've been expecting an important call all morning and he wouldn't let me take my mobile into our meeting.
Dave: Well you know how obsessive he is about going by the book.
Lin: I know – he's so blinkered!

4
Ed: Nisha's driving Dave up the wall, you know. She's so fussy.
Jo: Poor Dave – I certainly wouldn't like to be her manager!
Ed: Me neither – that sort of misplaced perfectionism really gets my goat!
Jo: Yeah – how long d'you think it'll be before Dave hits the roof?

5
Dave: Oh, for heaven's sake! Jo, look at this!
Jo: What now?
Dave: Tintex have got our order wrong again, and accounts have already paid the invoice! Those people get away with murder!
Jo: Right – that's the last straw! Next time we'll take our business elsewhere!

6
Lin: Has Dave told you about that student he's got shadowing him?
Ed: No, why?
Lin: Well, he's really rubbed Dave up the wrong way already! Keeps interrupting him – and you know how Dave loves the sound of his own voice!
Ed: Yeah right, I'm amazed the kid can get a word in!

7
Jo: Hey, Ed!
Ed: Yeah?
Jo: How's the inspection going with that bloke from head office?
Ed: Oh don't ask! He just doesn't listen. I'm at the end of my tether!
Jo: Not interested in any of your new ideas then?
Ed: No. He's got his own agenda and doesn't want to know about anything else.

8
Dave: So, Jo, what did you think of the strategic thinking session with Katrina?
Jo: It was OK but she wasn't prepared to take on other people's opinions. It was supposed to be a workshop not a lecture.
Dave: Really?
Jo: Yeah. She always has to have the last word. People like that really make me sink!

4 Do this task with the Student's Books closed. Write the five conflict strategies on the board and clarify the meanings. You will need to pay careful attention to the shades of meaning between: *collaborating* (working together), *compromising* (solving a problem or ending an argument by accepting that you cannot have everything that you want), *accommodating* (changing your attitudes and behaviour in order to deal with a new situation).

Elicit / pre-teach the following: *manoeuvre* (action or movement), *lay your cards on the table* (to tell people exactly what you are thinking and what you are intending to do), *to mull something over* (to think carefully about something over a period of time) and *to not take something lying down* (to show that you will not accept unfair treatment by complaining about it or trying to change it).

Drill the words for pronunciation, paying particular attention to stress.

Read each piece of advice out to the class and get students in pairs to identify which strategy the advice refers to. Elicit suggestions. Once you have read out each piece of advice, give students a few moments to read through the exercise and to check and amend their answers.

After students have conferred in pairs, take whole-class feedback and go through the answers with the class.

ANSWERS:

a 1   b 5   c 4   d 3   e 2   f 3   g 5   h 2   i 4   j 1

Collocations

5 Students can work on this cloze exercise individually by referring back to the previous exercise. Give them time to briefly check in pairs and then check through the answers with the class.

Now ask students to work in pairs to discuss the meaning of each collocation from the contexts. Where possible, provide extra information by drawing students' attention to the idiomatic meanings of the expressions, e.g.

To blow over: This idiom is related to the weather. We talk about storms blowing over.

ANSWERS:

1 blow   2 cards   3 air   4 work   5 towel   6 away
7 stand   8 manoeuvre   9 through   10 inevitable
11 way

Roleplay

6 Elicit / provide some expressions for advice giving, e.g.
If I were you I'd + infinitive ...
You could try + verb + ing ...
How about + verb + ing ...?
It might be an idea to +infinitive ...
Put these expressions on the board. Now allocate one of each of the eight problems to each student in the class (for classes of more than eight students, either prepare a few additional problems, or allocate a problem to pairs of students). Ask each student to memorize his / her problem (they can note it down on paper if they prefer). Now explain to the class that they should mingle and ask their classmates for advice. The objective is to get a piece of advice from every member of the class. Once students have mingled, ask them to return to their seats. Now ask them to decide which piece of advice is the best. Take whole-class feedback and get students to tell the class what advice they were given and which advice they think is the best.

Strong language

7 If you feel it is appropriate, set up a pre-reading discussion on the topic of swearing by providing some lead-in questions on the topic, e.g.
Do you ever swear?
In which situations do you sometimes swear?
Do you know anyone who swears?
What kind of things do they say?
Can you give some examples of swear words in your language?
How is swearing treated on television?

Note: Your decision to open this topic up for discussion will depend on the make-up (i.e. the cultural, demographic and gender mix) of your class and you may therefore decide to omit this activity. Explain the meaning of *Bleeping Word* in the title of the article (a reference to the 'bleep' sound that is dubbed over swearwords on TV). Ask students to read through the text and to underline or highlight the references to swearing. Give students a few moments to check in pairs before going through the answers.

ANSWERS:

profanity, swearing like a trooper, cursing, swear, profane language, swearing, bad language, profanity, four-letter words, colourful language, expletives, strong language, indecent, obscene, innocuous, vulgar, foul language, foulest mouths

Note: *innocuous* means *harmless* and is not directly related to swearing.

8 Pre-teach *to give as good as you get* (to fight back with equal strength to the attack). Get students to complete the statements by referring back to the words they highlighted in the previous exercise. Check through the answers.

ANSWERS:

1 Swearing, trooper
2 cursing, profanity
3 colourful, innocuous
4 four-letter, expletives
5 vulgar, obscene
6 foul

Discussion

9 Ask students to work alone to think about whether they agree of disagree with the statements. Ask them to note the reasons for their answers and any example situations they can think of. Put students into groups of three to discuss their views.

4.4 Management skills
Assertiveness

This module looks at strategies for improving one's assertiveness in the workplace and provides opportunities for students to practise expressing themselves assertively in English.

Internet research

In addition to the activity suggested, The World Business Culture website has lots of useful information on cultural differences around the world. Each country has an entry for 'communication styles' in which students can find information about body language and ways of speaking. Give each student a country or two to investigate and to present to the class.

Discussion

1 Check students understand the meaning of *assertive*. Extend this by eliciting the verb form (*assert*) and noun form (*assertiveness*).
Dictate the following for students to write down: *Your assertive rights in the workplace include the right to ...* Elicit the phrase and put it on the board. Ask students to work in pairs to write down as many continuations of this sentence as they can. Demonstrate with a model phrase of your own. Set a time limit for this and monitor. Then elicit suggestions from the pairs and write them on the board (or ask the class to dictate while a student writes them up). Next, ask students to discuss the suggestions and to say whether they agree or not and why.
Get students to read through the rights shown in the illustration and to check how many are similar to those they have already suggested. Now ask students to discuss the following questions in pairs:
Why is each of these rights important?
Could any of these rights cause problems for staff or managers?
Throw the discussion open to the class.
Read each of the four extracts out loud to the class and after each one, ask students to identify which rights are being contravened. This will give you an opportunity to inject some emotion and intonation into the spoken quotations and to provide useful paralinguistic clues.

SUGGESTED ANSWERS:

1 The right to hold your own opinions, and the right to a fair hearing for those opinions.
2 The right to need and want things that may differ from other peoples' needs and wants, and the right to refuse a request without feeling guilty or selfish.
3 The right to ask (not demand) that others respond to your needs and wants, and the right to have feelings and to express them assertively if you want to.
4 The right to be wrong sometimes, and the right to have others respect your rights.

2 A fun angle on this activity is to ask students to work in pairs and to enact the dialogue extracts together. Either put the responses on an OHP / IWB or get students to read them from the page. Elicit and model appropriate intonation for each response, e.g.

A: *When I want your opinion, I'll ask for it!* (short and snappy)

B: *Sorry, I didn't mean to interrupt you.* (apologetic, appeasing)

B: *I think exchanging views will help us move forward.* (calm, rational)

B: *You're so opinionated, why don't you ever listen to me?* (fighting back, angry).

Drill each sentence with the class, focusing particularly on intonation, pitch and stress. Give students plenty of time to practise in pairs, ensuring students have a chance to take both roles. Monitor and check pronunciation. Next, get students to decide which response they would choose and why. Open this up to a full-class discussion.

3 The discussion stimulated by the previous activity should lead easily into the discussion questions presented here. For question 2, you could guide students by asking them to consider posture, eye contact, gesture and voice. Students discuss the questions in pairs or small groups. Open this up to a full-class discussion.

ANSWERS:

1 a) answers = non-assertive/passive
   b) answers = assertive
   c) answers = aggressive
2 suggested answers:
   non-assertive / passive – no eye contact, nervousness, hunching, small gestures, soft voice
   assertive – direct eye contact, good posture, confident gestures, clear voice
   aggressive – intense eye contact, tense posture, intimidating gestures, loud voice
3 suggested answers:
   Aggression is likely to lead to threatening, verbal abuse and even violence.
   Non-assertiveness is likely to lead to withdrawal, accepting abuse and even depression.
4 Student's own answers

Listening

4 💿 1.59–1.62 Be prepared to explain or pre-teach *to have a bone to pick with someone* (to have a dispute / disagreement to settle).

The first time you play the extract, ask students to make notes about what the problem is and how Linda deals with it. Get students to compare in pairs and elicit their answers. Then ask students to read through the six techniques provided and ask them to tick the boxes based on what they recall from the recording. Play the extracts again to check, pausing after each one to allow students to check in pairs.

ANSWERS:

1 Marc is upset and aggressive because his holiday dates have been changed.
   Linda uses techniques 1, 2 and 4.
2 Linda has not been given the raise she was promised: Jerry is non-assertive and evasive.
   Linda uses techniques 3, 5 and 6.
3 Carmen is upset and aggressive because Linda has switched the TV off.
   Linda resists the temptation to answer aggression with aggression, and uses techniques 1, 4 and 5.
4 Moritz invites Linda to spend the weekend on his Dad's boat. Linda doesn't want to hurt his feelings.
   Linda uses techniques 2 and 3.

5 Ask students to try this exercise from memory, before playing the extracts a third time. As an extension activity, ask students in pairs to generate mini-dialogues using the phrases, e.g.

A: *Can I get back to you later on?*
B: *Well, I'd rather discuss it now.*

ANSWERS:

1   back to you later on?
2   that you feel upset,
3   something out this afternoon?
4   to ask you this,
5   maybe not the best time,
6   see it is like this
7   your own agenda,
8   an acceptable compromise
9   to think it over
10 the offer, but no thanks.

6 Write the five categories as five headings on the board. Ask students to copy them down. Dictate all the phrases from the table, as well as the previous exercise, in random order and ask students to write them under headings as you do so. Allow students to confer in pairs before eliciting the phrases and putting them on the board. Once the phrases are on the board, drill for pronunciation and intonation.

ANSWERS:

asking for time: 1, 9
acknowledging and being heard: 2, 5, 7
offering compromise: 3, 8
expressing feelings: 4, 6
saying no: 10

RECORDING SCRIPT

 1.59–1.62

1

Marc: Linda, I've got a bone to pick with you about my holiday dates. You promised I could have three weeks in June, but now I'm down to cover for Haley ...

Linda: Sorry Marc, can I get back to you later on? I'm just about to go into a conf-call.

M: But you don't understand, I've already booked my flights and everything! It's not good enough!

L: Marc, I understand that you feel upset, but I'd much rather take time to talk this through properly. Can we work something out this afternoon? What time would suit you best?

2

Linda: There was one other thing, Jerry.

Jerry: Yes?

L: Well, I hesitate to ask you this, but I was due for a raise after my last appraisal, and that was nearly six months ago.

Jerry: Oh, well, I don't know ... I'd have to find out – Finance are trying to keep costs down, you know.

L: Well I realize that this is maybe not the best time, but it was validated in the appraisal report.

Jerry: Yes, but it's not really my decision, you see. Um, I'll look into it, but I can't promise anything. OK?

L: Not really, Jerry. The way I see it is like this: I met my objectives, so it's only fair the bank should respect its commitments.

3

Carmen: Did you switch the damn TV off again, Linda?

Linda: Yes, Carmen, I did. I'm writing an important proposal here, and I need to concentrate.

C: Why can't you go someplace else?! I'm waiting for the market news.

L: Why can't _you_ ...

C: What was that?

L: Carmen, I appreciate that you have your own agenda, but there are eight of us in this office, and I feel strongly that we should respect each other's space. Now, what would be an acceptable compromise? Can we turn the sound off and just leave the picture until the market news comes on?

C: All right, I suppose so.

4

Moritz: Hi Linda!

Linda: Oh, hi.

M: So; what do you think about my idea?

L: Sorry Moritz, which idea would that be?

M: Spending a weekend on my Dad's boat, of course!

L: Oh, right. Well, it's a nice idea, but, erm, I need some time to think it over.

M: Come on, Linda, it'll be great! I know some really nice places to go – just the two of us!

L: Erm, look, Moritz: I appreciate the offer, but no thanks.

M: But you don't ...

L: Moritz: it's really sweet of you, but no.

M: Really?

L: Really.

M: Oh.

Speaking

7 In pairs, get students to decide on some suitable reformulations of the dialogues. Monitor and provide input, using the suggested answers below. As extra practice, get students to practise the dialogues orally in pairs.

A: Can we talk? I realize that this may not be the best time, but I didn't get an answer about taking Wednesdays off.

B: I'd love to talk about this later, but right now I'm in a bit of a hurry. Can I get back to you later on?

A: I think we should decide now; I know you're busy, but I feel it can't wait.

B: I understand that you feel strongly about this, but I need to deal with my customer's problem first.

A: OK, I understand the customer is your priority, so at what time can we meet to discuss this?

B: Um, let me see. How about 3 o'clock this afternoon?

A: Great. 3 o'clock will be fine. Thank you.

C: I hesitate to ask you this, but could you possibly lend me €50 until next week?

D: I'm sorry, but I don't have any spare cash.

C: Didn't you say you were going to buy a pair of shoes? Could it wait a few days?

D: Look, I'm sure you have a good reason, but this isn't the first time. To be perfectly honest, I just feel I'm being taken advantage of.

C: Oh dear, I didn't realize you felt this way about it. I'm sorry. I just thought that as you'd lent me money before, you wouldn't mind.

D: That's OK. I don't mind from time to time, but this month I really can't afford it, I'm sorry.

C: I understand. Not to worry and thanks anyway.

E: I'm surprised to see you wearing jeans to work again.

F: I realize that jeans are not allowed, but these are actually very high-quality designer trousers by Jean-Paul Gaultier.

E: I understand that they're very fashionable and very expensive, but I'm not allowed to make exceptions to company rules, do you see what I mean?

F: I appreciate you're just doing your job, but it seems a bit unfair to me. I only speak to customers on the phone, so they can't see what I'm wearing.

E: Yes, I know. But if I agree to let you wear jeans, then I'll have to make exceptions for other members of staff as well. And I really don't have the authority to change company rules.

F: Oh, I see what you mean. Do you think it would be possible to raise this at your next management meeting, to see if the rules can be changed at all?

E: OK, I'll put it on the next agenda.

Roleplay

8 Give students plenty of time to read their role cards and the situations. Get them to highlight the key information and to make notes on the points they want to make and what, if any, compromises / concessions they are prepared to accept. Also suggest students make a note of key phrases to use from the preceding tasks. Monitor the roleplays and make notes for post-correction.

4.5 Writing

Giving bad news

This module deals with the issue of giving bad news in writing. Advice for doing so is reviewed and discussed, models are provided and there is an exercise focusing on register. Students draft a short memo or email, then engage in a longer piece of writing which conveys information the recipient will not be pleased to receive.

Discussion

1 In pairs, students discuss which pieces of advice would appear to be most appropriate to each of the situations described. A number of the pieces of advice are contradictory (e.g. *make small talk* versus *get straight to the point*) and there are no right or wrong answers here, only opinions. In number 4, students may like to consider whether they would handle the situation differently depending on whether the news about the loss of the tender has to be conveyed to one's superior or to the team. You may like to personalize the discussion by asking about the ways bad news has been delivered to members of the class, although this would need to be handled sensitively. Remind the class that *advice* is an uncountable noun and that *tip* is the informal way of saying *a useful suggestion*. Other lexis to check includes *scenario* /sə'nɑːriəʊ/ (a situation that could possibly happen), *lucrative* /'luːkrətɪv/ (profitable), *tender* (a formal written offer to provide goods or services at a particular price), *succinct* (expressed in a very short but clear way) and *to couch* (to express in a particular way).

2 Students can be encouraged to add to the list with ideas of their own, but do not worry if they are not very forthcoming because this is the topic for Internet research in this module.

Analysis

3 Students work individually to match the sentences to the tips above. Elicit the meaning or pre-teach *conceivably* (possibly), *a sticky situation* (colloquial, a difficult or dangerous situation), *salvage* (to succeed in saving something in a situation or action that has been a failure) and *to put something on the back burner* (idiom, to decide not to deal with something until later).

1 approach the issue sensitively and slowly
2 offer some suggestions to overcome the bad news
3 give the background to the situation before stating the bad news
4 convey the bad news in writing; maintain a professional distance
5 lay out the facts clearly and succinctly
6 arrange a meeting to discuss the matter
7 approach the issue sensitively and slowly
8 tell those involved face to face

Reading

4 and **5** Students read the emails and discuss with a partner what the bad news is in each case. They then are to match the emails to the tips in exercise 1 above. Draw students' attention to the formal expression *rest assured* (feel certain about something) and clarify *knock-on effects* (the indirect result of something).

SUGGESTED ANSWERS:
The first email concerns interior design or architectural plans which have met with a bad reception. It uses bullet points, which indicates an attempt to be succinct.
The second sounds ominously like the closure of UK offices, with resulting redundancies. It attempts to give as much background to the decision as possible.
The third is the news that promotion is not going to be offered to the unsuccessful candidate. It couches the bad news in positive terms.

Style

6 You could ask one student to read aloud the informal version of the bad news and another to read the more formal version. Students then work in pairs to match the formal examples to the strategies in the table.

ANSWERS:

Strategies	1	2	3
Use softeners, e.g. *I'm afraid / Unfortunately / Sadly, …*	✓		
Show empathy, e.g. *I realize / I appreciate / I understand that …*			✓
Use the passive to avoid personalization of the issue	✓		
Discuss consequences, e.g. *This'll mean … / As a result / consequence*	✓		
Use inclusive pronouns (*I, we, us*, etc.) to demonstrate involvement, support and / or team attitude	✓	✓	✓
Use less direct language	✓	✓	✓
Give specific feedback		✓	
Offer suggestions	✓		
Focus on future action			✓

Drafting

7 If you have facilities, students could write their emails on computers and email them to you (or each other for replies). Research has shown that using word-processing software makes students much less reluctant to write and less afraid to make mistakes (probably because of the greater ease with which they can delete mistakes). If you have access to a computer room you can discreetly monitor as students write. Alternatively they can email you from their home computers.

Writing

8 It might be helpful to bring in visuals here such as a map of the relevant area in Africa, visuals of meerkats, rhinos, etc. and an image of Carl, to try to bring the context to life for the students. Remind them to include all the key points in the notes. Set the writing for homework, or ask students to write individually as you monitor in class.

Internet research

This might be a good follow-up, or could be done as homework before the class.

4.6 Case study

Olvea Brasil

This module provides an opportunity for students to further develop their language skills by taking the role of a human resources manager dealing with problematic employee-manager relationships.

Internet research

For this task, split your class into groups and give each group a website of tips to read. Get students to gather 8-10 tips. Then back in class put students into small groups to discuss and rank the tips. Finally, get a class vote on the top five tips.

Discussion

1 Get students to brainstorm, in groups of three, what they consider to be the main qualities or characteristics of a good team leader. Elicit ideas and put them on the board. This will probably recycle a lot of vocabulary from the discussion in 4.1, exercise 1. From the characteristics on the board, ask students to select the seven characteristics they would like in their ideal team leader. Then ask them to rank the characteristics in order of importance, from one (the most important) to seven (the least important). Have students compare their rankings with a partner. Elicit suggestions from the class on what they consider to be the most important characteristics.

Now ask students to consider what their ideal team leader would do in the five situations listed. Encourage them to make a few notes next to each point. Then get them to discuss in groups of three what their ideal team leaders would do in each situation. Take whole-class feedback.

Reading

2 You may need to elicit / pre-teach *pensively* (thinking carefully about something, especially something sad or serious), *a tag* (a label), *competition was fierce* (competition was tough) and *to take precedence over* (to be more important or have greater status than someone or something else).
Give students a few minutes to read through the text and to answer the three questions. Get students to compare their answers in pairs before checking through with the class. Note: for question 2 you may need to prompt fuller answers by asking students to state what the 'official' management style is and what the 'real' management style is.
Once the answers have been checked, ask students if they would like to be in Eliana's position. Why? Why not?

ANSWERS:

1 Eliana's 'concerns' are four employees who have been identified by their managers as potential problems.
2 Officially a people-oriented style, but often in reality a results-oriented style.
3 Eliana likes to hear both sides of the story to put the issue into perspective and identify possible concerns with the manager's performance.

3 This exercise is designed to leave plenty of scope for discussion. Draw students' attention to the employee profiles and give them a few minutes to read through. To give students a reading focus, ask them to quickly identify the problem or issue the managers have identified. Elicit feedback. Now ask students to answer questions 1–5 and to check in pairs. Point out that there are few black and white answers, and any position students can defend is acceptable, especially for question 4. Finally, ask students to discuss what the information in the four documents suggests about the employees' relationships with their managers.

SUGGESTED ANSWERS:

1 Wilson (No problems in first year ... Since then he has consistently disregarded procedures ...) and Luigi (just recently he's become colder, not his normal friendly self)
2 Vitor and Susan have no direct communication (people in the department say ... Isabel Correia, my boss, said she asked to speak to her)
3 Natasha (disappointing) Antony (disappointed)
4 Wilson (refuses to follow instructions), perhaps Natasha (phones me several times a day), perhaps Luigi (has become almost secretive about his work), perhaps Antony (she is much more willing than the rest of my department), perhaps Carla (I explained it was not his job to make changes; if changes are needed I will make them.), perhaps Isabel (when I offer to look at the latest test results with him he keeps suggesting I have more important things to do.)
5 Wilson, perhaps Natasha (I am not sure that she possesses the qualities we expect ...)

EXTENSION ACTIVITY

Get students to work in pairs to suggest the questions Eliana might ask the employees when she meets them later in the day to discuss their files. Elicit suggestions and put them on the board. Provide extra input and correction as needed. Now ask students to choose one of the employee files. Get students to conduct the interviews in pairs, one taking the role of Eliana, the other that of their chosen employee. Then get students to change roles. Monitor and note language points for correction.

Listening

4 🔊 1.63–1.66 Students listen to the four extracts and make notes about what the employees say. Guide students to note down what the employee says about their own behaviour and what they say about their managers' behaviour. Students will find it interesting to compare the extracts with their own comments from the previous roleplay. Play the extracts through twice and give students the opportunity to compare their notes in pairs.

SUGGESTED ANSWERS:

1 Wilson accuses Carla of paranoia and autocratic management. Although this style was appropriate for his first few months in the job, it is now clearly counterproductive, and he suggests that other people in the department are as unhappy as he is. He needs to be given more responsibility and autonomy.
2 Susan claims that Vitor is an absentee manager, an 'invisible man' who gives her no support. Her problems are personal, not professional, but she recognizes that she needs help and has tried to obtain it from Vitor's superior. Clearly Susan needs sympathy, help and guidance, which a minimalist manager will not give her.
3 Luigi is frustrated by what he sees as unnecessary supervision from his manager, Isabel, who hopes to get the best out of Luigi by being very participative. She has not understood that with someone as experienced and independent as Luigi, this style is counterproductive. He is an experienced and competent employee who just wants to be allowed to get on with his job.
4 Natasha feels she needs more help and supervision from Antony Middleton. Afraid of conflict, he is reluctant to give Natasha clear instructions or criticism in case she rejects them. She cannot learn to perform well in her job if everything she does is no more than an acceptable compromise.

RECORDING SCRIPT

 1.63–1.66

Wilson Holden

OK, at first I thought, fair enough, I won't make trouble, I'll wait and see how things develop. I mean, it's normal when you're new, you expect to be told what to do. So I kept a low profile, and just did what what I was asked to do. But, you know, I didn't do five years at engineering school just to stand around and wait for orders from some woman who thinks she's God's gift to engineering!

I know the job, I know a lot about injection moulding, I'm ready to take more responsibility, and I think I can improve the way we do things here. But Carla is completely paranoid! She's a total control freak, and she flatly refuses to allow her people to take even the slightest initiative. Frankly, she's a pain in the neck! There are good guys in my team, guys with ideas and potential! But I'll tell you now, they won't stay here long with a boss who won't even contemplate the idea that she might be wrong!

Susan Shipley

I'm glad you set up this meeting – I really need to talk to someone. I can't talk to Vitor, he's never in the office – or if he is, he won't speak to me. I tried to go over his head, to talk to Isabel Correia, but she told me I had to speak to Vitor first. You see, I've been having problems at home; I feel depressed and demotivated, and Vitor just doesn't seem to care. In fact I'm surprised he even noticed there was a problem. He arrives late, leaves early, and sits in his office with the door closed. When there are problems, he never does anything; he just waits for them to go away. Or he passes the buck and leaves someone like you to pick up the pieces. In our department we call him 'the invisible man'.

Luigi Tarantini

When Isabel was appointed Plant Manager, she was new to the company; we did a lot of stuff together so she could get to know the way we work. That was fine, we got on well, we still do. She's a good manager, demanding, yes, but encouraging and understanding too; always very close to her people. And that's the problem; she's just too close. We have a monthly reporting meeting where I update her on everything that's going on, but no, that's not enough; she wants to be in the lab with me every day. That gets on my nerves! I mean, sure, there are some people that need constant contact with their boss – but I've been here for more than twenty years, and things are going fine – at least they would be if she'd let me get on with my work! I don't need someone constantly looking over my shoulder. If I have a problem, I know where to find her, and I know she values what I'm doing. So let's just get on with the job, shall we?

Natasha Gomes

Well, Antony, I mean Mr Middleton, is really nice, you know? I don't want to cause problems, it's just that, well, I don't have very much experience really – it's my first job, and I want to do it well. But when he gives me something to do, he never tells me exactly what he wants. You know, he seems to think I should know what to do. So when I call him and ask him a question, he just says 'what do *you* think?' It's not unkind or anything, it's just like we have to negotiate everything, he can't just say, 'do this' or 'do that'. I just need to know what he wants. When I make mistakes, he doesn't even tell me off – he always looks for something positive first before talking about the problem. Other people in the department are always taking advantage of him – they do whatever they want, because they know he'll always compromise.

Discussion

5 Students work in small groups to discuss the questions, using their notes and other information gathered in the module.

SUGGESTED ANSWERS:

1 Students' own answers
2 Carla Hartmann – Produce or perish, Isabel Correia – Team, Vitor Martins – Impoverished; Antony Middleton – Middle-of-the-road
3 Students' own answers
4 Carla Hartmann – probably needs gentle persuasion and coaching to move towards a more flexible style of management
   Isabel Correia – delicate, as she is the Plant Manager – probably some discreet advice and counselling on moving towards more delegation
   Vitor Martins – probably needs either participation and support, if his impoverished management style is the result of personal problems, or perhaps telling, directing, or even disciplining if it is due to professional incompetence
   Antony Middleton – probably needs coaching or perhaps directing to encourage a more proactive approach and higher standards of performance

Presentation

6 Tell students to work in groups of three to draw up an action plan. If necessary, you could provide help by suggesting they consider moving employees / managers; promotion; counselling; training and disciplinary measures. When students are ready, they present their action plans to the class.

Review 3 and 4 answers

Review 3

(page 56 in the Student's Book)

3 Supply chain

1

1 power
2 supply
3 Difficulties
4 backdrop
5 suppliers
6 reform
7 chains
8 consumers

2

1 It remains unclear which particular countries are affected.
2 The report focuses particularly on coffee retailers that meet the refreshment needs of office workers in cities worldwide.
3 Our aim is to find an inexpensive piece of software which offers practical solutions.
4 The reason (why) so many great team leaders are gathered here today is to celebrate the life and achievements of Santiago Gabrielli.
5 Your key job responsibility involves promoting and achieving high standards of personal and social welfare.
6 Dr Stephen James is a successful and outstanding manager (who was) educated at Harvard.

3

1 choose
2 validate
3 source
4 consider
5 decide

4

1   b
2   a / e
3   d
4   a / e
5   c
6   g
7   h
8   j
9   f
10 i

5

1 The image we are trying to project is one of timeless quality.
2 In order to appear more cutting edge we have recently diversified our product portfolio.
3 The reason we decided to offshore our production facility to the Far East was to cut costs.

6

1c Returns
2d Stales
3a Unsaleables
4f Stockouts
5e Scan-based trading
7b Cradle-to-grave

Review 4

(page 57 in the Student's Book)

4 Managing conflict

1

1 g   5 h
2 d   6 c
3 e   7 b
4 a   8 f

2

1 You need to keep a backup copy in case the original gets mislaid.
2 While some tasks are too difficult, others are weird. / Some tasks are too difficult, while others are weird.
3 Unless you meet the deadline I won't be able to assess your work.
4 Reach for the mic and start speaking as soon as you step up on the podium. / As soon as you step up on the podium reach for the mic and start speaking.
5 I missed the deadline because I didn't actually know about it.
6 You can take Friday off provided you make up the time next week.
7 Although Simone had flu and was run down, she managed to give an excellent presentation.
8 He behaves as if he owns the place. / He thinks he owns the place, and acts as if he does too.

3

1 position   5 compromise
2 guilty   6 understand
3 appreciate   7 love
4 hesitate   8 prefer

4

1 put up with
2 get away with
3 stand up for
4 laying out
5 mull, over
6 face up to
7 talk, through
8 smooth, over

5

1 d   5 g
2 a   6 i
3 b   7 f
4 c   8 h

5 | Strategic marketing

Strategic marketing starts with an internal and external audit of the company. Together with other analyses, this allows the company to develop a strategic plan. Taking each of these areas in turn:

Internal audit

The company looks at its customers and the service and internal focus they receive. It looks at its distribution channel. It benchmarks its business process against competitors. It assesses its competitive position, and any special advantages it has. It checks that its business practices are in line with its mission. It takes into account any company-specific critical factors. All of this leads to a strength / weakness analysis.

External audit

The company analyses its market and its competitors, if necessary conducting new market research to get up-to-date information. It looks at market trends: which areas are growing, which are shrinking, and which areas offer new opportunities in the future. Again, it takes into account any company-specific critical factors. This leads to an opportunities / threats analysis.

Other analyses

Before developing its strategic plan, other analyses will be necessary. Financial information will be needed, in particular the profit margins for different product lines. Information about product life cycles will be needed. Organizational issues may need to be addressed: How integrated are the sales and marketing operations? Employee issues may need to be addressed: Are talented marketers being attracted and retained by the company?

Strategic plan

Now the company is ready to produce its marketing strategy. This may include some or all of the following:
Objectives for each business unit, product or brand (e.g. grow market share, introduce new products, increase profitability).
Target markets going forwards: types of customers, product areas, geographical areas.
The positioning of products (high-end or value-for-money).
Key elements of the marketing mix it will use for each product line: features and benefits, pricing, advertising and promotional plans, the distribution channels. A special focus needs to be given to areas that will change or need to be developed.
A selling plan: targets for areas and offices, how to develop relationships with the distribution network, merchandising materials, information systems for monitoring sales, roles and responsibilities of the sales force, and the billing procedures and accounting mechanisms.
A risk assessment: What could go wrong? Do we need a 'plan B'?
A timetable.
Expenditure and budgets.

The strategic plan has one overriding aim: to develop the brand. The brand is not just the name and logo, and it is not even the image of the product created by advertising. Rather, it is the whole impression left behind after any contact with the company. Customers can usually go elsewhere for a similar product – they will return to you only if they have brand loyalty. With a successful brand you can even charge a premium price – customers develop an emotional affinity to the brand and are prepared to pay more for the same quality, just to own it. Successful brands are often focused on one specific market segment – this is where the product becomes differentiated and easy to identify. For many brands it is design rather than quality that affects the purchasing decision.

The following sites contain a lot of detailed information about strategic marketing:
http://www.businessplans.org/Market.html
http://www.businessballs.com/freebusinessplansandmarketingtemplates.htm
And for branding:
http://www.businesslink.gov.uk/ (type the word 'branding' into the on-site search engine)
http://www.designcouncil.org.uk/en/About-Design/Business-Essentials/The-power-of-branding-a-practical-guide/

5.1 About business

Strategic branding and partnering

In this module students read about and listen to texts on the topic of branding strategies. There are opportunities for research and discussion on the topic.

Preparation

Before the lesson, search the Internet for the top ten brands (in the world or in the country where you are teaching). Then do another search for *brand strategy* + *brand name* to check for which brands the information is available. This will prepare you for activity 7.

Internet research

This activity ties in well with the discussion activity 7. Please refer to the instructions for activity 7 for ideas on how to exploit the Internet research activity in class.

Discussion

1 You may find it useful to display the logos for each of the five brands listed here. Ask students to work in pairs to brainstorm as much as they can about each brand. Elicit ideas from the class. Next, ask students to discuss in pairs what they think is the secret of success of each brand and what the typical customer profile for each might be (ask students to consider the typical customer profile by reference to specific criteria, e.g. age, gender, social class, marital status, income bracket).

ANSWERS:

There are many valid reasons that students could put forward: perhaps what they all have in common is that they evoke and promise the benefits of belonging to a specific lifestyle group, not just a product, and the differentiation of their brand defines their corporate strategy.

Reading

2 Students have their books closed. Dictate the following words and phrases from the text, and ask students to write them down: *prerequisite* /prɪˈrekwəzɪt/, *preference* /ˈpref(ə)rəns/, *differentiation* /ˌdɪfərenʃieɪʃ(ə)n/, *transient* /ˈtrænziənt/, *circumstantial* /ˌsɜː(r)kəmˈstænʃ(ə)l/, *strategist* /ˈstrætədʒɪst/, *demographic* /ˌdeməˈgræfɪk/, *characteristics* /ˌkærɪktəˈrɪstɪks/, *irreplaceable* /ˌɪrɪˈpleɪsəb(ə)l/, *incomparable* /ɪnˈkɒmp(ə)reb(ə)l/, *unique* /juːˈniːk/ and *Ikea* /aɪˈkiːə/.
Get students to compare spellings in pairs and to discuss the meanings of the words if they know them. Next, get students to scan the text to check their predictions and to check / correct their spellings. Elicit the words back from students and put them on the board. Drill for stress and pronunciation and go through the meanings.
Ask students to read through questions 1–6 and identify which paragraph deals with each question. Next, ask students to highlight / underline the sentences or phrases in each paragraph that answer the questions.

ANSWERS:

1b Almost always, preference can only be achieved by differentiation.
2a Doing things well ... Doing things better ... not a strategy
3d A brand is the consumer's anticipation for a unique and defined experience or benefit.
4c Competitive strategy is always a simultaneous answer to two questions. Firstly, which consumer group has the potential to buy your product? Secondly, what could you offer them that would help you realize that potential?
5f devising and implementing a way by which to deliver a benefit to consumers
6e These brand strategies are also the differentiation – the competitive strategy itself!

Reading for detail

3 This can be a demanding and time-consuming activity. Therefore, depending on the time available, you might like to consider doing the first two or three questions in class and setting the remainder for homework.
Read through the first statement with the class and ask them to highlight the information in the text that relates to the statement. This is in the first paragraph. Now ask students to compare in pairs and to decide whether the statement is true or false. Elicit answers from the class.
Repeat this process for question 2 and as many questions as you deem appropriate for classroom work. Set the rest for homework.

ANSWERS:

1T Doing things well is a prerequisite, and commendable, but not a long-term strategy.
2F Nokia offered something different by offering products which were fashion statements, but there is no insurance in the world of business.
3T Preference can almost always only be achieved by differentiation.
4F This is circumstantial differentiation, which is not long-lasting.
5F Only a defined consumer group – it is not about trying to get the whole world to love your product.
6F It's just not a BMW.
7T In the sense that both experiences offer exclusive and attractive anticipation, experience and benefits.
8F It's essentially place.
9F Perhaps in the past, in cosmetic branding, but today it is not enough.
10T Devising and implementing a way by which to deliver a benefit to consumers.

4 Vary the complexity of this task according to the ability of your class. With an advanced group, ask students to paraphrase the meaning of phrases 1–5. With highly advanced groups, ask students to explain the significance of the phrases in the context of the article. Get students to do the exercise orally in pairs.

1 Running a company better than the competition is not sufficient to gain a long-term advantage.
2 If your brand is sufficiently attractive, customers will not want to buy anything else.
3 Strategic differentiation provides a competitive advantage which is not dependant on particular circumstances of place, time, price, etc.
4 Your success engine is the small group of opinion leaders who other consumers will follow.
5 Starbucks' premises, which have created a new 'buffer' between home and work, are cited as an example of a strategic concept which allows the firm to both create and satisfy a consumer need.

5 Get students to answer the questions orally in pairs. Allow students to look back at the text to check their answers or to assist them in the task if needed.

Listening

6 2.01 Dictate the following words / phrases from the recording: *mergers and acquisitions* (M&A) /'mɜː(r)dʒə(r)z ənd ˌækwɪ'zɪʃ(ə)nz/, *mutually compatible* /'mjuːtʃuəli kəm'pætəb(ə)l/, *complementary* (ˌkɒmplɪ'ment(ə)ri), *synergy* ('sɪnə(r)dʒi) and *enhance* /ɪn'hɑːns/. Get students to check spellings in pairs and then elicit words back from the students and put them on the board. Check meanings and drill pronunciation.

Play the recording through once and ask students to take notes and then to compare in pairs. Next, get students to read through the questions and to discuss the answers in pairs, based on their notes. Play the recording again for students to check and modify their answers. Finally, play the recording a third time, pausing after each question for final confirmation of the answers.

Note: Ari is being ironic when he says, 'these days marriage probably implies considerably less sharing and long-term commitment than business partnering! But, no, seriously ...'. Students may not pick up on the subtlety so you may need to draw students' attention to this.

1 Because unlike mergers and acquisitions, partnering does not involve sharing equity.
2 Apple's core market is creativity, and Nike's is sport. They both provide lifestyle management solutions.
3 They decided to promote running shoes and iPods together. Customers benefited from real-time performance data while they were running.
4 They set up websites to store, process and share performance data collected anywhere in the world, and to offer personalized music to accompany workouts.
5 Businesses which promise lifestyle benefits; fields like travel, entertainment, healthcare and finance.
6 Businesses must be able to develop synergy with an external partner's brands, to deliver added lifestyle benefits to their customers, and ideally, to enhance customer experience via the Internet.

RECORDING SCRIPT

 2.01

Interviewer: Ari, you specialize in business partnering. Am I right in thinking that that's a kind of marriage bureau for companies?
Ari: Well, these days marriage probably implies considerably less sharing and long-term commitment than business partnering! But, no, seriously, we're not in the business of M&A. Perhaps a better analogy would be the cocktail party host who hooks guests up with other people with mutually

compatible interests and complementary talents, who can help each other out.
I: I see. Can you give us an example?
A: Sure. Probably the best-known example and certainly one of the most successful, is the partnering strategy between Apple and Nike. These are two extremely influential corporations with, at first sight, very different product lines. But when you take a closer look at their strategies, you realize that they have something very major in common, because what both organizations offer their customers are lifestyle management solutions. Apple's core market – no pun intended! – is what could be called the 'creativity culture', and Nike's is clearly the 'sport culture'. Anyway, Nike wanted to provide their customers with performance data from their shoes in real time, and thought that sending data to an iPod was the obvious way to do it. Now, the people at Apple, knowing that around half of their customers use their iPods while they work out, were obviously interested. By making the connection with Nike, they created a fantastic opportunity for both companies to promote a whole family of integrated products and accessories for the 'sport-creativity' culture.
I: So they developed shoes which communicate with your iPod, and can tell you your speed, how far you've run, how long you've been running ...
A: ... how many calories you've burned...
I: AND play music?!
A: Right! But that's only the beginning! Very cleverly, they also exploited the Internet to make maximum use of the data collected from the shoes; so you can now feed your data into Nike's website, and connect with, or even compete against, other athletes anywhere in the world! What's more, Apple's iTunes will sell you music mixes with exactly the right tempos for your personal workout, or your favourite sports stars' recommended playlists!
I: And you can get special Nike running gear with iPod pockets, and so on?
A: Absolutely! Shirts, shorts, armbands, jackets ... you name it.
I: OK. So are other businesses picking up on this partnering model?
A: Yes, indeed, and in all sorts of sectors, but perhaps most of all in any business which promises lifestyle benefits; fields like travel, entertainment, healthcare, finance, and so on. If businesses believe that you can work with an external partner to develop synergy between your brands, and if you believe that you can deliver added lifestyle benefits to your customers, then partnering is for you. If, in addition, you can enhance your customer experience via the Internet, then you earn yourself a very, very significant bonus.

Discussion

7 This can be linked to the Internet research activity suggested in the Student's Book. First of all, ask students to work in pairs and create a list of what they think are the top ten brands. This could be the top ten in the world or the top ten in their countries. Then get students to search the Internet to compare their lists with the official lists.

Write the top ten brands onto ten slips of paper / card and ask pairs to choose one each. Now ask each pair to go to the Internet and to search for *brand strategy + brand name* (e.g. *brand strategy + Coca-Cola*). Students read the web pages and make notes on the companies' brand strategies and how these differentiate them from their competitors. Next, match pairs of students up to discuss ways in which they can build partnerships, create synergy and boost possible benefits to their consumers by using the Internet or related technology.

5.2 Grammar

Prepositions

This module focuses on the grammar of prepositions and provides opportunities for students to develop accuracy of use. The module also broadens out to introduce some idiomatic prepositional phrases.

Internet research

Before asking your students to search for the keywords *marketing failure*, provide some categories of information for them to note down (e.g. *company name, product, date of failure, reasons for failure, consequences of failure, other information*). Once students have collected their information, ask them to work in pairs to exchange information.

Did you know?

This information could be presented as a short quiz, e.g.
1 *How many prepositions are there in English? About 50, about 100, about 150, more than 150*
2 *Do you find English prepositions easy or difficult to learn? Why?*
Then get students to read through the information. The key things to stress here are that a) it is useful to learn prepositions as collocations at the same time as new lexis; and b) prepositions need to be memorized as there are no rules governing their use.

Dependent prepositions

1 Divide this exercise into two distinct tasks. First of all, present the first parts of the sentences either through dictation or on the board / an OHP. Get students to work in pairs to continue the sentences in their own words. This will provide an opportunity to test students' knowledge of the correct prepositions, whilst also personalizing the language. Elicit suggestions from the class. Next, dictate the prepositions and ask students to match them to the sentences they have been working on. Check students' answers. Finally, ask students to read through the sentence endings and match them to the beginnings.

ANSWERS:

1 for (h)   2 by (f)   3 about (g)   4 of (d)   5 on (b)
6 against (a)   7 with (e)   8 into (c)

Reformulating

2 This task reviews a sample of prepositions in context. Dictate the following to the class:
I'm not interested in ...
Ask students to write two or three endings for the phrase and to compare in pairs. Elicit suggestions and put them on the board. This may provide the structures presented in the three examples. Now draw your students' attention to the examples in the Student's Book. Ask them to rewrite the sentences using the appropriate structure, following the keyword prompts provided. Students can do this individually before checking in pairs. Elicit the answers from the class and provide additional input as necessary. Now ask students to identify the structures that follow the prepositions. As you go through the answers, elicit / check the meaning of *out of the blue* (happening in a way that is sudden and unexpected, and does not seem connected with anything that happened before).

SUGGESTED ANSWERS:

1 where you plan to go
2 out of the blue
3 to escape / when there is an emergency
4 what their main purpose is
5 the last few weeks / months / years
6 where our new markets are
7 getting the actual job done / exactly what we need to do (to get the job done)
Note: the grammatical structures that follow prepositions are:
noun clauses (your views; emergencies; getting; talking; what you're...; where to... etc.)
time adverbials (recently; last week)

Modifying meaning

3 Before starting this exercise, you might need to pre-teach / elicit definitions for the following expressions: *foundation* /faʊnˈdeɪʃ(ə)n/, *to feel out of it, you name it, price hikes, to hold up* (to be strong) and *across the board*.
As an alternative to simply doing the gap-fill, prepare the full sentences on halves of card to make a matching activity, e.g.

1 I'm afraid to say that these allegations	are entirely without foundation.

Jumble the cards and get students to match the halves together to make the nine sentences. Once these have been checked, pairs can then test each other by reading the first part of a sentence and getting their partner to say the second part back to them, e.g.
A: *I'm afraid to say these allegations ...*
B: *are entirely without foundation.*
Finally, give students a minute or two to complete the gapped sentences. Students can test each other as outlined above in subsequent lessons, and you can recycle the exercise into a progress test.

ANSWERS:

1 entirely   2 almost   3 rather   4 straight
5 particularly   6 at least   7 right   8 only

Listening for gist

4 🔊 2.02 Play the recording through once and ask students to make notes while they listen. Then allow a minute or two for students to compare notes in pairs. Elicit the key points from the class. Next, ask students to answer the questions from memory. Elicit answers from the class. Play the listening again if necessary to provide an opportunity for students to clarify their answers.

ANSWERS:

1 North America – California, Washington State and Arizona
2 To brief (and motivate) his team about the North American operation.
3 Only partially. There seem to be certain problems which his audience are aware of.

Listening for detail

5 Now ask students to read through the gapped sentences 1–10 and work with a partner to check how many of the expressions they may have noticed during the previous listening(s). Then play the extract one last time for students to complete the gaps. Give students a few moments to check with a partner before eliciting the answers from the class. If you prefer, students can check their answers from the tapescript in the Student's Book.

ANSWERS:

1 On balance
2 In other words
3 as it were, at a stroke
4 By the way
5 by and large, on the one hand, on the other
6 at large, as a rule
7 in particular
8 In effect, of course
9 at all costs
10 By the same token, as well.

6 Having checked through the answers, give students a few minutes to discuss the meanings of the phrases. Then read the definitions provided in the answer key below in random order (these definitions could be written on the board for clarification) and ask students to match these to the phrases. Finally, you can ask students to test each other in pairs using the definitions provided.

SUGGESTED ANSWERS:

1 on balance = all things considered, essentially
2 in other words = to put this another way, or
3 as it were = sort of, as you might say, so to speak; at a stroke = all at once, all in one go
4 by the way = incidentally / anyway (informal)
5 by and large = mainly / in the main; on the one hand / on the other = firstly, in one situation / conversely, alternatively, in contrast
6 at large = all around the place, generally, everywhere; as a rule = in general, generally this is true
7 in particular = particularly, especially
8 in effect = effectively; of course = naturally, certainly
9 at all costs = definitely / whatever we do
10 by the same token = for the same reason, in the same way, similarly, likewise; as well = also, additionally, in addition

RECORDING SCRIPT

 2.02

Right, if we could just focus a bit on our main strategy to grow our North America operation. On balance, what we need more than anything else is a joined-up strategy across our main western centres in California, Washington State and Arizona. In other words, we all need to be focusing on the same strategy, whatever part of the business we're working in. You know, all pulling in the same direction and making sure we all get the three 'Fs' sorted – Focus, Familiarity, and Follow-up. Is that clear? So, focus on our core strategy – we've been through all that, build up close familiarity with the local markets, and follow up all leads and opportunities. We can then, as it were, capture the whole market at a stroke. At least that's the plan, if you know what I mean. By the end of this financial year we need to have cracked the West and have our numbers looking good to give us any hope of the Mid-west, and, well, more of that next year.

By the way, have you all managed to have a look through the strategy document, you know, the one I sent round the other day? Did any of you have any particular questions you wanted to ask about it? Good.

So, our next step is to, well, make the strategy work. I guess that's the hard part. The strategy is, by and large, pretty straightforward – on the one hand focus on the new customer, convince them that they need us, and all that stuff; on the other, well, I'll come on to that in a minute. I should emphasize that we need to be careful with customers at large. They can be a bit demanding so as a rule just fall back on the 'customer is king' thing – you know, just say yes to whatever they want. Within reason anyway – don't leave me with any massive clean-up bills. I don't really foresee anything in particular that can go wrong. In effect it's just like what we've been doing in Eastern Europe, though on a bigger scale of course. I expect it will go like a dream. Oh, one more thing. We must all avoid mentioning that glitch in the software, at all costs. By the same token, make sure you all keep quiet about the temperature thing as well – I still can't believe a bit of heat has such a terrible effect on …

Writing

7 Ask students to refer to the notes they made during the previous listening exercise and to recap the points made by Carl Edmonds at the meeting. Then ask students to read through the writing task. Ask the following questions:
What is your job? (Regional Marketing Negotiator, North America)
Who are you going to write to? (The MD of Rainbow Software Solutions)
What mode of written communication should you use? (email)
What is the purpose of writing this email? (to defend yourself and explain why you think you were let down by Carl)
What points do you need to include? (the strategy document was ineffective; the software was faulty; the hardware failed; lack of support from Carl Edmonds)
Check through these points with the class. If possible, bring in an example of an email of a similar type as a model to raise students' awareness of useful language, structure and layout of such emails.
Give students a time limit to write their emails. If possible, you could get students to do this for homework by writing the emails on a computer and then emailing them to you.

5.3 Vocabulary

Marketing

This module focuses on marketing vocabulary, with particular attention paid to collocations.

Preparation

For this lesson you will need a class set of dictionaries (preferably business English editions) and a set of blank pieces of postcard-sized card.

Internet research

This activity can be done either immediately before or after the reading activity, exercise 3.

Discussion

1 Put the following table on the board. Ask students to copy it and make notes for each point.

	Products that I / they aspire to own	The way I / they buy products	My / their attitude(s) to advertising
Me			
My parents			
My grandparents			

Monitor and offer help as necessary while students do this task. Next, ask students to read through the discussion questions and to make notes. Finally, ask students to work in groups of three to discuss the questions. Monitor and make notes of language points for correction. Take whole-class feedback.

Collocations

2 Write the word *brand* in large letters in the centre of the board. Ask students to work in threes and write down as many words as they can think of that go with the word *brand*. Set a time limit for this. Then elicit suggestions from the class and add them to the board, around the word *brand*. This will build up a collocation map. Now ask students to check against the collocations in the exercise and to identify the incorrect collocations. Note: *brand new* is a correct collocation, but is not directly related to the topic of brands and brand names. Go through the answers with the class.

ANSWERS:

1 brand new   2 to devise a brand   3 a flaming brand
4 to detect a brand

Reading

3 Before students read the text, write *generation Y consumers* on the board and clarify what this means. Next, ask students to brainstorm in small groups what they consider to be the characteristics of this particular consumer group, and ways in which marketing professionals can connect with them. Elicit ideas from the groups and write suggestions on the board.
Next, dictate the following words from the text: *savvy, covet* /ˈkʌvət/, *scrutinize* /ˈskruːtɪnaɪz/, *nurture* /ˈnɜː(r)tʃə(r)/, *peers, a buzz, to rocket, potent, to fine-tune, empowerment* /ɪmˈpaʊə(r)mənt/ *and to foster*. Ask students to write the words as they hear them, but not to worry about meanings at this stage. Next, ask students to compare their spellings in pairs and to discuss the meanings if they know them.

Now ask students to scan through the text to find the words, to check their spellings and guess at the meanings from context. Go through the meanings with the class and drill for pronunciation as needed.
Finally, ask students to read the text again and to answer the reading comprehension questions 1 and 2. Take whole-class feedback.

SUGGESTED ANSWERS:

1 An extremely marketing-savvy group that understands how numerous companies actively covet their business, they greet new brands with intense scepticism.
Brands have a tremendous effect on Gen Y-ers because they want to share in and exploit brands' emotional appeal. They use the brands they support as important forms of self-expression that communicate to peers exactly how they define themselves as well as how they want others to view them.

2 It is imperative for Gen-Y businesses to focus on brand strategy and to connect on an emotional level, to create brand endorsers, who recommend brands to friends and create the necessary buzz that drives sales and increases market share. They need to define precisely what Gen Y-ers care about and what benefits will motivate them to buy the brand, by using the steps suggested.

4 Write the three categories on the board:
action by brand managers
consumers or their reactions
brands themselves
Ask students to scan through the text and to find all the *brand* collocations and to note them down under the three headings. Allow students a few moments to compare in pairs before eliciting answers from the class.

SUGGESTED ANSWERS:

action by brand managers: brand strategy, brand-building strategy, to build a brand, fine-tune a brand
consumers or their reactions: scrutinize a brand, influenced by brands, support and recommend brands, brand endorsers, brand ownership
brands themselves: youth-oriented brands, top brands, emotionally driven brands, strong brand, emotionally potent brand, successful brand

5 For this activity you might like to get students to work in small groups. Divide the collocations amongst the groups, so that each group has three to four collocations. Distribute blank postcards to each group. Ask the groups to provide definitions and example sentences for each collocation (allow them to use dictionaries if necessary), and to write the definitions and sample sentences on the cards. Monitor and help as needed. Once this stage is complete, get the students to mingle and to test each other by providing the definitions. Students can then provide example sentences for their classmates as an extension.

6 This exercise will recycle the vocabulary pre-taught in exercise 3. Give students an opportunity to check answers in pairs before taking whole-class feedback. Once the answers have been checked, ask students to work in pairs to test each other on the meaning of the words. This vocabulary can later be recycled into a progress test.

ANSWERS:

1 c   2 a   3 a   4 c   5 c   6 b   7 a   8 b

Discussion

7 Ask students to refer back to the article and to highlight the key ideas that are described for tailoring brands to Generation Y consumers, e.g.

> *establish an emotional connection with the consumer*
> *project an emotional appeal*
> *consider Gen Y-ers' values*
> *try to own the 'lifestyle empowerment' brand position*
> *create a sense of brand ownership*

Next, ask students to work in pairs and choose one of the markets. They then brainstorm ways they could apply the ideas in the article to tailor the brands for Generation Y consumers. Monitor and note any language points for post-correction. When the pairs have generated some ideas, ask students to form new pairs and tell each other about the markets they chose and the strategies they would use. Finally, take whole-class feedback.

Listening

8 2.03–2.10 If possible, find some examples of real-life advertising blunders. An Internet search for *advertising blunders* will return some interesting ideas. Also, ask students if they know of any famous advertising blunders to tell their classmates about.

Next, ask students to work in pairs to brainstorm a list of dos and don'ts of advertising and marketing. Then get pairs to combine with other pairs to put their ideas together. Elicit suggestions from the class and put them on the board.

Next, tell the class they are going to hear eight extracts from a talk on how to avoid the biggest mistakes in advertising. Ask students to make a note of the advice given. Play the extracts through once. Then let students compare in pairs before eliciting answers from the class.

Now ask students to read through the list of dos and don'ts in their books and to match them to the extracts according to the notes they made during the listening.

Play the extracts through a second time for students to check their answers. Finally elicit answers from the class.

ANSWERS:

Do use image guidelines and templates to ensure a consistent company image in all communication. 4
Don't waste your budget by airing messages on radio or TV for an under-performing product. 1
Do separate long-term schemes from short-term measures; develop and implement a well thought-out marketing plan. 6
Don't omit to inform, remind, and inspire customers, and give them reasons and incentives to come to your business. 5
Do maximize ROI by highlighting a single major consumer benefit in your promotional text. 2
Do remember to continue to satisfy and delight your current clientele; cross-selling or up-selling to your loyal customers is much less costly than attracting new business. 8
Do be sure to lead with your strengths: don't make people wait for the pay-off. 3
Don't imagine that online business is yours for the taking: you also need to invest in traditional media to develop a successful web store. 7

RECORDING SCRIPT

 2.03–2.10

1 The first trap to avoid is running more ads if your product isn't selling well. If there's something wrong with your product, throwing money at it isn't going to help. As Bill Bernbach, who devised Avis' famous 'We try harder' campaign once said, 'Nothing kills a bad product like a good ad.'

2 The next mistake is to pack as many bells and whistles as you can into your advertising copy in the hope of getting 'more bang for your buck'. Consumers don't remember more than one main idea.

3 An ad is not a joke or an after-dinner speech, so deliver your message up-front: avoid keeping the best till last, or expecting people to wait for the punch line: four out of five people will only read the headline.

4 Don't let anyone persuade you it's a good time to redesign your logo or rethink your advertising tagline. You want customers to believe your business is well established and reliable: constantly changing your image will send the opposite message.

5 Build it and they will come. It worked for Kevin Costner in the movie *Field of Dreams*, but it doesn't work in business. Just opening a store or a website isn't enough; you have to inform customers and drive them to your business.

6 It's easy to confuse tactics and strategies; some people always want to jump on every new promotional bandwagon that comes along, instead of following a coherent policy.

7 Even now, long after the dot com bubble burst, many people still can't resist going for the low-hanging fruit. But just like bricks and mortar stores, E-businesses require time and money to develop.

8 Finally, don't ever be tempted to believe that your customers are captive. If you devote all your attention to converting new prospects, your existing customer base can quickly fade away.

9 This exercise focuses on some of the idiomatic collocations that occurred in the extracts. Begin by dictating the ten words from the box. Elicit the words and put them on the board, then check pronunciation and spelling. Give the students a few minutes to fill the gaps, then play the extracts once more, asking students to listen out for the collocations in order to check their answers. Go through the answers with the class.

ANSWERS:

1 throwing, jumping
2 running, getting
3 redesigning
4 providing
5 up-front, copy
6 captive, converting

Discussion

10 Elicit or provide some useful phrases for giving advice and criticism, e.g.
It's a mistake to ..., You should avoid ..., If I were you I'd ..., You shouldn't ..., It is/isn't a good idea to ..., Try (not) to ..., Make sure you (don't)...,
Ask students to discuss the points raised in the extracts using the phrases provided. If time is short, divide the extracts amongst the class and ask students to work in small groups to provide constructive criticism or advice for the situations. Then put the students into new groups to share their advice and criticism.

5.4 Management skills

Active Listening

This module focuses on the topic of active listening and provides opportunities for reading, listening and discussion around the topic.

Internet research

Searching for images using the keywords *active listening* returns some humorous and interesting visual representations of the topic of this unit. Use these images as a stimulus to promote lead-in discussions to the topic.

Discussion

1 Put the questions on the board and ask students in groups of three to discuss the questions and to make some notes. Monitor and, if necessary, provide guiding prompts using the answer key. Elicit ideas from the groups and put them on the board, then feed in ideas from the answer key.

SUGGESTED ANSWERS:

1 language difficulties, accent, dialect, vocabulary, inaudible speech, noisy environment, listener is unreceptive, listener is doing something else at the same time, listener talks or interrupts too much, not being 'on the same wavelength', listener makes assumptions because of the speaker's personality or hierarchical position, prejudice, listener is distracted, etc.
2 a) 7% b) 38% c) 55%, according to research by Dr Gerard Egan (*The Skilled Helper*, 1975).
3 TV presenters, politicians, religious leaders, sports commentators, managers or teachers students know, etc. Words, tone of voice and body language are coherent and consistent, eye contact is good, language is well chosen and pitched at the audience level, voice is clear and pleasant to listen to, questions or interruptions are treated with respect and listened to actively.

Reading

2 Pre-teach / elicit the meanings of *a barrage* /ˈbæraːʒ/ *of options*, *to elicit* /ɪˈlɪsɪt/, *one's convictions* /kənˈvɪkʃ(ə)nz/ and *a trap*.

Ask the class the following questions:
What do you understand by the term 'active listening'?
Can you give an example of each of the following question types: closed, open, multiple, supplementary, leading, trick?
Can you think of a reason for using each type of question?
Ask students to discuss these questions in pairs or threes. Monitor to check progress. Then elicit answers from the class. Now ask students to read through the text, to fill the gaps and to check their answers to the lead-in questions they discussed at the start of the exercise. This can be done individually, but allow students to check in pairs. Elicit answers and clarify as necessary.

ANSWERS:

1 open
2 supplementary
3 Closed
4 multiple
5 Leading
6 trick

3 This exercise provides examples of each question type. Give each student in the class one of the questions on a slip of paper (with classes of more than six, divide the class into two or more groups; with smaller classes, give one or two students more that one question or take one yourself). Now ask each student to dictate their question to the class. Their classmates have to write each question down and to decide which question type it is. Students then compare in pairs. Finally, ask students to read the questions in the Student's Book and go through the matching activity. As a follow-up, you could ask students to write their own examples of each question type.

ANSWERS:

1 supplementary
2 trick
3 open
4 leading
5 closed
6 multiple

Simulation

4 Ask students to work in groups of three. Tell them that they are market researchers for an online store selling books, music and software, and that they are going to interview customers about new products or services they might be prepared to pay for. Ask the groups to prepare a set of questions to ask the customer. Monitor and provide input and guidance as needed. When the groups have compiled their questions, split the students into new groups of three to interview each other according to the instructions. Give all students an opportunity to take each role. Monitor and note any language points for review.

Brainstorming

5 This exercise follows on naturally from the previous exercise. Ask students to briefly repeat the simulation from the previous exercise, but to use physical gestures and body language to show they are not listening. Then ask the pairs to note down the gestures they used. Elicit ideas from the class and put them on the board.

SUGGESTED ANSWERS:

In many Western cultures: No eye contact, turning or leaning away from the speaker, defensive posture, e.g. arms folded, fidgeting, clock-watching, touching wrist, eyes glancing around room, yawning, scratching, rolling eyes, doing something else at the same time, interrupting, talking to someone else. Behaviour and interpretation may be different in other cultures.

Listening for gist

6 2.11 Establish the context of the dialogue (an estate agent and a customer). You could use a visual to help. Play the recording through once and ask students to make notes as they listen. Then ask students to compare notes in pairs. Now ask students to read through the questions and to discuss the answers in pairs. Play the listening through a second time if needed for students to check their answers. Go through the answers with the class.

ANSWERS:

1 his flat is too noisy and too small, parking is difficult
2 He is fond of the street where he lives, and he seems nervous about borrowing money.
3 She uses appropriate responses to what Mr Garcia says: she paraphrases, reflects, empathizes, clarifies, echoes, encourages, summarizes and focuses.

Listening for detail

7 Ask students to read through the extracts from the dialogue and to complete the gaps as best they can from memory. Then play the recording through one last time, pausing at the appropriate points for students to check their answers.

ANSWERS:

1 understand correctly, basically
2 My guess is
3 too clear, have in mind
4 Too soon?
5 Uh-huh?
6 we've established
7 what I would suggest

RECORDING SCRIPT

 2.11

Mr Garcia: … and it's not far from the airport, which is handy of course, but it's not ideal. Then there's the traffic, parking is a nightmare these days, and then the neighbours playing music late at night; they're very friendly, but the walls are really thin, you know!

Agent: I know what you mean! So, if I understand correctly, Mr Garcia, you're saying that basically you'd like to move somewhere quieter?

Mr G: Yes. Twenty-two years I've lived here. I know everybody in the street, and all the shops and restaurants. But I really feel I need more space, and a bit of peace and quiet at night.

A: I see. My guess is that it'll be a wrench for you to leave, am I right?

Mr G: Oh yes, I'm quite attached to the old place. It'll be tough, but I'll work up the courage to make a move sooner or later.

A: Erm, I'm sorry, Mr Garcia, I'm not too clear about this. What sort of timeframe do you have in mind?

Mr G: Well, I don't know really. It depends if I find something I really like. It would be nice to move before the summer, but that's probably too soon.

A: Too soon?

Mr G: Well, there's the financial side to think of as well.

A: Uh-huh?

Mr G: Hm. I suppose I'll need to find out about getting a mortgage if I want something bigger than this place. I expect that'll take several months, you know what banks are like!

A: Yes, they do tend to drag their feet, don't they? But I have a very good friend who works in a bank as a Financial Advisor and sometimes helps me. I can introduce you, if you like? OK, do you mind if I recap? What we've established so far is that you'd like to move somewhere quieter if possible, next Spring, if we can find you something really nice to make it worth moving? And you'd like something a bit bigger, but for not too much more than you'll get for the sale of your flat. Is that a fair summary?

Mr G: Yes, you understand my situation perfectly. I can see we're going to get on really well, Miss …?

A: Irina. Yes, I'm sure we will, Mr Garcia! Now then, what I would suggest is that we start by doing a valuation of your flat. Then we'll have an idea of your budget for the new place, and, if necessary, we'll be able to start talking to the bank about how much you'd like to borrow. How does that sound?

8 This exercise extends the focus of exercise 7 and provides some additional useful responding techniques. Provide some meaningful contexts for the phrases yourself to help students identify the function, e.g. *OK, shall we tackle this year's budget first?* Read your phrases out to the class and ask them to note down the function of each phrase. Let students compare in pairs before taking whole-class feedback.

ANSWERS:

1=7   2=2   3=6   4=3   5=1

9 Pre-teach *to be in one's right mind*, *neurotic* /njʊˈrɒtɪk/, *overprotective* and *aesthetically* /iːsˈθetɪkli/. Get students to read through the dialogues quietly to themselves. Then ask them to work in groups of four and take the roles of Marketer and persons A, B and C. Ask the groups to act out the dialogues in their current form. Next, ask the groups to reformulate the dialogues using phrases from the unit. Monitor and offer input as required. When groups have finished, elicit suggestions and put them on the board, and feed in suggestions from the answers provided below. Now ask the groups to act out the dialogues again using the reformulated phrases. If students are enjoying the exercise and you have time, get the groups to act out the dialogues for the class.

SUGGESTED ANSWERS:

1 So if I've got this right, the main issue is communicating more clearly about the new product?
2 It sounds to me as if you're very concerned about your children's safety.
3 Sorry, I don't quite see what you're getting at. Can you be more specific?
4 Too expensive?
5 Well, let's just recap on what you've told me so far; you've expressed concerns about our product communication, child safety, design and pricing.
6 Shall we take a short break first, and then tackle some more tests?

Discussion

10 This activity provides an opportunity for freer practice. Ask each student to prepare a short talk on one of the topics. Encourage students to make notes about what they are going to say. Monitor and offer help as needed. When students are ready, put them into groups of three to carry out the discussions. Ensure that students swap roles, so that each student has an opportunity to take role A, B and C. When the groups have finished, take brief class feedback on how students performed and what they found easy or difficult about the task.

5.5 Writing
Advertising copy

This module focuses on the language of advertising copy and provides models of good advertising copy and guided practice in writing copy.

Preparation

Obtain some samples of real advertising copy from magazines, TV and the Internet. Prepare matching exercise 3 on slips of card, with one set for each pair of students in the class. If you have a computer lab, prepare the writing text for exercise 6 as a word-processed document. See the **Alternative activity** instructions after exercise 7 below.

Internet research

Search for *writing effective copy* for extra ideas to inform your lesson. Alternatively, get your students to search for tips on how to write good advertising copy. These can then be incorporated into exercises 3 and 6.

Discussion

1 Begin by asking students to define advertising copy and to describe the job of a copywriter. An Internet search will provide some useful definitions. Take some examples of advertising copy into class to help promote the discussion and to contextualize the unit. Next, tabulate the information in the lead-in discussion, e.g.

	Potential problems	Potential benefits
controversial images		
a large amount of text		
...		

Photocopy the table for the students or ask them to copy it. Now ask them to work in pairs or threes to discuss the points and to make notes in the table. Monitor and offer help as required. When the groups have finished, elicit feedback and put it on the board.

Reading

2 Pre-teach or elicit *differentiate* /ˌdɪfəˈrenʃieɪt/, *stunning*, *chassis* /ˈʃæsi/, *punchy*, *in unison* and *thoroughly* /ˈθʌrəli/. Ask students to read through the two advertisements and to highlight the USP of each product. Ask students to compare in pairs before eliciting answers from the class.

SUGGESTED ANSWERS:
Ford Ka – its size: a small car with big ideas; good things really do come in small packages.
Beetle Cabriolet – a thoroughly modern interpretation of our classic design.

Style

3 Have this matching exercise prepared on sets of cards, with one set for each pair of students. Give each pair a set of cards and a few moments to match the halves. Monitor to check progress. Elicit answers from the class. After the answers have been checked, collect in the cards. Now ask the pairs to note down as many pieces of advice as they can remember. Finally, ask students to go through the exercise in the book to consolidate.

ANSWERS:
1 c   2 f   3 d   4 b   5 e   6 a   7 j   8 l   9 k
10 h   11 g   12 i

4 If you have some authentic examples of copy available, distribute these to the class and ask students to identify examples of the tips. Alternatively, refer students back to the advertisements in exercise 2 to identify examples of the tips.

SUGGESTED ANSWERS:
solution: *a traffic jam as a sunbathing opportunity. (Text B)*
readers' needs: *if you're looking for more power. (Text A)*
Be specific: *just 13 seconds. (Text B)*
touch the audience: *this car's for you. (Text B) Whatever you're into, the Ford Ka wants to be part of the action. (Text A)*
Encourage the reader to take action: *Now you can make an even bigger statement with Ka-ligraphy. (Text A) request a test drive (Text B).*
Use language to excite and delight: *fun-loving, Catch-me-if-you-can. (Text A)*
Address the reader: *if you're looking. (Text A) this car's for you (Text B).*
Use action verbs: *lives for the moment, if you're looking for, made to get noticed. (Text A) folds down, can be opened. (Text B)*
Exploit language your target audience would use: *fun-loving, superb, feisty, whatever you're into, part of the action, There's just something about it. (Text A) this car's for you. (Text B)*

Dynamic language

5 This exercise raises awareness of the linguistic features of effective copy. This is a challenging exercise, as it requires a developed understanding of formal and informal registers in English. You could provide additional help for your students by supplying a selection of synonyms for students to match and to categorize as suitable or unsuitable for good copy, e.g.

appropriate language	*inappropriate language*
loads / tons of	a significant number of
clever / smart	sophisticated
punchy	powerful
plenty of space	ample room
we'll send it	it will be dispatched
at the same time	simultaneously

This could be done as a dictation exercise or as a card-matching activity. Draw students' attention to the table in exercise 5 and check the class understands the task. Give students plenty of time to rephrase the sentences and monitor, providing help and input as required. Ask students to compare in pairs before checking.
Note: If time is short, divide the six sentences among the class and ask students to transform one or two sentences each. This can be done individually and then in pairs. Students then read their solutions to the class.
Go through all the answers with the class. Give pairs an opportunity to test each other orally, e.g.
A: *The package will be dispatched within 48 hours.*
B: *We'll send off the package in less than 48 hours.*

1   We'll send off the package to you in less than 48 hours.
2   We'll reveal the strategies that will help you generate a $2m profit.
3   Press a central switch, and all the windows open at the same time.
4   Just click on the link below for more information!
5   Pay just £24.99 a month for complete access to all our online services.
6   The door chime function lets you know if anyone has come in or gone out.

Writing

6   This exercise extends the previous exercise. Set the following questions:
What product is being advertised? (the WayBeyond 250 sat-nav)
What new features are mentioned? (built-in receiver, thinner, weighs less, 'Where is it?' function)
Ask students to read through the text and to answer the questions. Elicit to check. Now ask students to highlight the language that could be improved. Get students to compare in pairs and then to discuss suitable replacement phrases to make the text more dynamic. Finally, give students time to rewrite the text in a more dynamic style. If time is short, this could be started in class and completed for homework.

Alternative activity

Input the text into a word processor. Take students to the computer lab and give them a copy of the text. Students can then edit and modify the text using the word processor.

5.6 Case study
Presnya Taxi

This module provides an opportunity for students to develop an improved marketing strategy for a Moscow taxi firm.

Internet research

The search for the keywords *limobikes* will return a number of sites promoting this new form of transport. These sites contain authentic examples of effective copy and can provide students with a helpful angle on the case study.

Discussion

1   To structure this discussion, you could write the following heading and sub-headings on the board:
the characteristics of taxi users
demographic (age, income)
reasons for travel
other info
Give the groups a few minutes to brainstorm some characteristics of taxi users, using the headings supplied. Then elicit feedback and put it on the board. At this stage you could feed in the following background information:
A survey of Australian taxi users produced the following information:
Demographic: Taxi users are evenly distributed between all age groups. They have predominantly medium or high incomes.
Reason for travelling: social 40%, professional 12%, airport 10%, shopping 6%
Other info: Business travellers are probably less sensitive to price than other users, and probably give better tips, but represent a surprisingly small segment of the market.
Once you have provided the background information, ask students to discuss the second question. Again, elicit answers and students' reasons for their answers.

2   Ask students to look carefully at the pictures and to read the copy. Now ask students in their groups to discuss how effective they think the advert is. Elicit comments from the class and prompt with ideas from the suggested answers as necessary.

The advert isn't very inspiring visually;
There are no USPs to the advert. For example, one would expect all taxi firms to provide airport transfers, so this is hardly a selling point;
The driver in the picture does not look friendly, although the copy claims the drivers are friendly; It isn't a good idea to advertise the limited operating hours of Mon-Fri 0600-2300.

Listening

3 2.12 Explain to the class that Volodya, the owner of the taxi firm, and his daughter-in-law, Ally, are discussing the company's problems. Ask students to note down the main points made by the two speakers. Play the recording through once. Then ask students to compare their notes in pairs or threes. Now draw students' attention to the questions and ask them to answer them using their notes. Play the recording through a second time for students to check and to add further details. Give students a few moments to check in pairs before taking whole-class feedback. Note: you may want to pre-teach *it's written all over your face* and check students know what a *Lada* is.

ANSWERS:

1 Volodya is worried because the accounts are not too good and turnover is falling steadily.
2 Competition from freelancers, minivans, other forms of transport and traffic jams.
3 To consider her ideas for rethinking the company's marketing strategy.

RECORDING SCRIPT

💿 2.12

Ally: Ah, there you are, Volodya. I wanted to ask you something … what's the matter?

Volodya: Oh, it's nothing. How can I help you, Ally?

A: Now come on, I can see there's something wrong; it's written all over your face. Are those the latest accounts?

V: Yes. I just got them today.

A: The drivers are saying we're losing money. Is it true?

V: You know Moscow taxi drivers, Ally. If you believe what they say, the end of the world is only hours away! But things are not too good. Turnover is falling steadily. The taxi business isn't what it was. Too much competition. In the old days, it was a real profession. These days, anyone who can beg, borrow or steal a car is a taxi – and a much cheaper taxi than ours.

A: Hm. And the minivans are a lot cheaper too.

V: Yes. We've lost half of our airport business to minivans. People don't seem to mind sharing if they're all going to the airport.

A: And the buses are getting faster and more comfortable.

V: Not to mention trains, trams, the underground – I've heard they even want to start one of those bicycle services like they have in Paris – you know, you pick up a bicycle in your street, ride where you want to go, and just leave it when you get there.

A: Well I'm not sure how popular that would be in the winter!

V: I don't know – with all the traffic problems we have, maybe it's not such a stupid idea. That's the other big problem. Even if you drive luxury limousines, nobody wants to spend hours on end stuck in the traffic – and I'm not pretending for a moment that our poor old Ladas are limousines, they're uncomfortable, inefficient and expensive to run. There's still some money in the bank, but we can't afford Mercedes or BMWs. In the old days, it used to take us twenty minutes to drive to Sheremetyevo – now it's usually two hours, or more! How's a taxi supposed to make money when it's not moving?!

A: Exactly. Listen, Volodya, Andrey and I have been doing some thinking about this.

V: Look, I know you went to business school, Ally, but after forty years in the taxi business, I think I know pretty much everything there is to know. If there was a solution, I'd have found it already. Andrey knows that.

A: Just let us explain our ideas, OK? It won't cost you anything, and it might just help. We think you need to completely rethink your marketing strategy.

V: Ally, this is a taxi company. We don't do marketing, we drive taxis!

A: And that's the root of the problem. Look, just give us a chance to explain our ideas – please?

V: All right, Ally. You know very well a Russian man can never say no to a beautiful woman!

Discussion

4 Give students a few minutes to read through the questions and encourage them to make some notes. Students should do this individually in the first instance. You could vary the classroom dynamic of the discussion by asking students to mingle to discuss the questions with other classmates. Monitor and offer support as necessary. Then ask students to work in pairs and collate the ideas they gleaned from their classmates. Finally, elicit ideas from the class and put them on the board.

Reading

5 Divide the class into two groups, A and B. Ask group A to read the information on page 111 of the Student's Book, and ask group B to read the information on page 113. Ask students to read through the information individually and to add their own ideas. Monitor and provide help as necessary. If students have difficulty generating ideas of their own, encourage them to work in pairs or threes to share ideas. Once the groups have read through the information and added some ideas, arrange the class into pairs, one student from group A and one from group B.

Discussion

6 Draw students' attention to the discussion points. The table can be copied onto the board or displayed on an OHP to help you clarify aspects of the task. Give the pairs plenty of time to discuss the ideas and to complete the table of information. Monitor and provide input or elicit ideas as necessary. When the pairs have finished this stage, take whole-class feedback and put the results on to the board.

SUGGESTED ANSWERS:

Strategy options	make current, *We do better* strategy more visible – how? go upmarket, e.g. limos, business-only or ladies-only cars? go downmarket: cut costs, salaries, service and prices, develop advertising revenue think laterally, e.g. taxi motorbikes, equipped with comfortable passenger seat, protective clothing and helmet, radio telephone, etc. – radical solution to traffic, comfort and image problems?
Branding decisions	change name, logo, etc. to something more in line with target customer profile? make clearer, more targeted promise to customers – what? develop new image and company values to match new strategy – what?
Partnering decisions	can we find a partner business to share resources and costs? e.g. hotel / restaurant chain, airline, railway, B2B, football club, other? can we use the Internet to enhance customer service / experience, perhaps with partners?
Promotion options	advertising – where, when, what? organize events – what? should we have a website? could we use direct mail? what about sponsoring a basketball team?

Simulation

7 For this simulation, students will use the information collated in the previous exercise to inform the discussion. The agenda forms a structure for the simulated meeting. Arrange students into groups of three or four. Ask the groups to elect a chairperson each to control and guide the meetings. Also, ask them to elect a member to take notes or minutes. Allow about fifteen to twenty minutes for the meetings, but do not let them overrun. Monitor and note language points for immediate or post-correction.

Presentation

8 Advise students that they can use the agenda structure as the presentation framework. Suggest that each member of a group take responsibility for presenting an aspect of the presentation. For example, student A presents the *Marketing Strategy*, student B presents *Branding* and so on. Give the groups time to rehearse their presentations. Depending on the time you have available, give the groups an opportunity to prepare PowerPoint™ slides for their presentations. As the groups make their presentations, make notes for feedback. Here are some suggested headings: *pronunciation points, vocabulary points, grammatical points, coherence of structure, use of visuals, body language.*

6 | Risk management

Subject background

What is risk, from a business point of view? Four broad categories of risk can be identified:

Strategic risk

This is the highest level of risk, where the whole business activity is at stake. Examples might include long-term changes in demand for the company's products; political or economic instability in a key market; the entry of a major new player in the market; and integration problems arising from a merger or acquisition. It is the responsibility of the Board and the senior management team to monitor strategic risk and respond to it.

Operational risk

This is risk that needs to be controlled on a day-to-day basis. Examples include the breakdown of key equipment; supply chain problems; IT issues; recruitment difficulties; and poor reporting procedures that fail to show management where a project is going overbudget, or that costs are rising, or that sales are below target. It is the responsibility of line managers to monitor operational risk and respond to it.

Financial risk

Financial risk is a necessary part of any business. In fact there is a direct relationship between the level of risk of a business venture and the potential reward. However, some areas of financial risk need to be monitored particularly carefully, and these include cash flow problems; the level of bad debt; more expensive credit due to banks raising their interest rates; changes in foreign exchange rates (for an importing or exporting company); and internal fraud.

Financial risk is the hardest form of risk to monitor because the devil is in the detail – you need to work through pages of spreadsheet printouts to spot an anomalous or suspicious figure. Also, financial information is compartmentalized within a company: accounts receivable, accounts payable, internal budget control, relations with the bank – in a large company all these may be handled by different people working in different offices. Ultimately it is the Finance Director who has responsibility for controlling this risk, but the external auditors called in every year to verify the firm's accounts also have a role to play.

Compliance risk

This is risk associated with failure to follow government rules and regulations. The two most important areas here are employment legislation and health and safety legislation. In both cases the HR Director will have a strong role in keeping up-to-date with the law. This is an area where an international company may find that there are significant differences between countries. For example, in some countries it may be easy to dismiss people for poor performance alone, whereas in others it might be almost impossible. Again, some countries may have strict policies regarding equal opportunities, others not. These differences can have a direct impact on company culture locally.

What happens when careful risk management is not enough, and a crisis has developed? With luck and good planning there will be a contingency plan. This will involve a well-defined decision-making process, with escalation procedures if the situation deteriorates. But usually a crisis is unexpected and there is no plan in place to deal with it. Managers have to respond to fast-moving events and take remedial action on the spot. It feels like stamping out a bushfire – you put out the flames in one place only to see new flames arise in another. Sometimes the situation gets out of control, and you are involved in a damage-limitation exercise. Here, the role of the Public Relations Officer is key – issuing statements, talking to the media and trying to project an image of focused action combined with calm and stability. A company that does well in a crisis can actually come out of it with its reputation enhanced. For example, a quick recall of defective or dangerous products can actually build trust in the brand.

Useful websites

The single best source for further study is this downloadable pdf:
http://www.theirm.org/publications/documents/Risk_Management_Standard_030820.pdf
For the specific area of health and safety, the following site is very useful:
http://www.hse.gov.uk/risk/
And for a short review of crisis management look here:
http://tutor2u.net/business/strategy/crisis-management-planning-and-action.html

6.1 About business

Crisis management

This module focuses on the topic of crisis management and provides stimulating listening and reading texts on the topic, which can be further exploited for vocabulary building.

Internet research

As preparation for the lesson, ask students to search the Internet using the keywords *bad crisis management* and to find one or two examples of crises that have been badly managed. Ask them to make notes on what the crisis was, when it happened, where it happened, who was involved and what the outcome was. Students then share their findings at the start of the lesson. Alternatively, you can conduct a similar search to gather some additional authentic examples to share with the class.

Discussion

1 Pre-teach *psychopath* /ˈsaɪkəʊpæθ/, *cyanide* /ˈsaɪənaɪd/, *to recall a product*, *to relaunch* /ˈriːˌlɔːntʃ/, *tamper-proof* and *provocative* /prəˈvɒkətɪv/.

With large classes, the quiz can be made into a class survey. Divide the class into four groups (A–D) and give each group one question each, so that group A has question 1, group B has question 2 and so on. Give the groups a moment to check they understand their questions. Monitor and clarify as needed. Now split the class into new groups of four, comprising a student from each group A–D. Give the groups a few minutes to discuss the four questions and to note down the answers their classmates give. Once each group has discussed all four questions, ask the students to return to their original groups and to collate the answers they obtained in the previous stage. Take whole-class feedback.

Next, draw students' attention to the four discussion questions in the Student's Book and ask them to circle their answers, before turning to the exercise key on page 114.

Listening for gist

2 **2.13** Check students understand the gist question, particularly the idea of a *philosophy* (an underlying theory) and *conventional wisdom* (ideas or beliefs generally accepted as true). Ask students to take notes under the following two headings:
Dezenhall's philosophy of PR
conventional wisdom
Play the recording through once. Ask students to compare their notes in pairs and to answer the gist question.

SUGGESTED ANSWER:

Dezenhall rejects the dogma of traditional PR rules; he feels that attack is the best form of defence.

Listening for detail

3 Ask students to read through the detail questions and to answer as much as they can from their notes and what they recall from the previous exercise. Play the recording again. Give students a few minutes to compare answers in pairs, then take whole-class feedback.

ANSWERS:

1. In the White House under Ronald Reagan. His approach to crisis management is political rather than commercial.
2. Always apologize, always show concern, always instantly recall your product.
3. People think that a sincere apology will be accepted and the wrongdoing will be forgiven, but Dezenhall feels that apologies are usually ineffective.
4. He recommends fighting the accusations, because he believes whoever attacks, wins; whoever defends, loses.
5. He gave it as an example of how by defending himself against a false accusation, Steve would still be generating negative publicity.
6. A villain, a victim and a vindicator. In a crisis, if you can find a vindicator and be seen as a victim rather than a perpetrator, you are forgiven far more easily.

RECORDING SCRIPT

2.13

Steve: If you're in the student loan industry, or in another industry under pressure, you may call in the services of our next guest. Eric Dezenhall is in the business of making bad news go away. He's co-authored a new book called *Damage Control – why everything you know about crisis management is wrong*. Mr Dezenhall was initiated into the world of public relations in the Reagan White House, and he has some different advice for his clients about how to deal with a crisis.

Dezenhall: One of my chief criticisms of crisis management is, there are these rigid, 'Mother Goose' rules that the PR industry applies that are wrong …

S: Such as …

D: Always apologize, always show concern, always instantly recall your product – this rigid dogma is simply wrong. Now there are certain general rules that we follow …

S: Let me just check out why they're wrong – always apologize? That's something that's often said about politicians for example, if you get in some scandal, just say you did something wrong, say you're sorry, get it over with, don't let it go on and on and on, why's that the wrong advice?

D: Well, sometimes it's the right advice, but often it's wrong. What we would like to believe is that apologies are effective. The fact is, we don't see a lot of evidence of that; the Reverend Jim Baker apologized, lost his pulpit. Imus apologized, lost his job.

S: Don Imus, the radio talk-show host – did say he was sorry, many many times, what should he have done, if he was going to you for advice?

D: Well first of all I think he was toast the minute the words came out of his mouth. The track-record of recovering from racial remarks is awful. Basically because corporate advertisers do not want to be in a battle with Al Sharpton or Jesse Jackson. Never ever, ever – because they know they won't win.

S: Well, talk a little about some of the techniques you do apply.

D: Well, I think in our culture, whoever attacks, wins, whoever defends, loses. If I came into your studio and I said, look, listeners, I want everybody to know that Steve stole my wallet, well, suddenly all eyes and ears are on you.

S: And even if I say – I didn't steal your wallet! – I'm still talking about stealing your wallet.

D: Exactly. Every crisis has the three characters, there is a villain, there is a victim and there is a vindicator. And the only way the story, the crisis changes, is if you are able, and you're not always able, to change the characters. Example, Wendy's, the fast food company, was accused of selling chilli that had a finger in it. The narrative of that story didn't change until it was revealed that somebody put a finger in the chilli.

S: Initially Wendy's was the villain, somebody out there eating was the victim, and you're waiting for a vindicator, some investigation …

D: That's exactly right. And so, a lot of times, when you are not seen as the perpetrator of the crisis, you are forgiven far more easily than if you are seen as the villain.

S: You mean, they held on long enough to get out of the perpetrator role, and maybe become sort of a victim after a while.

D: They were essentially a corporate victim, it's hard to be a corporate victim, but the pundits were saying, recall the product, and they didn't, and they were absolutely right not to.

S: If you're truly innocent, you're saying, fight it out, insist on your innocence, because you may lose your chances otherwise – but I would imagine there are people who would take that advice, and even if they're totally guilty, they're going to deny it, stonewall, lie …

D: Well, you're dealing with one of the most sensitive points of my business, which is the clients I don't take. You can't take someone who is hateful and who is totally guilty, and who has no interest in repenting, and put lipstick on that pig.

S: There must be colleagues in your business who feel otherwise, who might say for example, even a guilty person needs a lawyer, and maybe a guilty person also needs a PR agent.

D: And I disagree. I believe that the Constitution allows you a right to a legal defence, the Constitution does not allow you the right to a good reputation.

S: Eric Dezenhall is the author of *Damage Control*. Thanks very much for coming by.

D: Thanks for having me.

Inference

4 This exercise requires students to deduce the meanings from context. As a lead-in to this, ask students to close their books. Play the recording again, pausing at each vocabulary point, and ask students to note down the words they hear. Ask the class to open their Student's Books and to read the sentences to compare. Ask students to guess the meanings from context. Note: *Mother Goose*, *Al Sharpton* and *Jesse Jackson* are all cultural and historical references that rely on additional schematic knowledge.
Go through the answers, providing additional input as required.

ANSWERS:

1 Traditional rules handed down from generation to generation without questioning – *Mother Goose* is a traditional book of stories that every child learns at his / her mother's knee.
2 He was 'burnt', he had no chance of recovering from the mistake.
3 Al Sharpton and Jesse Jackson are black religious leaders and human rights activists.
4 *To stonewall* means to refuse to give information, i.e. to obstruct progress like a stone wall.
5 *To put lipstick on a pig* means to try to make something unpleasant look more attractive by artificial means.

Reading

5 Dictate the following items: *to grieve* /griːv/, *to be toppled* /tɒp(ə)ld/, *perch* /pɜː(r)tʃ/, *canard* /ˈkænɑː(r)d/, *redemption* /rɪˈdempʃ(ə)n/, *grandiose* /ˈɡrændiəʊs/, *to purport* /ˈpɜː(r)pɔː(r)t/, *a lucky break*, *to lionize* /ˈlaɪənaɪz/, *messianic* /ˌmesiˈænɪk/, *to be exempt from* /ɪɡˈzempt/, *scrutiny* /ˈskruːtɪni/, *plaintiff* /ˈpleɪntɪf/, *to opine* /əʊˈpaɪn/, *to torpedo* /tɔː(r)ˈpiːdəʊ/, *stalker* /ˈstɔːkə(r)/ and *whistleblower* /ˈwɪs(ə)lbləʊə(r)/.

Students write down the words and phrases, then compare in pairs. Next, ask students to scan through the text on page 71 to locate the words and to check their spellings. Elicit the words back from students and put them on the board. Elicit or explain meanings. Drill for pronunciation.

For the reading exercise (questions 1–5) give students plenty of time to read through the text and to answer the questions.

Monitor while students do the task and provide help and support as needed. Give students time to compare in pairs, then take whole-class feedback.

ANSWERS:

1 The cell phone manufacturer's stock dropped by 20%, Merck lost roughly $750 million in the fourth quarter of 2005 alone and was expected to have to pay between $4 billion and $18 billion in damages, Perrier lost its position as market leader, and Audi had very few sales in the US market for ten years. Dezenhall refers to them as examples of how crisis management can be crucial to a company's survival (and by implication, how easily his PR company's fees are justified!).
2 *strong leaders* – survivors are able to take difficult decisions
feel-good gurus – survivors do not blindly follow conventional wisdom on reputation management
climate shifts – survivors are flexible enough to adapt when necessary
guarantees – survivors know there are no guarantees, even when major investments are made
pain thresholds – survivors accept short-term losses in return for long-term gains
baby steps – survivors do not try to solve everything at the same time
self-knowledge – survivors are realistic and objective
the little guy – survivors believe that the ordinary citizen does not automatically have more rights than the corporation
luck – survivors sometimes get lucky breaks
3 In the past, crisis management was judged by financial and ethical standards; now a company's handling of a crisis is judged by its stock price, its advertising campaigns, its success or failure in court and its image on TV.
4 The political model of crisis management assumes that a crisis is motivated by an opponent and must be resolved by fighting, rather than being the result of accident or misfortune and resolvable through good communications.
5 Dezenhall seems to be rather cynical about the media: he refers to the *hostile scrutiny* used to *fill the media vacuum on twenty-four-hour-a-day cable news*, and suggests that radio and TV encourage experts to criticize crisis management on the grounds that successfully resolving crises *doesn't make for very good TV*.

Discussion

6 Pre-teach / elicit *an indictment* /ɪnˈdaɪtmənt/ (an official statement accusing someone of committing a crime), *sensationalism* /senˈseɪʃ(ə)nəˌlɪz(ə)m/ (a way of writing or talking about events that makes them seem as exciting and shocking as possible) and *savvy* /ˈsævi/ (knowing a lot about something and being able to make good judgements about it). Ask students to read through the discussion questions individually and to note their answers and opinions. When students have prepared their answers, ask them to work in groups of three to discuss the questions. Monitor the discussions and make notes of language points for later correction and comment.

6.2 Grammar

Perspective and stance

This module focuses on the grammar of perspective and stance, with a range of activities to raise students' awareness and to provide opportunities to practise these grammatical categories.

Preparation

In advance of the lesson, prepare the reading texts (page 73) on an OHT or IWB. This will enable you to highlight relevant sections of text throughout the reading tasks.

Did you know?

Write the words *perspective* and *stance* on the board and ask students to define the meanings in general terms. Provide input based on the information given in the 'Did you know?' box and supply some concrete example sentences to illustrate the point, e.g. *Looking at it from a technical standpoint, it's my view that we need to install at least one new web server.*

Listening for perspective

1 2.14 Ask students in pairs or threes to brainstorm as many 'perspectives' as they can think of. Get the ball rolling by providing a few yourself, e.g. *technical, financial.* Elicit suggestions and put them on the board. Next, write the list of words from exercise 1 on the board in phonemic script (ˌiːkəˈnɒmɪk, ˈkʌltʃ(ə)rel, pəˈlɪtɪk(ə)l, faɪˈnænʃ(ə)l, ˈbɪznəs, ˈgləʊb(ə)l, ˌɪndɪˈvɪdʒuəl, ˈbæŋkɪŋ, ˈeθɪk(ə)l, ˈhjuːmən, ˌsaɪkəˈlɒdʒɪk(ə)l, hɪˈstɒrɪk(ə)l, ˌmænəˈdʒɪəriəl, ˌfɪləˈsɒfɪk(ə)l, ɪnˌvaɪrənˈment(ə)l).
Ask students to work in pairs to practise reading the phonemic script and pronouncing the words, then ask them to write the words down in plain text. Next, ask students to read through the list of words in their books. Check students understand the task. Note: they have to listen for explicit mention of the perspectives, but also have to consider which may be implicit. Play the extract through once. Give students a few moments to check in pairs, then take whole-class feedback.

ANSWERS:

explicit: financial, business, global, banking, human, managerial
implicit: (suggested answers) economic, ethical

2 Ask students to read through the incomplete sentences and to insert any words or chunks they can remember from the previous exercise. Allow some time for pairs to confer. Then play the recording through again, pausing at the appropriate points if necessary to give students time to write in their answers. Ask students to check in pairs, then take whole-class feedback.

ANSWERS:

1 in simple terms
2 if you put this in simple human terms
3 From a human point of view
4 Financially speaking
5 in global terms
6 From the point of view of the banking industry

RECORDING SCRIPT

 2.14

Interviewer: So Li, you're an expert in risk management. Could you start giving us a definition of what risk management is?

Li: Risk management is the attention that organizations must pay in simple terms to things that can and do go wrong. It covers the financial context, technology, human activities, professional and expert activities, and the interface between all of these things.

I: So it's quite wide-ranging then.

L: Oh, absolutely.

I: Do you have a specific example – you mentioned the financial context.

L: Well in 2007 the United States sub-prime mortgage market crashed. This market was created to help those who either did not have much money or who had a bad credit risk to get onto the mortgage and property ladder. If you put this in simple human terms, if somebody is a bad risk, you would not lend them money. This market turned that idea on its head and the worse the risk effectively the more the banks lent them, not just in terms of the sum of money but also the interest rate that was charged to it.

I: So you mean the banks charged these people higher interest rates? Why did they do that?

L: To make more money out of those who could not pay in the first place. The logical thing would be that, if you haven't got much money, you stand little chance of making a repayment. If you haven't got much money and you are asked to repay a huge sum of money at a higher rate of interest, logically, you are never going to make those repayments and the bank is never going to get its money back.

I: What kind of risk management systems did these banks have in place?

L: They simply assumed that these people would make the repayments, and that is the extent that they went to. From a human point of view, they never studied the likely behavioural response that somebody who is short of money with a large loan will have huge difficulty repaying it. Financially speaking, some of the banks saw the problem coming, and did their best to parcel up the bad debts and sell them on, in some cases to banks in other countries.

I: So in global terms this affected everyone?

L: Yes, it was a global phenomenon and its effects were felt worldwide. The debt parcels had a high asset value because there were high repayments attached to them, but in many cases there was a minimal chance of realizing those assets. So it became a global problem. From the point of view of the banking industry, you can see the logic but if you look at it from the point of view of the ordinary human being, it was a disaster.

I: I see. Could you just sum up the banks' mistake for us, in one sentence?

L: The mistakes were that they assumed the money would be repaid once it had been contracted, and they also assumed that the asset value could be sold on, meaning that if anything did go wrong they would be absolved of all responsibility, and also all comeback.

I: That's very interesting …

Reading for stance

3 Dictate the words in the list to students and ask them to write them down as they hear them. Give students a few moments to compare their words with a partner, then elicit the words and put them on the board. Elicit / input the meanings. Ask students to generate example phrases to convey each stance, e.g. *tentative: I think it might be an idea to cut interest rates.; confident: I'm absolutely certain our profits will be higher this quarter.* Finally, drill the pronunciation of each word (ˈtentətɪv, ˈkɒnfɪd(ə)nt, ˌɒptɪˈmɪstɪk, ˌpesəˈmɪstɪk, əˌpɒləˈdʒetɪk, səbˈdʒektɪv, əbˈdʒektɪv, ˈkrɪtɪk(ə)l, sɑːˈ(r)ˈkæstɪk, ˈskeptɪk(ə)l).

Some students may find the reading task quite demanding. Tell students to read through each text and identify some of the stances conveyed. Let pairs confer before eliciting answers from the group and inputting the suggested answers.

> **SUGGESTED ANSWERS:**
>
> Text A: confident, pessimistic, initially more objective, later more subjective / critical / subjective
>
> Text B: fairly confident, quite critical, subjective
>
> Text C: quietly confident (despite tentative language), partly optimistic, partly pessimistic, objective / sceptical
>
> Text D: objective, apologetic, confident

Identifying stance expressions

4 Ask students to underline the language that conveys stance in each text. Display the texts on an OHP or IWB. Ask students to point out the language conveying stance and highlight it on the board. Alternatively, highlight relevant sections of the text and ask students to identify the stance conveyed in each case.

> **SUGGESTED ANSWERS:**
>
> Text A: seem likely to continue (tentative); across the board (confident); generally (fairly confident); there remains little doubt (confident); not to mention (confident); rapidly deteriorating / wholly unpleasant / in tatters (pessimistic); in my view (subjective)
>
> Text B: to make matters worse (pessimistic); she is now promoting so forcefully were ... the opposition (sarcastic); surely that is an example of hypocrisy, is it not? (critical)
>
> Text C: on balance / it could be argued / seems somewhat limited /may lie ahead (tentative); some grounds for optimism (optimistic); considerable doubts remain (pessimistic, objective)
>
> Text D: we recognize that our standards clearly fell short (apologetic); we remain confident that (confident).

Expressing stance

5 This is another task that some students may find challenging. Before asking students to transform the sentences, brainstorm ways of expressing categories of stance, e.g.

Confident:
It's surely the case that ..., We're absolutely certain / confident that ..., ... is bound / certain / sure to happen.

Tentative:
It's a possibility that ..., ... might happen, it could be argued that ..., On balance ..., It seems that ...

Objective:
It's a well-known fact that ..., There remains little doubt that ...

Critical:
You should(n't) have ..., It was wrong / inappropriate to ...

Subjective:
In my view ..., As I see it ...

Apologetic:
We realize that ... fell short of expectations, We regret to announce that ..., We're sorry to say that ...

Get students to brainstorm ideas in pairs or threes. Elicit suggestions and put them on the board. Provide extra input as necessary.

Once you have collated an array of suitable ways of expressing each stance, ask students to rewrite the sentences provided using the expressions. Go through the answers with the class. Then ask pairs to test each other, e.g.

A: *Your risk management plan is without doubt full of holes. (confident)*

B: *We're absolutely certain that your risk management plan is full of holes.*

> **SUGGESTED ANSWERS:**
>
> 1 Without doubt your risk management plan is absolutely full of holes.
> 2 On balance the strategy has been reasonably successful.
> 3 It looks increasingly likely that prices may rise.
> 4 I must say that you really should have paid more attention to the risks involved.
> 5 There are strong reasons to believe that the product is firmly taking hold.
> 6 There is little likelihood of the same thing happening twice.
> 7 We may have made mistakes, but we have learned some useful lessons.
> 8 In some cases sales have maintained a satisfactory level.

Internet research

As risk management is a broad area, you could break the Internet research activity into sub-categories (e.g. *identifying risk; risk assessment; risk treatment*). Divide the class into three groups and assign a topic for each group to investigate using the Internet. Then reform students into groups to exchange information.

6.3 Vocabulary

Risk Management and digital risk

This module presents and reviews key vocabulary related to risk management through engaging reading and listening tasks.

Lead-in

Draw students' attention to the photograph and the quotation. Ask students to discuss the meaning of the quote. Prompt with questions, e.g. *In what ways is risk good?*, *What is the danger of not properly managing risk?* Encourage a brief class discussion.

Brainstorming

1 Use picture or photo of a coffee shop as a stimulus for this activity. Ask students to work in threes. Explain that they are planning to open a coffee shop near a university and that their task is to identify the key risks facing their new business venture. If necessary, prompt with some key areas to consider, e.g. *money, staff, products, supply chain, premises*. Monitor and offer help as necessary. Elicit all suggestions and put them on the board, then ask students to classify the risks if they can.

SUGGESTED ANSWERS:

hazard risks: fire, theft, flood, vandalism
operational risks: overheads exceed income, suppliers fail to deliver, coffee is sub-standard, staff problems
financial risks: cash flow problems, customers don't pay, bank refuses overdraft
strategic risks: coffee is too expensive or too cheap for the market, students prefer other drinks, competition

Reading

2 The text contains the following vocabulary items, which you may decide to pre-teach or post-teach depending on time available and the structure of your lesson: *myriad* /'mɪriəd/ (very many, especially too many to count), *proactively* / prəʊ'æktɪvli/ (in a manner of taking action and making changes before they need to be made, rather than waiting until problems develop), *in a nutshell* /'nʌt̩ʃel/ (used for saying that you are going to express something in a simple direct way), *viability* /ˌvaɪə'bɪləti/ (being likely to succeed or make a profit), *fluctuations* /ˌflʌktʃu'eɪʃ(ə)nz/ (frequent changes in the amount, value or level of something), *misaligned* / mɪsə'laɪnd/ (incorrectly matched), *a holistic approach* / həʊ'lɪstɪk/ (thinking about the whole of something, and not just dealing with particular aspects), *to have one's bases covered* (to be fully protected) and *be detrimental to* / ˌdetrɪ'ment(ə)l/ (to be harmful to).
Ask students to scan through the text quickly and highlight all of the risks mentioned, and add these to the list of risks they identified in the earlier brainstorming session. Elicit students' answers. Next, give students a few minutes to read through the text again and to highlight the four categories of risk mentioned. Allow pairs to confer before eliciting answers. Finally, ask students to identify the three advantages of enterprise risk management. Again, allow students to check in pairs, then take whole-class feedback.

ANSWERS:

1 students' own answers
2 hazard, financial, operational and strategic
3 makes risks more prominent and real to managers; expands a company's definition of risk; improves perception of 'good' risk that can help a company grow, and 'bad' risk that will only lead to loss

3 For this exercise, refer students back to the four categories of risk and put them on the board in tabular or mind-map form, e.g.

RISKS			
Hazard	Strategic	Operational	Financial

Ask students to copy the table (or mind map), locate all the risks mentioned in the article and enter them under the appropriate headings. Elicit answers and put them on the board.
If you have time, extend this activity by asking students to add their own examples of risks in each category. This could also be tied into the Internet search activity suggested on page 75 of the Student's Book.

ANSWERS:

hazard: fire, theft, flood, property damage, smashing a company car
strategic: competitive pressures, customer shortfall, misaligned products
operational: supply chain problems, cost overruns
financial: interest rate and foreign exchange fluctuations

4 This is a fun anagram activity that students should be able to complete fairly quickly. Provide models of pronunciation for *manage* ('mænɪdʒ), *mitigate* ('mɪtɪɡeɪt), *quantify* ('kwɒntɪfaɪ) and *prioritize* /praɪ'ɒrɪtaɪz/. Then elicit / input the meanings of each expression in relation to risk.

ANSWERS:

1 face   2 deal with   3 examine   4 manage
5 mitigate   6 identify   7 quantify   8 prioritize

Describing risks

5 Ask students to close their books. Dictate the verbs and expressions 1–12 to the class and ask students to write them down. Give students a few moments to compare in pairs. Ask students to read through the phrases and to check their spelling. Next, ask students to read through the article again and to locate the phrases within the text and to identify what the phrases refer to, e.g. *to trace to – 58% of companies traced their stock drops to strategic risks.* Go through the answers then ask students to categorize the verbs and expressions according to the three categories provided. Take whole-class feedback.

ANSWERS:

1 a   2 c   3 b   4 a   5 c   6 b
7 a   8 c   9 b   10 a   11 c   12 b

6 With lower-level or very mixed ability classes, be ready to supply the words in mixed-up order to help students accomplish this task. This would also be a useful intermediary checking activity for stronger groups, that is, once they have attempted the cloze for the first time, supply the answers in random order for students to confirm, check and modify their answers before you provide the solution. Ask students to look carefully at the words around each gap to provide clues to the word form, tense and meaning required in each case.

Note: for number. For point 4, 'reduce' is also acceptable.

ANSWERS:

1 dealing   2 detrimental / material   3 account
4 reduce / mitigate   5 steps   6 performance / viability
7 cited   8 continuity   9 managing   10 bases
11 impact 12 face

Listening

7 🔊 2.15 Write the phrase *e-business* on the board and ask students to provide some examples of e-businesses that they are familiar with. Now ask students to work in threes for a few minutes to brainstorm possible risks facing e-businesses. Encourage students to consider hazard, strategic, operational and financial risks. Elicit suggestions and put them on the board. Play the recording through once and ask students to make notes. Give a few moments for students to compare in pairs, then take whole-class feedback.

8 Ask students to read the two comprehension questions and to answer the questions based on the notes they made during the listening. Play the recording through again for students to check and modify their answers. Go through the answers with the class. Check the pronunciation of *cybersquatting* /ˈsaɪbe(r)ˌskwɒtɪŋ/.

ANSWERS:

1 passing off – the unauthorized commercial use of a company's brand, name, logo, etc.
cybersquatting – registering a domain name featuring another company's brand name
hacking – malicious security incidents or breaches
protest issues – manipulating Internet users to protest, boycott or attack a company product or site
2 by using software and specialist analysis to locate, report and act on abuse

9 Dictate the words provided and ask students to write them down. Tell students to check in pairs, then elicit the words and put them on the board, paying attention to meaning, stress and pronunciation. Ask students if they noticed the contexts in which the words were used in the listening, then play the recording through again if needed as a reminder. Next, ask students to complete the gapped text using the words supplied. Take whole-class feedback.

ANSWERS:

1 abuse   2 perpetrators   3 reversal   4 monitor
5 issue   6 desist   7 litigate   8 pursue

RECORDING SCRIPT

 2.15

Interviewer: Steve, your website, Brand Intelligence, claims that digital infringements are costing e-businesses $90 million a day!

Steve: That's right.

I: So, what sort of risks are you open to these days if you're doing your business online?

S: Well, if you have a successful e-business, one problem you're very exposed to is passing off, or ambush marketing. You wake up one day to find someone else has a website which is masquerading as your company, and making money by trading on your company's name – often they will even pirate your own text, images and logo.

I: Nasty!

S: Yeah, and not very easy to deal with. Another classic is cybersquatting – that's when you have an established offline brand and you decide to start an online business to reach more customers. Much to your surprise, you then find out that someone else is freeloading on your reputation by using a domain name featuring your brand name!

I: Hm. And what about hackers?

S: Yes, of course, they're a major problem, and it's still growing as the Internet gets larger and larger – everything from simply defacing web pages to cracking credit card and information databases. Every year nearly half of UK businesses suffer a malicious security incident or breach. But there are also more unexpected risks, what we call

protest issues. If your business relies on the Internet to reach an instant worldwide audience, you are vulnerable to protests and rumours of all kinds. It's incredibly easy to incite customers to boycott a company or its products, to try to manipulate your stock price or simply to bombard a defenceless mailbox with hate mail!

I: Sounds like it's a real jungle out there! But you have solutions, right?

S: Right. We use a combination of unique, highly sophisticated software and specialist analysis to locate and report areas of brand risk, damage and abuse online. For instance, we can scan the Internet to find anyone who is illegally using your logo, even if it has been modified.

I: But what can you do to stop this kind of abuse?

S: Once we've identified the problem, there are lots of solutions, we track perpetrators, we initiate reversal, and then monitor progress.

I: Initiate reversal? Can you be more specific?

S: Each individual case is different, and we adapt to each customer's needs and wishes. At a basic level we issue 'cease and desist' orders to infringing site owners, to get them to remove their sites: we can also get sites removed from ISPs and search engines.

I: So if someone googles my brand, only the real site will come up, not the fakes?

S: Yes. And in more serious cases we get our expert legal trademark partners involved to litigate for damages or pursue criminal and civil action.

10 Check students understand the meaning of *to masquerade*, *to deface*, *to infringe* and *malicious*. Encourage students to justify and explain their choices.

SUGGESTED ANSWERS:

(students may be able to defend other choices)
1 trading   2 scan   3 malicious

Discussion

11 Allow plenty of time for this activity. Get students to do this in groups of three. Groups should note down their ideas and prepare short presentations for the class. Suggest that groups use a presentation programme and that each member of the group present a different strategy (e.g. student A: strategic and operational risks; B: financial and digital risks; C: managing the risks). Set time limits for the presentations of ten minutes maximum. Note language points for post-correction.

Internet research

The suggested activity here can be linked in with the categorizing risks activity in exercise 3 of the Student's Book.

6.4 Management skills

Communicating in a crisis

This module provides opportunities for the development of speaking skills around the topic of crises, with a particular focus on dealing with media interviews.

Discussion

1 Take in some pictures of an outdoor party and fireworks to introduce the discussion. Explain the context as described in exercise 1. Tell students that you are going to read out a series of ways of dealing with the press and that as you do so, they are to write *I agree*, *I disagree* or *it depends* in their notebooks. Read each sentence to the students, allowing them enough time to think about their answers and to note down their responses. Then ask students to briefly compare their answers in pairs. This should stimulate some recall of the six situations you read out as students discuss their responses. Next, arrange students in groups of three and ask them to read through the statements on page 76 of the Student's Book. Ask them to come to a unanimous group decision on each point. Encourage students to justify their choices. Finally, take whole-class feedback.

SUGGESTED ANSWERS:

1 This is preferable to giving an insufficiently prepared interview.
2 Experts advise smiling unless someone has died.
3 It's usually a good idea to be as positive as possible.
4 Do not argue with journalists; it is better to focus on the safety measures which were taken.
5 Never ask journalists to reveal their sources.
6 Do not be led into speculating about things you do not control.

Reading

2 Pre-teach or elicit the following vocabulary: *to strangle* /ˈstræŋg(ə)l/ at birth (to stop something as soon as it has begun), *the essence of* (the central meaning or theme), *toxic* /ˈtɒksɪk/ (poisonous and harmful), *a sound bite* (a short comment that is taken from a longer conversation or speech and broadcast alone because it is very interesting or effective), *to be drawn into* (to become involved in a conversation or situation), *outcomes* (the final results of a process, meeting, activity, etc.), *alliteration* /əˌlɪtəˈreɪʃ(ə)n/ (the use of the letter or sound at the beginning of words in a sentence, especially in poetry), *reinforce* /ˌriːɪnˈfɔː(r)s/ (to make an idea, belief or feeling stronger) and *analogies* /əˈnælədʒiz/ (comparisons between two situations, processes, etc. that are intended to show that the two are similar).
Set the following comprehension questions related to the first part of the text:
What is the secret of dealing effectively with a crisis? (preparation)
What kinds of crisis are you unlikely ever to have to deal with? (major national crises, such as starving refugees or poisoned water supplies)
What kinds are you likely to have to deal with? (small-scale crises, such as projects being behind schedule or orders not being delivered on time)

Ask students to read the first section of the text and to answer the three questions you have supplied. Then ask students to close their books and in pairs or threes to brainstorm the 'dos' and 'don'ts' of communicating in a crisis. Elicit ideas from the class, before asking students to read through the text and to compare their ideas with the pieces of advice given in the text. Finally, ask students to decide whether *do* or *don't* is more suitable in each case and to discuss with a partner. Go through the answers before asking students to decide how each piece of advice corresponds to the situation outlined in exercise 1.

ANSWERS:

1 Do   2 don't   3 Do   4 Do
5 don't   6 don't   7 Do   8 Do
Tip 1 applies to response 1
Tips 3, 4, 6, 7 and 8 could apply to response 3
Tip 5 applies to response 6

Listening

3 2.16–2.23 To help structure this listening task, put a table on the board and ask students to copy it and use it to note down their answers, e.g.

Extract	Kind of crisis	Tips applied / not applied
A		
B		

Explain the task and play the extracts through once, pausing after each one for students to make notes. Give students an opportunity to check in pairs, then take whole-class feedback.

ANSWERS:

A) Crisis: the need to keep paying for risk management, Tip: 8
B) Crisis: making sure competitors do not win, Tip: 3
C) Crisis: old machinery threatens productivity, Tip: 7
D) Crisis: industrial action / strike, Tip: 2 / 6
E) Crisis: natural disaster (hurricane), Tip: 1X
F) Crisis: allegedly harmful effects of drug, Tip: 5
G) Crisis: suspected corruption or insider trading, Tip: 4
H) Crisis: poor sales, Tip: 6X

4 Ask students to read through the gapped texts and to complete as much as they can from memory. Allow students to confer in pairs. Then play the recording through again a second time for students to complete the task. Go through the answers with the class, drawing attention to the key elements of each extract. Drill for stress, intonation and pronunciation. Give students an opportunity to practise each phrase with the modelled intonation, stress and pronunciation.

ANSWERS:

1 is like   2 legitimate, issue   3 to the point
4 focus, positives   5 important, remember   6 forget, as yet
7 briefly sum up   8 quietly confident

RECORDING SCRIPT

2.16–2.23

A)
A: Do we really need to keep forking out on risk management?
B: Well, running a business without risk management is like walking a tightrope. It's only a matter of time before you fall off!

B)
C: How on earth are we going to find space for another big development project?
D: It's a legitimate question, but I think the bigger issue here is really how we make sure that our competitors don't beat us to market.

C)
E: I don't see why we should fix something that's not broken!
F: Quite simply, although the machines we have at the moment aren't broken now, we know they won't go on for ever. Even more to the point, the new machines will improve precision, productivity and profitability.

D)
G: What sanctions are you planning to take against the strikers?
H: Let's focus on the positives, shall we? The really important thing to remember is that talks are underway, and we hope to be able to release details of an agreement in the next few hours.

E)
I: How do you intend to finance rebuilding the homes that were lost in the hurricane?
J: To be honest, I don't really know. We haven't thought about it yet, it's too early to say.

F)
K: What sort of compensation will you be offering people who suffer from side effects?
L: Let's not forget that as yet there is no evidence of patients suffering any ill effects: we are simply withdrawing the drug temporarily as a precaution.

G)
M: Can you confirm that several company Directors sold large blocks of shares shortly before the profit warning?
N: Let me briefly sum up the current position. An inquiry is currently being conducted with the full cooperation of all staff. The results will be announced in due course, and we are quietly confident that the commission will report that there was no wrongdoing. Thank you.

H)
O: Why are you asking us to pump up the advertising budget when the product is hopeless?
P: Well, it's not completely hopeless; of course we haven't sold as many as we'd like, but the market isn't exactly helping us at the moment.

Alliteration

5 Provide some examples of alliteration as illustration of this literary device, e.g. *the fickle finger of fate* and *a lover's last lament*. Ask students if they can supply one or two examples themselves.

Ask students to provide an alliterated word for each sentence. Monitor to check progress. Then ask students to work in threes and to put their ideas together. Take whole-class feedback and put students' ideas on the board. Drill for pronunciation, rhythm, rhyme and intonation.

SUGGESTED ANSWERS:

1 better 2 sun / surf 3 bank / business 4 staff
5 products 6 food / fish / fruit 7 happy
8 effort, risk / emissions

Analogies

6 Remind students of the meaning of *analogy* (a comparison between two situations, processes etc. that is intended to show that the two are similar). Explain that one way to make an analogy is by using the structure *... is like ...* Dictate the first set of sentence halves (1–6) to students and explain that their task is to provide suitable endings for each one. Demonstrate the task by modelling the first analogy using the endings provided. Monitor while students do the task. Then get pairs to compare their answers before eliciting suggestions from the class. Get the class to vote on the best endings.

Next, draw students' attention to the exercise in the book and ask them to match the sentence halves provided.

ANSWERS:
1 c 2 f 3 a 4 e 5 b 6 d

7 This exercise builds on exercise 6, and can be conducted in the same way. Again, elicit ideas from the class and get students to vote on the best suggestions.

As a fun alternative, get students to search Google using the stems as whole search strings, e.g. *"Learning English is like ..."* (Note: the double inverted commas are required for this search in order to return the whole string unbroken). Get students to note down the funniest or most appropriate analogies that they find and to share them with the class.

SUGGESTED ANSWERS:

1 climbing a mountain, the higher you get, the harder it is to make progress.
2 acting, if you haven't learnt your lines, you're in trouble.
3 bees, tolerable when there are only one or two, but deadly when they swarm.
4 underground trains, if you miss one, the next is never far behind.

Speaking

8 Ask students to work in pairs. Ask each pair to select a crisis situation from the list 1–6. Try to ensure if possible that each pair has chosen a different situation. Ask the first pair to prepare for the interview using the bullet points for guidance. Ask the rest of the class to formulate questions to ask the interviewees.

9 Ask the class to conduct the interview as a press conference. Make notes on students' language performance for remedial correction and comment. Repeat stages 8 and 9 until all pairs have been interviewed.

6.5 Writing

Press statements

This module focuses on the linguistic features of press statements and provides practice in writing this form of business correspondence.

Preparation

Search the Internet for examples of press releases and press statements as authentic materials to use for this lesson. It would also be useful to have one or two examples on an OHP, an IWB or a laptop and projector for highlighting textual features during the lesson. The texts on page 78 of the Student's Book could also be displayed on an OHP or an IWB to draw students' attention to the features of the text.

Internet research

As suggested, ask students to search for press statements and releases from a range of companies and to summarize these to their classmates. Useful search terms for these include *company name + press statement / release*. The press releases / statements collected by students can also be referred to throughout the lesson to identify the key linguistic features.

Discussion

1 Bring some examples of press releases and press statements to the class. Divide the class into two groups. Give group A copies of the press releases and group B copies of the press statements. (Note: if you cannot access any authentic examples, use the texts provided in the Student's Book instead). Give students a few minutes to read their texts and to highlight the key information. Provide some guiding questions, e.g. *Who wrote the press statement / release?, What is the purpose of the press statement / release?, When was it written?, What's the topic?, Is it positive or negative?* Next, ask students from each group to form pairs (A and B) and summarize their text for their partners. Then ask the pairs to identify any similarities or differences between their documents, e.g. layout, tense, voice and aspect. Ask students to discuss these points and then conduct a class discussion to highlight and summarize the key points. Draw students' attention to the box defining a press release and a press statement and ask them to identify which is which. Note: the key difference is that press statements tend to be in response to criticism or attack.

ANSWERS:

a) press release
b) press statement

Reading

2 Allow students to refer to the authentic examples you have provided as they do this exercise. Give students a few moments to check in pairs, then take whole-class feedback.

ANSWERS:

Students' own answers

3 Before asking students to read through the list of collocations for this exercise, ask them to read through the texts carefully and to think of suitable words to fill each gap. Give students a few minutes for this and then ask them to confer in pairs. Elicit suggestions from the class. Next, ask students to read through the list of words and to match them to the gaps. Again, allow a few moments for checking in pairs, then take whole-class feedback. Go through the answers and provide feedback as needed.

ANSWERS:

1 Tremendous progress 2 preventing (violent) disorder 3 posing a risk 4 wholeheartedly agree 5 secure environment 6 targeting (anti-social) behaviours 7 openly admit 8 utterly convinced 9 minute traces 10 fully informed

Analysis

4 Ask students to read through the two example texts in the Student's Book to confirm their answers before you provide the solution. Allow a few moments for students to check in pairs, then take whole-class feedback.

You may need to pre-teach the following vocabulary from the texts: *to clamp down* (to make a determined attempt to stop people doing something bad or illegal), *a banning order* (a decree that prohibits something), *traces* /treɪsɪz/ *of* (a slight sign that someone has been present or that something has happened) *pesticide* /ˈpestɪsaɪd/ (a chemical used for killing insects, especially those that damage crops), *residue* /ˈrezɪdjuː/ (the part of something that remains after the rest has gone or ended).

ANSWERS

address, city, the context, background info on the situation, quotations, date

5 This exercise is fairly straightforward, so give students a minute or two to answer the questions individually, then to check in pairs. Go through the answers with the class, drawing attention to the sections of text that the questions refer to.

ANSWERS:

1 A   2 A   3 B   4 B

Style

6 Ask students to close their books. Dictate the following words for students to write down: *outbreak* (ˈaʊtˌbreɪk), *circular* (ˈsɜː(r)kjʊlə(r)), *allayed* (əˈleɪd), *quelled* (kweld), *allegations* (ˌæləˈɡeɪʃ(ə)nz), *cruelty* (ˈkruːəlti), *misleading* (mɪsˈliːdɪŋ), *acknowledge* (əkˈnɒlɪdʒ), *rumours* (ˈruːmə(r)z), *fraudulent* (ˈfrɔːdjʊlənt), *quash* (kwɒʃ), *dispel* (dɪˈspel) and *resolve* (rɪˈzɒlv).

Ask students to compare their answers in pairs. Next, elicit the words from the class and write them on the board in phonemic script. Drill the pronunciation of each word. Now ask students to read through the seven sentences on page 79 and to check the spelling of each word. Next, ask students to work in pairs and to discuss the meaning of each word, if they know it. Elicit meanings from the class and provide prompts to guide students, e.g. *The company sent a circular to all shareholders – what do you think a circular might be? What sort of information do you think the circular would contain?* Once you have checked the meaning of each word, ask students to identify the words that cannot be used in each gap. Check through with the class and clarify as needed. You can then ask students to test their partners on suitable words to fill the gaps, e.g.
A: *The organization _____ responsibility for ...*
B: *accepts*
The gapped sentences can also be recycled into a weekly progress test with the options removed. Students have to fill the gaps from memory with two suitable words.

ANSWERS:

1 c   2 c   3 c   4 a   5 b   6 c   7 c

Writing

7 For the writing task, students are required to write a press statement, incorporating the information in the bullet points. Make it clear to students that they are not to copy the bullet points verbatim, but have to express the key points in their own words. Remind students that their press statements must be laid out in a suitable document format and include the features identified in exercise 4. Encourage students to use suitable phrases from exercise 6. Give students time to brainstorm ideas in pairs and to make notes before they begin writing. If you have a computer lab available you could make the task more authentic by getting students to word-process their documents.

6.6 Case study
Périgord Gourmet

This module deals with the case of a company that produces *foie gras* and an attempt to sabotage it. The students' task is to identify the risks this company faces and to deal with a potentially damaging case of poisoning.

Preparation

If you can, obtain some items related to foie gras (pictures, tins, etc.) to introduce the theme of the module and to help contextualize the activities.

Internet research

The Animal Enterprise Terrorism Act is a controversial U.S. law that came into force in 2006. It is designed to protect enterprises that use animals from acts of force, violence or threats committed by animal rights activists. As the Internet research instruction suggests, searching for the key words will return a good deal of information about this law. Divide your class into two groups and ask one group to search for arguments in favour of the law and the other group for arguments against. When the groups have done this, pair students from each group to discuss the topic before holding a whole-class debate.

Discussion

1 Ask students to work individually to read through the bullet points and consider how they would feel about working for the types of company listed. Ask students to consider their answers primarily from an ethical point of view and to justify their reasons. Monitor to check progress and provide help or guidance as needed. Next, ask students to work in small groups to discuss their answers. While the discussions are in progress, monitor and note any language points for post-correction or comment. Finally, hold a brief whole-class discussion of the points.

2 Ask students to close their books. Show them some of the pictures / realia related to foie gras that you have brought to the class. Ask students to work in threes to brainstorm everything they know about foie gras. You could also provide students with a few discussion questions about the topic, e.g. *Have you ever eaten foie gras? Where is it produced? How is it produced?*
Elicit ideas and put them on the board to build up a picture of your students' knowledge of the product.
Next, draw students' attention to the photos on page 80 of the Student's Book and ask them to read through the encyclopaedia extract. Ask students one or two comprehension questions, e.g. *Why is foie gras 'a subject of controversy'? Where is production of foie gras banned?*
Elicit / pre-teach the following lexis: *a truffle* (a fungus that grows under the ground and is very expensive to buy because people consider it a special food), *to be unashamed* (to feel or show no remorse or shame), *to withdraw* (to remove or take back) and *direct action* (the use of immediate acts, such as demonstrations or sabotage).
Draw students' attention to the Périgord Gourmet web page and ask them to read through the information. Next ask students to check the true / false statements that follow and to confer in pairs. Elicit answers from the class. Note: the solutions to the true / false statements are mostly neither true nor false and are intended to promote discussion and interpretation of the information provided.

ANSWERS:

1N (We do not know if PG actually produces foie gras, or just distributes it, and we do not know, although we may strongly suspect, that force-feeding is used.)

2F (Production is banned in these countries, but not purchasing or consumption; and PG delivers worldwide, so no problem for the UK and Germany.)

3T (Europe + France = more than 50%)

4N (Possibly, but the threat is vague – direct action against PG and its suppliers, contractors or customers.)

5N (Possibly, but imports come from Hungary, and the warehouse may be more difficult to protect.)

6N (Probably not, since several steps in the production process appear to be outsourced, so more of these jobs would be lost than in the company's administrative departments.)

Discussion

3 This task will require some clarification before you ask students to start brainstorming. It might be helpful to break this task down into independent stages to ensure that your students accomplish each stage fully before proceeding to the next.

Write the four categories of risk on the board: *hazard, financial, operational, strategic*. Ask students to work in groups of three to brainstorm all of the risks facing PG at this stage. Monitor as the groups do this and provide help as needed.

Once all of the groups have brainstormed the risks, explain that their task now is to assess the potential impact of each risk on the company's long-term future. Again, monitor to check the groups understand what to do and to provide help and support as needed.

When the groups have identified the potential impact of each risk, explain that they now have to decide how they should react to each risk, using the categories *tolerate, treat, terminate* and *transfer*. Check students understand these concepts in this context. You may need to clarify by providing examples as a model, e.g. *tolerate by carrying on business as usual, treat by increasing security, terminate by closing one of your production plants, transfer by outsourcing production to third-party contractors*. Again, monitor to check progress and provide help.

When groups have finished this third stage of the task, ask groups to compare their ideas, then take whole-class feedback.

SUGGESTED ANSWERS:

hazard risks:
damage or sabotage of production facilities: short-term impact, can probably be transferred by insurance
theft or 'kidnap' of animals from farms: short-term impact, treat by increased security
kidnap or attacks on staff by animal rights groups: major impact, treat by increased security or terminate by giving up sale of foie gras

financial risks:
exchange rates make products too expensive in foreign markets: limited impact for luxury product, tolerate or treat using financial instruments and / or outsourcing
exchange rates make Hungarian imports too expensive: short-term impact, treat by sourcing alternative suppliers

operational risks:
raw materials: quality problems, disease: short-term impact, treat by improving quality systems, sourcing alternative suppliers
processing and warehousing: sabotage of finished goods: major impact, treat with increased security or terminate by giving up sale of foie gras
distribution: website breakdown or sabotage, transport or postal strikes, picketing: impact could be major, treat with redundant systems and increased security

strategic risks:
sale of foie gras banned or limited in Europe, or customer boycott: major impact, treat by lobbying, developing alternative products and markets
damage to company's image by association with animal cruelty: major impact, treat by advertising or changing production methods

Listening

4 🔊 2.24 Explain the context of the listening: that Pierre receives a call from the US. Play the extract through once and ask students to take notes. Ask students to compare notes in pairs, then elicit from the class. At this stage you may want to elicit and clarify the meaning of: *muscle spasm* (a sudden, involuntary contraction of a muscle or group of muscles), *a physician* (a medical doctor), *strychnine* (a very poisonous white crystalline compound).

Next, ask students to read through the four questions in the Student's Book and to answer the questions using their notes. Allow pairs to confer and play the extract a second time for students to check their answers. Go through the answers with the class.

ANSWERS:

1 Washington Police Department
2 Two French citizens have been taken to hospital with suspected food poisoning
3 Are you aware of any other similar cases? How difficult would it be for someone to get access to your product?
4 Strychnine poisoning

RECORDING SCRIPT

 2.24

Pierre-Yves Gaget: Âllo, oui?

Cindie Hauser: Is this Monsieur Gaget?

PYG: Speaking – how can I help you, Madame?

CH: Cindie Hauser here, from the Washington Police Department.

PYG: Yes?

CH: I'm afraid I have rather bad news for you. Two French citizens living here in DC have been taken to hospital with suspected food poisoning. It seems they'd been celebrating their wedding anniversary with a jar of your foie gras. They're quite seriously ill.

PYG: Oh my God!

CH: We're optimistic they'll recover quickly – fortunately they went straight to the hospital when they started having muscle spasms. But I'm really calling you for two reasons. The first is to ask whether you are aware of any other similar cases?

PYG: No, no, nothing like this has ever happened before! We have very, very strict quality controls ...

CH: Hm. How difficult would it be for someone to get access to your product before it's shipped?

PYG: Well, not very – there are any number of people involved in cooking, packaging, warehousing and shipping – but why do you ask?

CH: We're still waiting for the lab report – but the physician in the ER room said they had all the classic symptoms of strychnine poisoning.

PYG: Strychine?!

CH: Yeah, it's one of the easiest poisons to acquire – it's found in rat poison.

Discussion

5 Ask students to work in small groups (threes or fours) and to discuss the following questions:

What problems does Pierre now face?

If you were Pierre, what would you do?

Elicit ideas from the class. Now ask students to read through Pierre's notes on page 81 and to discuss the question: *How do you think Pierre and PG should handle this crisis?*

Elicit ideas from the class and conduct a brief open-class discussion of the current status of the crisis and the best courses of action.

Listening

6 2.25 Pre-teach / elicit the following lexis: *fatal* /ˈfeɪt(ə)l/ (causing or capable of causing death), *leads* /liːdz/ (information that may help someone to solve a problem or to find out the truth about something, especially a crime), *to cover up* (to hide the truth about something by not telling what you know or by preventing other people from telling what they know) and *carte blanche* /ˌkɑː(r)t ˈblɑːnʃ/ (the freedom to do what you want in a particular situation).

Explain to students that they are going to receive a voice message from Pierre and that they should note down the key points as they listen. Play the message through once. Ask students to compare their notes in pairs, then take whole-class feedback.

Draw students' attention to the questions for exercise 6 and ask them to answer the questions using their notes. If required, play the recording again for students to check, before going through the answers with the class.

RECORDING SCRIPT

 2.25

PYG: Hi, this is Pierre-Yves. Sorry to call you in the middle of the night, but it's urgent, and I need you to be working on this first thing in the morning. The good news is, the two people in Washington are making a good recovery. It seems the strychnine dose was too low to be fatal. The bad news is there are three more cases – in Hong Kong. Plus, the animal rights people have hacked into our website and left a message about the poisonings – but they claim they didn't do it. The police are on the case, but no leads yet. The thing is, it's out in the open now, so we can't afford to be seen to be covering up. I want you to call a press conference for tomorrow afternoon. I won't be there – I'm flying out to Hong Kong – so I want you to make a short statement, and then take questions. You know much more about these things than I do, so I'm giving you carte blanche. Good luck.

7 This exercise is preparation for the simulation that follows. Make sure students understand that they will be calling a press conference tomorrow afternoon.

Ask students to work in threes to prepare for the press conference for tomorrow afternoon. Refer the groups to the bullet points for exercise 7 and encourage them to use the information they have gathered throughout the unit to inform their press statements. Monitor and provide guidance and ideas during this stage of the preparation. Set a time limit of about 20 minutes for this stage.

Next, ask the groups to imagine that they are the journalists who are going to attend the press conference, and brainstorm questions they would like to ask the representative of Périgord Gourmet. Again, monitor and provide guidance and ideas as needed. Set a time limit of 10 to 15 minutes for this.

Simulation

8 If possible, arrange the tables and chairs in the classroom to represent a typical press conference layout, with company representatives sitting at the front facing the journalists. Give each group a few minutes to make their press statements and to answer questions from the journalists. Listen and make notes of language points for later attention, correction and comment. Once all groups have held their press conferences, ask the class to take a vote on which team handled the crisis most effectively.

Review 5 and 6 answers

Review 5

(page 82 in the Student's Book)

5 Strategic marketing

1

1 Where do you think branding comes from?
2 Whose marketing strategy seems less attractive than what you can offer?
3 How does your brand strategy differentiate you from the competition?
4 Which socioeconomic or demographic characteristics define a group? / Which characteristics define a socioeconomic group or demographic?
5 What do you mean when you say strategy is power? / When you say strategy is power, what do you mean?
6 Why is strategic thinking a better choice than fire fighting? / Why is fire fighting a better choice than strategic thinking?
7 How, then, are you supposed to compete? / How are you supposed to compete, then?
8 What can you do that would ensure you succeed?

2

1 across
2 until
3 without
4 except
5 on account of
6 in accordance with
7 in the light of
8 With regard to

3

additional, supplementary
advantage, edge
adapt, tailor
anticipation, hope
concerns, worries
constitutes, forms
create, devise
evoke, suggest
hikes, increases
temporary, transient

4

1 a brand
2 an impression
3 prices
4 appeal / problem
5 question
6 text
7 a solution

5

1 c
2 e
3 b
4 d
5 a
6 j
7 g
8 f
9 i
10 h

6

1 clarifying
2 echoing
3 paraphrasing
4 focusing on the next step
5 reflecting what the other person feels
6 summarizing
7 not saying anything

Review 6

(page 83 in the Student's Book)

6 Risk management

1

1 relaunch
2 recover
3 fight
4 occupy
5 refer
6 practise
7 speculate
8 commit

2

1 circulate
2 charged
3 accused
4 accept
5 deny
6 pose
7 determined
8 committed

3

1 e
2 g
3 b
4 d
5 c
6 f
7 h
8 a

4

1 bombarded
2 abuse
3 vulnerable
4 tolerate
5 strategy
6 identify
7 monitor
8 damage
9 impact
10 resources

5

1 incorrect: 'tremendously' does not collocate
2 correct
3 correct
4 incorrect: 'necessarily' does not collocate
5 correct
6 incorrect: 'simply' does not collocate
7 incorrect: 'explicitly' does not collocate
8 incorrect: 'forcefully' does not collocate

Subject background

There are four main ways that people invest:

Stocks

(Also called *shares*.) You can buy stocks in any publicly traded company. When you buy stocks in a company, you become one of its owners. If the company does well, you receive a part of its profits as dividends and you also see the price of your stock increase. Of course the company can also do badly, and in this case the value of your investment will drop.

A stock has no absolute value – at any given time its value depends on what other investors are willing to pay for it. This depends on the likely future profits of the company and the overall state of the economy. Investors try to find stocks that are undervalued, which means that they are available on the market for less than they are really worth.
But this is subjective and very difficult to know – at any one time all available news and information about a company is already built into the stock price. If company A has good products in a growing market and is led by an experienced management team, then everyone knows this and its stock price is already high. Past performance is also no guide as to whether a stock will do well in the future – there is a strong effect of sector rotation in the economy, so if financials or consumer electronics or healthcare have been doing well for the last few quarters, they are unlikely to continue to be leading sectors for the next few quarters.

With stocks, there are two basic strategies: buy and hold (which means buying a stock and then keeping it for many years until money is needed for retirement, college fees, etc.) or trading (waiting until the stock has reached a target price and then taking profits and looking for a new opportunity).

Bonds

Bonds are loans made to corporations or governments. Unlike buying stocks, which make you a part-owner in a company, buying bonds makes you a creditor. You buy a bond and the company or government takes your money and uses it to invest. In return, they pay you a specified amount of interest over the life of the bond and repay the original loan (the principal) at the end. There are many types of bonds, of which the best known are government bonds (called *treasury bonds* in the US and *gilts* in the UK), high-quality company bonds (called *investment-grade bonds*), and riskier low-quality company bonds that pay more interest (called *junk bonds*).

Mutual funds

(Called *unit trusts* in the UK). For many ordinary investors, buying individual stocks or bonds makes no sense. The time and knowledge required to do the research and minimize the risk is too great. Instead, they invest in a mutual fund which holds a basket of stocks or bonds. The choice of what and when to buy and when to sell is left up to a team of fund managers (who receive a commission for their work). The investor can just leave his / her money with the fund and relax, with no need to constantly monitor it.

Real estate

(Also called *property*.) Some people invest by buying property and then letting it to tenants. They hope that the underlying value of the property will rise (creating a capital gain) while at the same time receiving rent from the tenants. The danger here is that the property market is cyclical, and there may be unexpected costs such as repairs, or periods when the property is empty but a bank loan still has to be repaid. It is also true that many people consider their own home where they live as an investment, and so are prepared to take on a high level of debt (a *mortgage* from the bank) to live somewhere bigger and better than their salary allows. This strategy works well while property prices are rising, but can be a disaster while they are falling.

The basic principle with all investments is the balance of risk and reward. Take more risk, and the potential rewards are higher. Choose safety and your returns will be slow and steady.

Useful websites

The following site has useful sections under the tabs 'Tutorials' and 'Dictionary':
http://www.investopedia.com
For general financial news and analysis there are many sites such as:
http://www.bloomberg.com
http://www.moneyweek.com

7.1 About business

Investing responsibly

This module introduces the topic of responsible investment with a thought-provoking reading text on the topic accompanied by a series of engaging tasks to promote active reading.

Preparation

Copy the article on page 85 onto an OHT or scan it onto an IWB / projector. This will enable you to easily draw students' attention to key areas of the text during input and feedback around the exercises. Also, prepare a cut-up version of the text if you intend to do one of the alternative tasks suggested in exercise 2 below.

Internet research

Prepare the Internet search activity by searching for the key words *our social investment policy*. Make a note of the companies whose social investment policies you find. Divide your class into pairs and assign one company to each pair. Ask the pairs to search for that company's social investment policy, to make notes and to report back to the class.

Discussion

1 Ask students to work individually. Explain to the group that they are investors with a large sum of money to invest in stocks and shares (provide a figure in local or foreign currency, e.g. £250,000). Ask students to rank the four criteria (a–d) on a scale of 1–4 according to which is the most important (1) and which the least (4). Stress that it is important for the students to justify their reasons. Once students have produced their rankings, ask them to work in pairs to explain their rankings to one another. Conduct an open-class discussion of students' opinions on the issues raised.

Reading

2 Before starting the reading exercises, you may like to try one of these alternative reading tasks:
a) Prediction of content based on the title. Write the title of the text on the board and ask students to work in pairs or threes and to brainstorm words and ideas they think the text will contain. Elicit suggestions and put them on the board. Ask students to explain their suggestions and use this as an opportunity to extend, clarify and discuss the ideas. Then ask students to scan through the text to check their predictions.
b) Cut the text up into meaningful sections (e.g. paragraphs) and label each one (a, b, c, etc.). Distribute one section to each student in the class (for larger classes, divide the class into pairs). Ask students to read their section and to write a comprehension or true / false question for their section. Also, ask students to note down any new vocabulary in their section and to look up the meaning. Give a reasonable time limit for this, but do not expect students to look up every new word. Next, ask each student to write their question on the board along with the new vocabulary and to briefly explain the meaning of the words to the class. (An alternative approach is to ask students to dictate their questions to the class and for the class to write the questions out. You then write the questions on the board for students to check). Once all students have done this, draw their attention to the text on page 85 of the Student's Book and ask them to read through and answer the questions provided. Next, ask students to compare in pairs before taking whole-class feedback.

Once students have completed these student-centred activities, ask them to complete exercise 2 on page 84. Again, allow checking in pairs before going through the answers.

ANSWERS:

1 True
2 False. Change *like* to *unlike*.
3 False. Example rewrite: The philosophy was formulated by fund donor Charlie Michaels and Haas professor Kellie McElhaney.
4 True
5 False. Example rewrite: The main aim is for students to learn how to fund and work with the development of small enterprises.

3 Give students enough time to read through the suggested summaries and to select the most appropriate. Next, ask students to compare in pairs and to try to reach a mutual consensus. Next, ask each pair to discuss their answers with another pair and again to reach a consensus. Finally, ask the class to vote by show of hands on which is the best summary. You may need to clarify the answer by reference to certain salient details of the text, e.g. the frequent references to particular American universities.

ANSWER:

b

4 Students should now have a comprehensive enough understanding of the text to be able to write an effective summary. However, encapsulating such breadth of meaning into a single sentence is a linguistically sophisticated skill. The task can be approached in a number of ways. For example, you could cut the provided answer into sections and ask students to put the text in order. Or create a mini-cloze of the provided answer and ask students to fill the gaps by reference to the main text.

SUGGESTED ANSWER:

Managed by university students, socially responsible university investment funds aim for a positive impact by adopting social, environmental and financial selection criteria.

Focus on evaluation

5 Dictate the three sentences to the class and ask students to write them down. Next, ask students to read through the text and to locate the three sentences and to check spelling. Now ask students to identify the words in each sentence that convey evaluations or opinions (*typically, definitely, obviously*). Go through the answers and clarify any points that arise. Next, ask students to read through the text and to highlight / circle four further examples of sentences conveying evaluation / opinion. After checking through and discussing the answers, ask students to write a few example sentences of their own expressing opinion or evaluation. You may like to set a few mini topics for this, e.g. *health care – it's definitely the responsibility of the state to ensure that all citizens have fair and equal access to adequate health care*, or *the credit crunch – the current financial crisis in the banking sector is obviously the result of global economic conditions*.

Extracts expressing an evaluation / opinion:
It is definitely a new concept for business-school students to be doing this
This is obviously a real-life example of putting your money where your mouth is
Words indicating evaluation: *definitely, obviously*
Further examples of opinion and evaluation:
'it's not huge money, but even giving a loan of $25,000 to such a small institution can make a big difference.' (lines 68–71)
Raymond Fisman, a faculty adviser to the group, applauds the approach. (lines 77–78)
Note: this is reported evaluation.
'Business students have become more socially oriented, and they realize that it is not just about making money,' (lines 97–99)
'It's about having an impact in a positive way in the rest of the world.' (lines 99–100).

Collocations

6 This exercise raises learners' awareness of strong collocations with the words *social* and *socially*. If students have read through the text several times already, set a contest: ask students to work in teams of three to see how many collocations with *social / socially* they can recall from the text without looking. Set a two- to three-minute time limit. See which team has the most answers and ask them to read them out to the class. Encourage teams to challenge each other. Next, ask the class to read through the text to check and to identify any collocations they did not remember during the game. Elicit the collocations and put them on the board and drill pronunciation. Now ask students to work in pairs to produce some working definitions in their own words for each collocation, e.g. *social returns means gaining a sense of social responsibility instead of purely financial gain.*

ANSWERS:

social returns (lead)
socially responsible business practices (line 7)
socially responsible investing (lines 12–13)
social and environmental issues (lines 17–18)
the Haas Socially Responsible Investment Fund (lines 35–36)
most socially responsible investment funds (lines 43–44)
socially responsible activities (line 55)
socially responsible investment techniques (lines 63–64)
their social, environmental, and financial performance (lines 68–69)
social investing (line 73)
social entrepreneurship (lines 90–91)
Socially responsible investment funds at universities (lines 120–121)
socially oriented (line 130)

Vocabulary

7 By this stage in the reading, students may already have asked about or checked the meanings of these interesting idioms, so this exercise provides a good opportunity for revision and further work on these. Ask students to close their books. Dictate the following words from the phrases: *steam* /stiːm/, *flurry* /ˈflʌri/, *clamouring* /ˈklæmə(r)ɪŋ/, *lamented* /ləˈmentɪd/, *stake* /steɪk/ and *dent* /dent/.

Ask students to compare their word lists in pairs. Write the phonemic transcriptions for each word on the board and drill. Next ask students to scan through the text and to find each word and the phrase in which it occurs. Ask students to work in pairs and, using the context of the text, to work out the meaning of each idiom and to express it in their own words. Elicit suggestions from the class and provide guidance through concept questions, e.g. *With what vehicles / form of travel do you associate steam? Can you give me another word for gain?* Once you have checked through the answers and students have some working definitions, give students a few moments to test each other in pairs.

ANSWERS:

1. gaining steam (line 9) achieving momentum (like a steam train)
2. a flurry of new electives (line 15) a sudden or short rush of students opting to take an academic course
3. students are clamouring to apply their knowledge in this field (lines 23–25) students are very eager (demanding) to put their knowledge into action
4. putting your money where your mouth is (lines 32–33)
5. they both lamented the way socially responsible funds are run (lines 43–45) they expressed sorrow or regret about the way socially responsible funds are managed
6. put our stake in the ground (line 72) to claim or secure something as one's own (from the activity of staking out a plot of land)
7. make a dent in global poverty (line 80) reduce global poverty

Discussion

8 Ask students to work in groups of three for this discussion task. Ask the groups to discuss and to draft their investment plans. Set a reasonable time limit (15 to 20 minutes). Monitor and provide help, support and ideas as necessary. When the groups have prepared their plans, depending on the size of the class, either ask them to present their plans to the class (small classes) or ask the threes to split up and join up with members of other groups to tell each other about their investment plans.

7.2 Grammar

Inversion and emphasis

This module reviews emphatic structures and provides a range of controlled and freer practice activities within the context of financial language.

Internet research

Before asking students to research the topic of *intellectual investment*, you may like to discuss the concepts of *intellectual property* and *intellectual capital*. An Internet search using the term *define intellectual investment* is a useful starting point.

Did you know?

Prepare a few additional examples of the types of emphatic structures mentioned in the *Did you know?* information box. This will help to illustrate and clarify the information presented in the box. You may also like to add that students should be cautious of over-using inverted structures, as they can sound overly theatrical or rhetorical. Remind students that such structures are often used by politicians and in advertising language. Note also that students can inadvertently make mistakes with these forms, for example when beginning a sentence with *only*.

Inverted conditionals

1 This first exercise revises and reviews the use of inverted conditional structures to provide emphasis. If students have difficulty with this exercise, be prepared to assist by drawing attention to the verb structures in each sentence that provide clues to the solutions. For example, in sentence 1, the words *not be met* indicate that a modal verb fits grammatically, and *will be* provides a clue to the conditional form being expressed.

With lower level groups, you could also provide assistance by supplying the missing words in random order and asking students to fit them into the appropriate sentence. Finally, it might be useful to elicit or provide the full conditional forms that are conveyed. For instance, for number 1, *If the conditions are not met by the end of May, the submission will be rejected.*

ANSWERS:

1 Should 2 were 3 Should 4 Had 5 Were 6 had

Emphatic structures

2 The second exercise reviews other forms of emphatic structure. Please note that the exercise covers cleft sentence structures (1, 2 and 9), conditional forms (7) and negative inversions (3, 6, 8 and 10), a modal (5) and the determiner *such* (4).

If your students find this exercise too challenging, you could simplify it by creating pairs of sentences, one of which is correct and one erroneous, and ask students to identify the correct / incorrect structure in each case, e.g.

a) *What I want to focus on today is ...*
b) *What do I want to focus on today is ...*

Alternatively you could incorporate the incorrect sentences into a 'grammar auction', in which pairs or teams have to bid for the correct sentences and avoid purchasing incorrect ones. You could then recycle the exercise as it stands on page 86 into a progress test. Allow students a few minutes to check in pairs, then take whole-class feedback. Be prepared to extend and elaborate with extra examples to clarify and reinforce the structures.

ANSWERS:

1 What I (do) want to focus on today is the importance of evaluating risk.
2 Short-termism is (the reason) why many investors fail.
3 Scarcely had she made her investment when the global markets crashed.
4 He was such a charismatic person that he inspired absolute loyalty in his team.
5 May you have the best of luck when you're out there – you'll need it!
6 Only by focusing closely on risk was he able to avoid huge losses.
7 Were the markets really to / to really take off, we'll be set to make major gains.
8 Not only did you fail to make any gains, but you also lost nearly all our money.
9 Why I (do) disagree with you is that you ignore fundamentals.
10 On no account must we give in to their demands.

Reformulating for emphasis

3 This exercise provides freer practice in applying appropriate structures in a sentence transformation exercise. Go through the example with the class to ensure students understand the task. To make the exercise more interactive, write the first sentence on the board and the first key word below, e.g.

We need action rather than words.
Words ...

Ask students to work in pairs / threes and predict the next word. Elicit suggestions from the teams until one gets it right. If no one can provide the correct word, supply it yourself.

We need action rather than words.
Words are ...

Repeat this process with each subsequent word until the sentence has been completed. Then repeat this process with the next key word (*Action ...*) and so on until the exercise is completed.

You can recycle this exercise in subsequent lessons and progress tests. For instance, in the next lesson as a warmer, ask students to take out paper and a pen. Read aloud one of the sentences, e.g. *First of all I want you only to listen.* and call out one of the stem words, e.g. *All ...* and ask students to rewrite the sentence using the word provided.

ANSWERS:

1 Words are not what we need, it's action.
  Action rather than words is what we need.
  What we need is action rather than words.
2 The reason why I'm here today is to discuss my promotion prospects.
  What I want to discuss here today is my promotion prospects.
  My promotion prospects are the reason why I'm here today.
3 No market is more important for raw commodities than China.
  Without doubt the most important market for raw commodities is China.
  China is undoubtedly the most important market for raw commodities.
4 What impresses me more than any other quality is your attention to detail.
  The quality that most impresses me is your attention to detail.
  I am more impressed by your attention to detail than any other quality.
5 All I want you to do first is only listen.
  The only thing I want you to do first of all is listen.
  Just listen – that's all / what I want you to do first.

Emphatic words

4 Dictate the list of words taken from the cloze text and ask students to write them down. Ask students to compare in pairs, then elicit the words and put them on the board for students to check. Next, ask students to work in pairs and to discuss the meaning of each word and to provide a sample sentence or phrase containing each. Supply some examples of your own, e.g. *I have never heard such utter nonsense! It's such a nice day, why don't we go out for a walk?* Monitor to check progress and make a note of the example sentences being produced.

When the pairs have finished this stage, elicit examples from the class and clarify and discuss these examples. Use this as an opportunity to highlight grammatical patterns and collocations and to provide additional examples of your own.

Next, draw students' attention to exercise 4 in the Student's Book and ask them to complete the cloze using the words provided. Allow a few moments for checking in pairs, then take whole-class feedback. Use the cloze text with the list of words deleted for revision and testing later in the course.

ANSWERS:

1 absolutely 2 indeed 3 utter 4 such
5 whatsoever 6 Regrettably 7 do 8 rather

Listening

5 2.26 Explain the scenario to the class, as presented in the rubric. Ask students to note down the key points made in the talk. Play the extract though once. Ask students to compare their notes in pairs. Elicit points from the class. Next, draw students' attention to the notes in exercise 5 and ask them to complete as many answers as they can from memory. Play the extract through a second time for students to check their notes and to add to or modify their answers accordingly. Finally, go through the answers with the class and clarify as needed, playing sections of the recording again if needed.

ANSWERS:

1 investment
2 ways of finding investment to fund new business ideas
3 what they tell you in business school does not work
4 that of the person seeking investment / the person with the idea for a new business plan
5 that of the investor
6 intellectual
7 finding a core group of people to complement your skills
8 social networking site
9 a programming wizard / (e-commerce) lawyer / someone to market and sell the product
10 traction / that you've got customers already / you're on the ground, you've already started and you're ready to go

6 Ask students to work in pairs to recall as many emphatic structures as they can from the listening and to note them down. Elicit ideas from the class. Next, ask students to listen to check and to note down as many structures as they can. Play the recording through, but pause at appropriate moments to give students time to note down the phrases used. After the recording has been played, ask students to compare notes in pairs, elicit answers and put them on the board. Highlight and discuss the grammatical features (e.g. inversions, verb forms, word order) and drill the phrases for stress, rhythm and intonation.

Ask students to work in pairs to practise forming their own example sentences using the stems provided, e.g.
What I particularly want to talk about today is the performance of our shares' portfolio over the past twelve months.
The reason for wanting to focus on this is mainly because there are rumours of a takeover bid.
Leave the phrases on the board for the negotiation exercise that follows.

ANSWERS:

What I particularly want to talk about today is …
The reason for wanting to focus on this is mainly because …
What we've found over the years is that …
Were the business schools to focus on …
I do want to emphasize at this point that …
Should you have access to a huge amount of money …
Under no circumstances should you …
What you need above all … is …
No sooner do you … than …
What you're doing is …
Not only do you need programmers and lawyers, but also …
Only then do you have …
What investors want to see is …

RECORDING SCRIPT

2.26

Well, good morning ladies and gentlemen and thank you for inviting me to talk to you. What I particularly want to talk about today is investment, or to be more specific, ways of finding investment to fund new business ideas. The reason for wanting to focus on this is mainly because what we've found over the years is that the philosophy that's been traditionally taught in business schools, which you could simply say is: write a brilliant business plan, raise two million dollars, hire some very expensive executives, doesn't actually work for most of us. Were the business schools to focus on the alternative approach, which I'm going to tell you about, business entrepreneurship would be quite different. I do want to emphasize at this point that I'm speaking from the point of view of the person seeking investment, in other words the person with the idea for a new business plan. Indeed, the perspective of the investor is quite different.

So, to start off. For most of us aspiring entrepreneurs: you've got a good idea but really no track record so you've really got to do everything yourself. Should you have access to a huge amount of money, you're laughing, but unfortunately most of us don't. When you're talking about investment there are really two types of investment. There's the financial investment that you need to, you know, buy a computer, build some code, but more important is what you might call intellectual investment – how do you find a group of partners that you actually work with together and actually build something and bootstrap it into existence? Under no circumstances should you go it alone – you won't succeed. What you need above all, before getting your hands on any investment money, is a core group of people to complement your own skills. For example if you want to build a social networking site, you might have a brilliant idea, say to build one for the fashion industry.

However, if you can't programme then the first thing you need to do is to find a programming wizard so that you do this. No sooner do you start doing something on the Internet than you need a lawyer. So where can you find an e-commerce lawyer to help you who's prepared to work for equity in the future company? Basically you haven't got the money to, well, pay anybody, so instead you offer equity. What you're doing is putting together a credible team. Indeed, you're looking for people that can do everything. Not only do you need programmers and lawyers, but also people who can market and sell, people who know about your target market. Only then do you have a credible team and you can actually build something. What investors want to see is what they call traction. They want to see that you've got some customers already. You're on the ground, you've already started and you're ready to go.

Negotiation

7 For this task students are required to negotiate the most favourable business alliance on behalf of the companies they represent. First of all, explain the scenario as outlined in the rubric. Arrange the class into three small groups (A, B and C) of equal size (if you have a very large class, divide your class into six small groups of equal size). Ask each group to read through their assignment role cards on pages 113, 114 and 116 of the Student's Book. Monitor and provide help and clarification as necessary and check that all students understand what they have to do. During this preparation stage, encourage the groups to discuss the points they are going to make at the negotiation, using the bullet points on the role cards, and to make notes on these. Ask students to practise expressing their ideas using the emphatic structures on the board from the previous exercise.

8 Reform the class into new groups of three with a student from each group A, B and C. Explain to the class that each student's job is to persuade the others to form an alliance with them. Set a time limit of about 15 minutes. Ask students to make notes about what the other company representatives say about their companies during the task. Monitor as the discussion take place and make notes of language points for later attention and feedback.

9 Once the negotiations are complete, ask students to reform into their original groups to discuss which of the other two companies they think would make the best ally. Explain that each group should reach a consensus. Set a time limit of five to ten minutes for this. Once the groups have made their decisions, ask each group to feed back to the class on their choices of ally and the reasons for their choices.

7.3 Vocabulary
Investment choices

This module presents and reviews vocabulary related to the field of investment and provides a varied and stimulating range of activities to practise using the vocabulary in context.

Preparation

Prepare a completed version of the text on page 88 with the interviewer's questions removed. Make enough copies to give one to each of your students for exercise 2, as described below. Prepare the vocabulary matching activity (exercise 4) onto cut-up cards, enough for each pair of students in the class.

Internet research

As the box suggests, the keywords *property investment* will return a lot of sites making bold claims. You could narrow the task down by asking students to locate two or three websites of companies offering property deals and advice, to note what types of property they are selling, the asking prices and the promised returns on investment. Ask students to bring their findings to class and in small groups to decide which they think is the safest investment and which the most risky.

Discussion

1 Before starting the discussion exercise, you may want to draw students' attention to the following: the meaning of *a property empire*, the use of *an* with a consonant in *an MBA* and the pronunciation of vintage /ˈvɪntɪdʒ/ and jewellery /ˈdʒuːəlri/. Next, present the scenario to the class. Ask students to work on their own and read through the list of options and to choose one of the investment choices. Monitor and provide help as needed. Next, ask the class to mingle and to discuss and explain their choices. Keep the discussion quite brisk and monitor to make notes of language points for post-correction. Conduct a show of hands to see which options have proven the most and least popular. Finally, ask students to work in pairs or small groups and discuss how else they would invest the money.

Reading

2 Dictate the questions taken from the text to the class in random order and ask students to write them down. Elicit the questions back from students and put them on the board. Next, distribute your prepared copies of the completed text and ask students to match the questions to each paragraph and then to compare in pairs. Go through the answers with the class. Ask students to turn the text over so that it is no longer visible.

Dictate the following items (minus the definitions) to the class and ask students to write them down: *diversity* /daɪˈvɜː(r)səti/ (range and variety), *to recoup* /rɪˈkuːp/ (to regain), *bricks and mortar* (houses), *buy-to-let* (the practice of buying a property in order to rent it out to tenants), *equities* /ˈekwɪtiːz/ (securities that represent ownership in a company, shares), *to entail* (to involve), *to be risk-averse* /rɪsk-əˈvɜː(r)s/ (to have a tendency to avoid risky investments), *a portfolio* (a collection of assets owned by an investor), *a plum property* (a good or fine property), *to plummet* (to fall or decrease very rapidly), *to wind up as* /waɪnd/ (to become, to end up as), *a mantra* (a commonly repeated word or phrase; a Hindu incantation), *take a tumble* (to fall), *to be quids in* /kwɪdz/ (to make a profit, a *quid* is one pound sterling), *mattress* (the part of a bed made of thick soft material that you put on the bed's base to make it more comfortable).

Ask students to compare their answers in pairs. Provide phonemic transcriptions on the board. Next, ask students to read through the text and to locate the words. Now ask students to consider the meaning of the words from the context. Use guiding questions to lead to the solution, e.g. *Is the meaning positive or negative? What does the word refer to in the text?* Go through the answers with the class. Finally, ask students to provide some example sentences of their own using the newly presented lexis, e.g. *Although it's important for companies to diversify, they must be sure to maintain a strong core brand.*

Do not ask students to complete the cloze at this stage, but reserve the exercise until the end of the lesson. Also, if possible, recycle the cloze into a progress test later in the course.

ANSWERS:

1	value
2	equities
3	companies
4	recession
5	recoup my losses
6	portfolio
7	buy-to-let
8	risk-averse
9	diversify
10	exposed
11	entails
12	bricks and mortar

3 As with the preceding exercise, dictate the idioms and ask students to scan the text to locate them in context. Ask students to paraphrase the meanings in their own words. Elicit interpretations from the class, prompting with guiding questions to lead students to the solutions, e.g. *If you put all your eggs in one basket, what would happen if you lost or dropped the basket?*

Ask students to produce an example sentence incorporating each of the idioms and to read these out to the class. Finally, ask students to discuss whether they have the same or similar idioms in their own languages, and also whether they have other idioms to express the same meanings.

ANSWERS:

have your head screwed on: *be sensible, practical and aware*
put all your eggs in one basket: *rely on just one thing for success*
go pear-shaped: *go wrong*
the other side of the coin: *the opposite angle or viewpoint*

Vocabulary

4 Be prepared to explain / elicit the meanings and pronunciation of the following: *to boost* (to increase or raise), *to adopt* (to take on, assume), *a stance* (attitude or position), *a buffer* (a cushion), *volatility* (wide variation, instability), *diversified* (varied), *herd* (a group of cattle), *command a price* (to get or receive a price), *sure-fire* (certain).

Distribute the cut-up cards to your students and give them a few minutes to match the expressions. Go through the answers with the class, providing additional examples and explanations as required. Next, ask students to test each other in pairs on the meanings of the jargon. Recycle the matching activity later in a progress test.

ANSWERS:

1 d   2 f   3 b   4 h   5 c   6 g   7 a   8 e

Listening

5 🔊 2.27 This task presents some of the expressions from exercise 4 in context. Ask students first to listen to the recording and to take notes on the key points as they listen. Then ask students to compare their notes in pairs and then elicit answers. Next, ask students to recall as many of the expressions from exercise 4 as they can. Check through with the class, but do not provide definitive answers just yet.

ANSWERS:

The items mentioned are 2, 3, 4, 5, 6, 7 and 8.

6 Present your class with the topics listed under exercise 6 and ask them to make notes on the points using the notes they took during the listening. Play the extract a second time for students to check both exercises 5 and 6. Go through the answers with the class, putting the advice given on the board.

ANSWERS:

Retirement is going to come one day and the earlier you invest for it, the better
Investing in different currencies is going to offer you a buffer against market volatility
Go for property: 'Properties To Die For Ltd' is a sure-fire investment

RECORDING SCRIPT

🔊 2.27

Right then ladies and gentlemen you're going to be thankful that you came along here today. From what I can see, there's a lot of different age groups among you – some more mature ladies and gentlemen if I may say so, rich in experience, quite a few younger ones here, and it looks like one or two teenagers even.

What I want to emphasize to you all today is the importance of investment. The younger ones among you may not want to think about it, but retirement is going to come your way one day, oh yes, the eighth age of man as they say, it won't go away. And the earlier you start investing for your retirement, the richer you'll be when you retire. It really is something that you can't start doing early enough, the more mature customers amongst you will back me up on that one, won't you?.

So, what can you do to make sure you have enough money to see you through your retirement? You may have heard all sorts of investment advice, both good and bad, ranging from topping up your pension pot to buying bottles of vintage wine. And who exactly is going to buy a load of wine years from now? Don't ask me. Well, you may have heard that you should build up a diversified portfolio, all sorts of different investments in different kinds of products, in different currencies even. And I won't disagree with that advice. I know it's going against the herd instinct these days, but investing in different currencies is going to offer you that buffer against market volatility, a bit of protection against the ups and downs of the market.

Ladies and gentlemen more than anything I would recommend adopting a defensive investment stance to do just that. I reckon if you invest in several currencies you'll actually reduce your overall risk – ever heard of putting all your eggs in one basket? I thought so: all your money in one currency and if it goes down, well, you don't need an expert like me to tell you which way your investment is going to go.

So where was I? Market volatility. Whilst you can't prevent the markets going all over the place, what you can do is go for property, ladies and gentlemen, which is why I'm here, as a representative of Properties To Die For Limited. Investing in property means putting your money in bricks and mortar. They're a sure-fire investment, believe me. People are always going to have to live in houses, and the world population is going up and up, so you'll easily find someone to rent your properties out to. The thing is, other property investments you might see here today charge what you might call a 'premium price'. They're a rip-off in the language of you and me. Now, with Properties To Die For Limited you know where you are. What you see is what you get, fantastic properties that you would actually die for. None of that lack of transparency you'll find if you wander across the floor to one of our lesser rivals. We can offer you prime properties in Spain, in Portugal, in Bulgaria, in Turkey, in the US, you name it. I said you name it – I didn't hear you say anything.

If you don't trust us all you need to do is ask one of Properties To Die For Limited's valued clients. Do you know I've even seen Felicia Turner here? Well between you and me she's bought one or two of our plum properties already. That's Ms Turner's retirement sorted. And she's very pleased with what we've sold her so far ...

7 Draw students' attention to the pieces of advice written on the board and ask them to work individually to decide which pieces they agree with and which not. Next, ask students to discuss their opinions in pairs, then take whole-class feedback.

Speaking

8 Put the following headings on the board: *attitude to risk, favoured geographical areas, expectations of future wealth, types of investment* (e.g. financial instruments, property, stocks and shares, exotic investments).

Ask students to consider the points on the board in relation to their own investment profile. Encourage them to make some notes under the headings provided. Monitor and provide support as needed. Next, tell students that they are to work in pairs to establish each other's investment profiles, preferences and plans. Ask students to work in pairs to generate questions to ask about each of the topics, e.g. *What is your attitude to risk? Are you generally risk-averse or do you prefer riskier investments with higher returns?*

Put students into new pairs to interview each other using the questions supplied. Ask them to make notes as they conduct the interviews. Monitor and note language points for post-correction. For feedback, ask students to briefly tell the class about their partner's investment profile.

Writing

9 Ask students to use their notes from the interviews to write a short (80-word) summary of their partner's investment profiles. Set a time limit and collect the summaries for correction and feedback. The information contained in the summaries can be incorporated into a *find someone who* activity for a later lesson.

7.4 Management skills

Decision making

This module presents grid analysis as a useful decision-making instrument and provides an opportunity for language development and speaking practice within the context of grid analysis.

Preparation

Adapt exercise 2 into a matching exercise by copying items 1–8 and a–h onto coloured card, e.g.

a)	Evaluating performance of the option you have chosen will be easier ...	1	define the objective
b)	Prepare a grid ...	2	identify the options

Prepare enough sets of cards for each pair of students in the class.

Internet research

As the box suggests, a search for the keywords *six thinking hats* and *plus minus interesting* will return some very interesting sites explaining how these decision-making tools work. Ask students to do some research to summarize how the tools work, with examples if possible.

Discussion

1 Ask students to work in pairs or threes to brainstorm common methods of making decisions. Provide an example from the list given, e.g. *tossing a coin*. Collate students' ideas and put them on the board, and discuss briefly with the class. Check which items from the list students have not included in their brainstorming and dictate any additional items from the list, asking students to add these to their lists. Go through the meaning and pronunciation of each item.

Now ask students to work individually and to consider questions 1–3. They should make notes of their answers. Next, ask students to work in threes to discuss the questions. Monitor and note language points for post-correction. Take whole-class feedback.

Grid analysis

2 Pre-teach / elicit the meaning and pronunciation of *plot* /plɒt/, *quantifiable* /ˈkwɒntɪˌfaɪəb(ə)l/, *remedial* /rɪˈmiːdiəl/, *facilitate* /fəˈsɪləteɪt/, *take something into account, optimal* /ˈɒptɪm(ə)l/, *to weight* /weɪt/ and *weighting.* /ˈweɪtɪŋ/.

For the matching exercise, you could copy the list of descriptions a–h and steps 1–8 onto pieces of card. Distribute a set of cards to pairs of students and ask them to match the items.

When providing feedback, display the text of the descriptions on an OHP or IWB, revealing each stage one at a time and highlighting the key words that indicate the answer for each. For example in a), the key words that indicate monitoring of performance are *plot* and *evaluation period*. This will provide a clear visual focus for your class and make it easier to clarify points that arise.

ANSWERS:

1 e   2 g   3 c   4 b   5 h   6 d   7 a   8 f

3 Draw students' attention to the grids and the map of France. Ask students to summarize briefly why the grids are being used in this case (possible answer: they evaluate the most suitable location for a new business venture or new factory). Next, ask students to label the features of the grids by referring to the previous exercise. For example, *Lille, Nice, Lyon* and *Nantes* are options; *cost, communications, climate* and *workforce* are criteria or conditions. Now ask students to identify which stage in the decision-making process each grid represents.

ANSWERS:

A 4   B 5

Listening

4 2.28–2.31 Explain to students that they are going to hear four extracts in which colleagues discuss the factory sites listed in exercise 3. Ask students to make notes while they listen. Then ask students to compare their notes with a partner. Next, ask students to read through and answer the three comprehension questions in exercise 4. If necessary, play the extracts through again for the class to check.

ANSWERS:

1 1 Define the criteria 2 Identify the options 3 Weight the criteria 4 Make the decision
2 Claire prefers Nice, Bernard prefers Lyon.
3 Yes. (*It's pretty black and white* and *It seems an open and shut case.*)

5 Write the first jumbled sentence onto the board (or display on an OHP / IWB) and ask students to work in pairs to order the words. Set a time limit. Do not go through the answers at this stage. Repeat with sentence 2 and so on until all 10 sentences have been completed.

Now play the extracts again to give students an opportunity to check or alter their answers. Go through the answers with the class. Displaying the answer key (using an OHP or IWB) will help at this stage. Next, drill the sentences focusing on stress, intonation and pronunciation.

ANSWERS:

1 What conditions would we need to satisfy to find the ideal solution?
2 We need to draw a distinction between essential requirements and desirable characteristics. (or) We need to draw a distinction between desirable characteristics and essential requirements.
3 Can we quantify that more specifically?
4 Let's consider all our options; can we draw up a list?
5 Does that cover everything, or are there other avenues we should explore?
6 Where would you put cost on a scale of one to five?
7 Cost isn't nearly as critical as workforce; I'd only give it a three.
8 It would seem that we can rule out Nice.
9 Do we go for Lille?
10 Lille it is then.

RECORDING SCRIPT

 2.28–2.31

1

Yann: OK, so what conditions would we need to satisfy to find the ideal solution?

Bernard: Climate for one: production start having problems when the temperature hits thirty degrees, so Nice is out of the running for a start, unless we splash out on an air-conditioned production unit.

Claire: Bernard, that's not fair! OK, high temperatures are inconvenient, but they're hardly a make or break factor. We need to draw a distinction between essential requirements and desirable characteristics.

Y: Point taken, Claire, but don't worry, we'll come to weighting in a moment.

B: Communications have to be our number one concern.

Y: OK, but can we quantify that more specifically? In numbers?

B: Sure. Distance from the airport, railway station, motorway; number of international flights per day ...

2

Y: All right, some of us have another meeting scheduled at five, so let's get on. What are the options for the new factory?

B: Lyon, period. It has the best communications, and that's our priority. It stands to reason.

Y: Hold on a minute, Bernard; we want to do this scientifically, OK? Let's consider all our options; can we draw up a list?

B: OK – I suppose Lille and Nantes also have to be considered.

Y: Right; so we have Lyon, Lille and Nantes. Does that cover everything, or are there other avenues we should explore?

C: Well, I still feel we shouldn't leave Nice out of the equation. OK, it'll be expensive, but it's a very attractive location for the workforce.

3

Y: Right then, next step: define the relative importance of each of our criteria, give them a weighting. Claire, where would you put cost on a scale of one to five?

C: I'd say, four. It's not the be all and end all of it, but it's pretty important nevertheless.

B: Hang on, Claire, don't you think communications are more relevant than cost? And cost isn't nearly as critical as workforce; I'd only give it a three. What do you say, Yann?

4

Y: So; it would seem that we can rule out Nice. Sorry, Claire, but I think the figures speak for themselves, don't you?

C: Yes, it's pretty black and white, I s'pose.

Y: And it appears that the overall winner is Lille: so, do we go for Lille?

B: Like Claire said, it seems an open and shut case.

Y: Lille it is then. Is everybody happy with that?

Vocabulary

6 Ask students to complete the expressions from memory and to compare in pairs. If students struggle with this, then dictate the missing words in random order and ask students to write them in. Go through the answers, then ask students to match the pairs of similar meaning. Check the answers and clarify the meaning of each expression. Finally, ask students to test each other in pairs, e.g.

A: *Out of the running.*
B: *Out of the equation.*

ANSWERS:

1 running   2 break   3 reason   4 equation
5 end   6 numbers   7 white   8 case
Pairs with similar meanings:
1 and 4, 2 and 5, 3 and 6, 7 and 8

7 Ask students to work in threes and to act out the dialogue as it currently stands. You may want to model the dialogue yourself first with the class.

Next, get the groups to re-work the dialogue in order to make it more appropriate. Demonstrate the task by providing the first modification yourself. Monitor to check progress and provide help and input as needed.

Once groups have completed their dialogues, ask them to rehearse their dialogues in their groups, paying particular attention to intonation, rhythm, stress, body language and gestures. Finally, get the groups to act their dialogues out in turn for the class.

A: Gentlemen, may I have your attention? The next item on our agenda is selecting a city for our annual conference. Let's consider all our options; can we draw up a list?

B: Well, we could consider Chicago, Palermo or Tokyo.

A: Does that cover everything, or are there other avenues we should explore?

C: We shouldn't leave Moscow out of the equation.

A: All right, what conditions would we need to satisfy to find the ideal solution?

B: We need to draw a distinction between essential requirements and desirable characteristics.

C: Well, I think the approval of the local authorities is a make or break factor.

A: Can we quantify that more specifically? Exactly how much will it cost?

Later ...

A: Now, where would you put casinos on a scale of one to five?

B: I'd say five. It's pretty black and white.

C: I'm afraid I can't agree. Casinos aren't nearly as critical as clubs; I'd only give them a three.

A: So, it would seem that we can rule out Palermo. As for Tokyo and Moscow, the figures speak for themselves. So do we go for Chicago? Is everybody happy with that?

B: Chicago it is then. After all, there's no place like home, is there, Sir?

Discussion

8 If possible, bring in some pictures of the types of vehicle in the text (saloon, sports car, station wagon, etc.) and ask students to brainstorm the pros and cons of each (e.g. *a sports car is fast and stylish; a minivan is practical*). Ask the groups to read through the background to the scenario. Ask a few brief comprehension questions, e.g. *What's your job? What's the name of the company you work for?*
Next, ask the groups to identify the options and criteria to form the basis of their grid analysis, e.g.

	Access to remote and rural areas	Long distances	Family car for holidays and weekends	Company advertisement
saloon				
sports car				

Once the grids have been established, ask the groups to refer back to the guidelines in exercise 2 and to discuss suitable gradings and weightings for their options. Finally, ask each group to make a decision based on the grid analysis they have carried out.
Get each group to briefly report back to the class on the decisions they have reached.

This module presents the genre of financial reporting and provides a range of awareness-raising and controlled practice exercises leading to a free-written production task.

Internet research

A general search for the key words *share tips* will return the latest reports on recent developments in various share markets (commodities, bonds, gold, property, etc.). Use this data to provide real examples of current good and bad investment choices. You could also ask your students to identify a few companies / markets to invest in / avoid.

Discussion

1 Explain / elicit the meaning of the word 'metaphor' (*a figure of speech used to illustrate a similarity between things*). Write the five topic words (*sports, water,* etc.) on the board. Explain that these are typical categories of metaphor often used when conveying financial information. Provide an example of your own, e.g. *Trignet was last past the post in the takeover bid for Corvex.* Ask students to work in pairs or threes to brainstorm as many metaphors as they can related to the topics listed. Elicit suggestions from the class and put them on the board, and add some more of your own. Draw students' attention to the phrases listed in exercise 1 and ask them to match these to the topics and also to answer questions 2–4. Go through the answers with the group.

ADDITIONAL ACTIVITIES

1 Search the Internet for company annual reports and scour the financial sections for authentic examples of metaphorical language in use. Use these to supplement this exercise.

2 Ask students to search the Internet using the following search terms: "*took another knock*", "*in good shape*", "*happy to take a punt*", "*now back on track*" and "*weather the storm*". Ask them to note down examples where these phrases are used in financial contexts. (Note: the double inverted commas are necessary to ensure the search engine searches for the entire phrase.) Collate students' findings into a financial metaphor word bank.

ANSWERS:

1 a) combat b) health c) water d) sports e) weather
2 Students' own answers
3 Students' own answers
4 Possible answers include,
   Sport: to be first past the post
   Water: to jump ship
   Weather: to survive the turmoil
   Combat: to trigger something
   Health: to be in good shape, to stunt growth, to have muscle, an early recovery

Analysis

2 Cut the text into two sections, i.e. one report per section. Divide the class into two groups, A and B, and distribute one report to the individuals in each group. Ask the students to read their reports, highlight the key points and answer the three comprehension questions. Next, tell students to work in pairs, one A and one B, and give each other a summary of their respective reports.

ANSWERS:

1 Text A: construction, Text B: tourism
2 Text A: booming industry in the Middle East and Carillion negotiates its own contracts, Text B: not given, but the recent acquisition of intrip20.nz may have affected it.
3 Text A: integration of McAlpine, Text B: demonstrating solid progress

3 Now ask the pairs to discuss the correct order for a report. Finally, ask the pairs to read through both reports quickly to check. Check through the answers with the class.

ANSWERS:

news / context, performance, outlook, recommendation

Style

4 This is a relatively straightforward collocations exercise. Write the six words (*forecast*, *generate*, etc.) on the board. Check students understand the meaning of each. Next, ask students to work in pairs to generate as many collocations or phrases as they can using each word. Provide a model example yourself first, e.g. *forecast a cut in interest rates*.
Elicit students' suggestions and put them on the board, providing feedback as needed. Next, ask student to work individually to complete the sentences, using the correct verb form in each case. Before providing definitive feedback, highlight the key collocates / clues from each sentence, e.g. *advantage*, *strong sales*, and *keeping, soaring ... £3m mark, next year* and *shares*.

ANSWERS:

1 take
2 generating
3 tucking away
4 reach
5 forecast
6 trading

5 Refer students back to exercise 3, the section labels for reports. Ask students to read through the six sentences and to identify which sections of reports they are taken from. Allow students a few moments to check in pairs before going through the answers.

ANSWERS:

1 recommendation
2 performance
3 recommendation
4 news / context
5 outlook
6 performance

6 Dictate the list of phrases from the left-hand column to the class and ask students to write them down. Then ask students to compare in pairs. Next, ask students to read through the texts on page 92 and to locate the phrases, checking spelling as they go. Elicit the phrases, put them on the board and drill for pronunciation and stress. Ask students to work in pairs to discuss possible meanings of the phrases from the contexts. Elicit suggested interpretations from the class. Next, draw students' attention to the meanings provided on page 93 and ask them to match the phrases to the meanings. Go through the answers with the group. Finally, ask students to test one another in pairs, e.g.
A: *a compelling investment opportunity*
B: *a very attractive investment opportunity, not to be missed*

ANSWERS:

1 e   2 f   3 h   4 d   5 a   6 b   7 c   8 g

7 Prepare some additional example sentences incorporating the phrases in bold. An Internet search for the phrases will provide a good source of examples, e.g. *Supermarket claims that profit recovery is now on track*.
Incorporate your own examples with those provided in the Student's Book. Ask students to work in pairs to discuss the meaning of each phrase, and whether the meaning is positive, negative or cautious. Go through the answers with the class and provide additional examples and explanations as needed. Ask students to complete the phrases a)– f) and take whole-class feedback. If you have time, extend the activity by asking students to produce mini dialogue extracts to illustrate the phrases, e.g. *With house prices falling we may as well sit tight until the market recovers*.

ANSWERS:

1 in the right place – positive / cautious
2 start to deal with an unpleasant or difficult situation – positive
3 used in horse racing: where the winners go after the race – positive
4 return – positive / cautious
5 stay where you are – positive / cautious
6 if things can get worse – negative
a) 6   b) 3   c) 1   d) 5   e) 4   f) 2

Writing

8 In preparation for the writing task, refer students back to the model reports on page 92 for guidance. To help students get started on the task, provide a model beginning, e.g.
Most know SourceMedia as a film production company, but as that sector has become increasingly unpredictable and risky, SourceMedia has established a strong portfolio of TV series and films. This is a less exciting, but more predictable and profitable line of business.
You may like to set some or all of the writing task for homework, or set a time limit of 20 to 30 minutes of class time for students to complete the task.

This module consolidates the language covered in the previous modules, providing opportunities for students to apply grid analysis techniques to make structured decisions on the launch of a new no-frills car.

Internet research

As the search box suggests, the keywords *no-frills chic* will provide a rich source of information on this developing trend. You could also ask your students to locate some companies that are cited as examples of no-frills chic.

Preparation

You may find it useful and helpful to copy the grid analysis table on page 95 onto an OHT or scan it onto your IWB. This will facilitate feedback during tasks 4 and 5. Also, photocopy and cut up the role cards on pages 111, 112, 114 and 116 of the Student's Book so that you have enough to distribute to the class for the final discussion activity.

Discussion

1 Draw students' attention to the photograph and read through the discussion rubric together. Provide a few comprehension questions to check understanding of the task, e.g. *Why do many customers feel 'oversold'? (Answer: because the product often has features they do not really want or need.) What do you think is meant by 'a no-frills product'? (Answer: A product that does not have lots of unnecessary added features.)*
You could also personalize the topic by asking students whether they have ever felt oversold and why, and whether or not they have purchased any no-frills goods or services. Next, ask students in threes to brainstorm further examples of no-frills goods and services. Prepare a few examples of your own as additional input, e.g. airlines, supermarkets, holidays, cinemas, hotels, buses, food and mobile phones. Elicit student suggestions and put them on the board. Discuss which ones students would (not) be prepared to buy and why.

Reading

2 Be prepared to pre-teach or elicit the meaning of the following vocabulary from the text (this could be set as a dictionary exercise for homework): *a sedan car* /ˌsɪˈdæn/ (American English, a typical passenger car, with two rows of seats; British English = saloon car), *emerging markets* (countries expected to experience substantial growth), *unpretentious* /ˌʌnprɪˈtenʃəs/ (simple, modest), *to retool* /ˌriːˈtuːl/ (to refit or modify the machinery and tools of a factory), *ailing* /ˈeɪlɪŋ/ (unwell, ill), *to stumble (onto/across)* /ˈstʌmb(ə)l/ (to find unexpectedly or by chance), *a vein* /veɪn/ (a source of supply, as in a gold vein), *utilitarian* /juːˌtɪlɪˈteəriən/ (functional, having a useful function), *mania* (intense enthusiasm), *to be stripped of* /strɪpt/ (to have something removed), *to be superfluous* /suːˈpɜː(r)fluəs/ (to be more than is needed), *to peg something at + price* (to fix the price at a certain level), *to slash* (to cut or reduce), *to ramp up* (to increase), *to turn heads* (to attract attention; to be attractive).
Dictate the following figures from the text for students to write down: $6,000, $9,300, $17,250, $18,264, $592, 1999, 80%, $,1,089, $2,468, more than 50%, $324, $3,650, $2,500.
Next, ask students to scan through the text to locate the numbers and to identify what each refers to, e.g. *$6000 is the price the Logan is designed to sell for.*

Monitor and check progress. Allow students a few minutes to check in pairs, then elicit answers from the class. Next, ask students to answer the questions in exercise 2 by referring to the text, and then to discuss their answers with a partner.

ANSWERS:

1 Because he aimed to produce a low-cost vehicle targeted at developing countries, but Western buyers clamored for the car.
2 It is a roomy five-seater with a passenger-side airbag and a three-year warranty which still sells for about half the price of its competitors. It meets a demand for utilitarian cars in the context of Europe's discount mania.
3 By stripping the car of costly design elements and superfluous technology, avoiding electronics, using an adapted platform which is cheap to build and easy to maintain and repair, slashing the number of components by more than 50%, assembling almost entirely without robots, and taking advantage of low labour costs in Romania.
4 Students' own answers: perhaps by following suit like Volkswagen, or cutting costs even further like Tata, or maybe just by strengthening their positions in their traditional markets.

Listening

3 🎧 2.32 You may need to teach the following items from the recording: *it's got a lot going for it* (it has a lot of advantages), *rebadging* /riːˈbædʒɪŋ/ (to give something a new name or logo), *badge* /bædʒ/ (emblem, logo), *to slap something on* (to put something on without much care), *to rule something out* (to preclude or dismiss an idea), *what's your take on all this?* (What is your opinion on this?). These items could be pre-taught, or you could focus on them after the listening comprehension exercises.
Explain the background to the task as outlined in the rubric. Play the recording through once and ask students to take notes on the key points. Next, ask students to compare notes in pairs. Then ask them to read through and answer the three comprehension questions. Take whole-class feedback before moving on to the next task.

ANSWERS:

1 Amelia is a member of the Lesage family, and presumably the President or CEO.
2 Mikhail is in favour of not going down-market, or if they do, stripping down an existing model. His suggestion of rebadging is ironic. Jack sits on the fence and gives very little indication of his preferences.
3 They are drinking 'affordable' coffee as part of Amelia's no-frills campaign.

4 Display the grid on the board and ask students to read through the incomplete options in the grid on page 95 and to complete as much of the information as they can from memory and the notes they made in the previous listening task. Elicit answers from the class and write them onto the grid.

ANSWERS:

1 refuse to go down market – invest in quality, style, service
2 produce a no-frills model in France
3 build own model in Eastern Europe
4 strip / take cheapest existing model down to essentials / and strip it down to essentials
5 joint venture with Russians using old-generation technology
6 import and rebadge cheap cars from India
7 target traditional markets in Western Europe
8 target developing markets in Eastern Europe / China / Africa

RECORDING SCRIPT

 2:32

Mikhail: There you go. No cream any more, I'm afraid, but there's this skimmed milk powder if you want?

Jack: No, thanks Mikhail. I'll take it black, like my soul!

M: OK, so how about baring that black old soul of yours, then? Are you intending to back Amelia on this 'no-frills' project?

J: Ah. Amelia wants a Logan. And what the Lesage family want, they generally get.

M: True. But don't you think there's a case for resisting the temptation to go down-market? Just keep investing in quality, style and service?

J: Maybe. But the Logan is certainly providing growth for Renault, so who am I to say they're wrong?

M: So you think we should produce our own no-frills model? In our French plants?

J: Or maybe go the whole nine yards – build it in Eastern Europe. No robots, no electronics, skilled workers on low wages: it's got a lot going for it.

M: Hm. More coffee?

J: Go on then.

M: But listen, Jack; developing a completely new model would take years – why not just take our cheapest existing model, and strip it right down to the essentials?

J: Uh-huh. Worth considering. Another option is a joint venture with the Russians. Basically, we send them the shell, and they put in their own power train. Old generation technology, but reliable – and cheap.

M: Well if you want cheap, what about rebadging? Just buy in cars from India, and slap a Lesage badge on them!

J: I wouldn't rule it out.

M: Really? I suppose it all depends whether you're targeting our traditional markets in Western Europe: I was thinking more in terms of developing markets in Eastern Europe, China, Africa ...

J: Yeah, maybe both.

M: Hm. And perhaps there are other options we haven't even thought of yet. So what's your take on all this?

J: Well, I don't know. I guess the jury's still out. There's a lot riding on this. We're going to have to think it through very, very carefully, look at all the options, weigh up the pros and cons ...

M: Yeah. I'm with you on that. You want some more of this?

J: No, I think I've had enough. Amelia's no-frills campaign has gone too far – there's only so much 'affordable' coffee a man can take!

Reading

5 Ask students to brainstorm possible criteria they think the Lesage team should consider in their grid analysis. Elicit a few ideas from the class.

Next, pre-teach / review the following vocabulary: *implications* /ˌɪmplɪˈkeɪʃ(ə)nz/ (significance), *incentives* /ɪnˈsentɪvz/ (rewards to increase motivation), *ROI* (return on investment), *tricky* (difficult), *morale* /məˈrɑːl/ (confidence), *liquidity* /lɪˈkwɪdəti/ (the rate at which an asset can be converted into cash), *to dilute* /daɪˈluːt/ (to weaken, usually by adding water), *equity* /ˈekwəti/ (the value of something above the amount owed).

Ask students to read through Amelia's note and to identify the six criteria she mentions. Allow a few moments for students to compare in pairs, before eliciting answers and completing the grid.

Discussion

6 Assign students to work in groups of four or five. Explain the situation – that they are going to take part in a meeting to discuss the implementation of the no-frills car project. Distribute the role cards on pages 111, 112, 114 and 116 of the Student's Book and ask students to read their cards. Provide an opportunity to answer or clarify any questions and points at this stage, to ensure everyone understands what they have to do. Next, refer students back to the grid completed in the previous exercises. Ask students to consider the points based on their respective roles and to decide what they are going to say in the meeting. Encourage students to make notes in preparation. Stress that it is important that each individual firmly puts the case assigned to their roles.

Monitor to check students are making sufficient preparation for the discussion and provide input and help as required. Once you are satisfied students are sufficiently prepared, explain that their task now is to work as a group to modify, quantify and weight the criteria and options in the grid and to reach an objective and unanimous decision to recommend to the board of Lesage. Set a time limit of 15 minutes or so. Monitor the discussions, provide help and input as needed and note language points for immediate or post-correction. Once all groups have reached a decision, ask each group to present its recommendations to the class, making reference to their revised grids.

Free trade is a system in which the trade of goods and services flows without restrictions imposed by governments. Free trade is generally considered to include free access to markets, free access to market information and the free movement of labour and capital.

Free trade can be contrasted with protectionism. Protectionist measures include:
Taxes and tariffs (tariffs are simply a tax on goods coming into a country).
Quotas (a quota is an amount of goods that is officially allowed over a period of time).
Government regulations designed to discourage imports and generally protect domestic industries from foreign takeover or competition.
Inter-government trade agreements such as NAFTA (the North American Free Trade Agreement) or those within the European Union or ASEAN (the Association of South East Asian Nations). Such agreements create barriers for non-members.

Early arguments about free trade go back to Victorian economists such as Adam Smith and David Ricardo. In the 20th century, key proponents of free trade were Milton Friedman and Friedrich Hayek. In recent years Thomas Friedman's book *The World Is Flat* has been central to many MBA courses and has influenced a new generation of business leaders.

Arguments for free trade

There have been two main types of argument in favour of free trade: economic arguments and moral arguments.

The economic argument is simply that free trade will make society richer. It increases living standards and reduces poverty – compare North Korea with South Korea, or indeed any ex-communist country with the situation today in the same country. At a global level, free trade permits specialization among countries – they can gain a comparative advantage. This may be low wages or high tech, but in either case the global level of production increases.

The moral arguments in favour of free trade include that it makes war less likely (countries that trade together are much less likely to go to war), and that it enriches culture (external influences have a positive effect on culture).

Arguments against free trade

Again, there are two types of argument against free trade: economic ones and moral ones.

The economic arguments against free trade include the fact that protecting young industries initially can be beneficial in the long term – local companies can compete on the world stage later, when they are ready; a developing country can get locked into serving the needs of the world market with a limited range of sectors – for example it expands its agricultural or commodity sector but then fails to diversify; and free trade increases the risk of economic bubbles.

The moral arguments against free trade include the fact that free trade causes too much social dislocation and economic pain – especially for older or less educated people in the community who cannot adapt to the changes; free trade benefits only the wealthy within countries (in developed countries factory workers have seen their jobs disappear, while in developing countries control over trade keeps autocratic regimes in power); free trade creates a 'race to the bottom' in terms of environmental and labour regulations; and local cultures are slowly destroyed.

http://www.adamsmith.org
http://news.bbc.co.uk/1/hi/business/533716.stm
http://www.globalissues.org/issue/38/free-trade-and-globalization
http://www.freetrade.org/faqs/faqs.html

8.1 About business

Free trade and multinationals

This module provides extensive guided practice in identifying and interpreting a writer's stance, within the context of a challenging *Financial Times* article on the topic of free trade.

Preparation

Copy the main text onto an OHT or IWB for ease of reference throughout the lesson.

Internet research

It is a good idea to do the Internet search before embarking on the remainder of this module. The trade blocs referred to in the article are the Free Trade Area of the Asia Pacific Region (FTAAP), the Asia Pacific Economic Community (APEC), the Mercado Común del Sur (Mercosur), the European Union (EU), the North American Free Trade Agreement (NAFTA) and the Association of South East Asian Nations (ASEAN). Divide your class into groups and assign a region to each group. Ask the groups to research their regions and to present their findings to the class. This will provide invaluable background knowledge for the reading tasks that follow.

Discussion

1 Write the words *free trade* on the board and ask students in pairs or threes to provide a definition of the term. Elicit ideas from the class and discuss.
Dictate the following vocabulary and ask students to write it down: *to impose* /ɪmˈpəʊz/ (to apply as compulsory), *unhindered* /ʌnˈhɪndə(r)d/ (not obstructed), *tariffs* /ˈtærɪfs/ (rates or charges), *to entail* /ɪnˈteɪl/ (to involve), *quota* /ˈkwəʊtə/ (a set number, quantity or amount of something), *liberalization* /ˌlɪb(ə)rəlaɪzeɪʃ(ə)n/ (the process of making something more liberal or less restrictive).
Ask students to compare their lists in pairs, then elicit the words back from students and put them on the board. Teach / elicit the meaning of each, providing example sentences to illustrate. Draw students' attention to the cloze text on page 96 and ask them to complete the text using the words supplied. Take whole-class feedback.

Alternative

An alternative approach to this cloze exercise is to present the completed definition as a 'dictogloss'. Complete the text yourself prior to the class. In class, read the text aloud, but slightly slower than a native speaker would speak, and ask your students to listen. Next, ask your students to take out a piece of paper and a pen. Read the text again at native-speaker speed and ask students to note down what they hear. Resist reading too slowly, as the objective is to get the main ideas. Next, ask students to work in pairs to share their notes and to start recreating the text. Then ask pairs to work in fours to continue constructing the text. If necessary, read through the text a third time at normal speed for students to make final modifications.

Once the answers have been checked draw two columns on the board, as follows:

Free Trade	
For	Against

Ask students to work in threes and to brainstorm as many arguments for and against as they can. Set a time limit of three to four minutes for this. Then elicit ideas from the class and write them under the columns on the board. Conduct a brief class discussion of the main arguments.

EXTENSION ACTIVITY

This is an Internet search activity. Divide the class into two groups and ask one group to search for the key words *for free trade* and the other group for *against free trade*, and to compile the arguments. Once the data has been collected, pair students from each group to tell each other what they have found and discuss the arguments for and against.

ANSWERS:

1) market
2) goods
3) restrictions
4) taxes
5) non-tariff
6) quotas
7) liberalization

Reading for gist

2 You may find it helpful to set a vocabulary research exercise for homework, in which you provide a list of the most challenging lexis from the text for students to find out the definitions prior to the lesson. Alternatively, you could provide a glossary of the words. Potentially problematic lexis includes: *weeds, to sprout, to wither* /ˈwɪðə(r)/, *to flourish* /ˈflʌrɪʃ/, *bilateral* /baɪˈlæt(ə)rəl/, *to span, to float* /fləʊt/ *a proposal, a laggard* /ˈlæɡə(r)d/, *inertia* /ɪˈnɜː(r)ʃə/ *to founder, to be recalcitrant* /rɪˈkælsɪtrənt/, *to sway, multilateral, strife, ridden, endgame, plausible* /ˈplɔːzəb(ə)l/, *to scupper, vein* /veɪn/, *to unleash, a debacle* /deɪˈbɑːk(ə)l/, *to polarise, to diminish, defy* /dɪˈfaɪ/, *abundant, moribund* /ˈmɒrɪbʌnd/, *dogged* /ˈdɒɡɪd/, *sui generis* /ˌsuːi ˈdʒenərɪs/, *replicable* /ˈreplɪkəb(ə)l/, *to pull off a deal, to rake over, a buffer, unilateral* /ˌjuːnɪˈlæt(ə)rəl/, *to reap, to buttress, lofty, futile* /ˈfjuːtaɪl/ and *to haggle* /ˈhæɡ(ə)l/.
You may also find it useful to provide a guided reading comprehension task to unpack the meaning of the text at paragraph level. Suggested questions (and answers) are:
Paragraph 1: *What image does the writer use in the first paragraph?* (gardening)
Paragraph 2: *What two plans are mentioned?* (Japan's big idea and Fred Bergsten's plan)
Paragraph 3: *Which American policy has contributed to the collapse of the Doha talks?* (agricultural protectionism)
Paragraph 4: *What was Europe afraid of?* (America unplugging itself from multilateralism, i.e. going bilateral or unilateral)
Paragraph 5: *Does the writer state that the effects of bilateralism were good or bad?* (bad)
Paragraph 6: *Have the objectives of APEC, Mercosur and ASEAN been a success?* (no)
Paragraph 7: *What 'ingredients' are missing from the regional schemes?* (committed leadership and drive)
Paragraph 8: *What is 'Plan B'?* (for governments to open their own markets)
Paragraphs 9 and 10: *Is the unilateral removal of trade barriers a good strategy?* (yes)
By approaching the text in this way you will provide an opportunity to discuss the content with your class before moving on to the more challenging exercises in the Student's Book.

Your students should by now have had sufficient exposure to the text to successfully complete exercise 2. Give students a few minutes to complete the sentences and then to compare their answers in pairs. Go through the answers with the class using the text on the board for feedback, and to highlight key points. If students need any additional help at this stage, you could ask them to locate the areas of text that contain the information, and check through before students write their answers.

ANSWERS:

1 the collapse of the Doha talks.
2 the 1993 Uruguay talks were stopped from failing only because APEC [prompted by the USA] proposed closer intraregional [as opposed to inter-regional] links, which got Europe back to the negotiating table.
3 that the reason for Europe's continuation in the talks was because Europe was afraid that the USA would 'unplug itself from multilateralism', i.e. turn to unilateralism.
4 APEC and Mercosur.
5 lack of leadership and drive.

3 Again, your students should have little difficulty answering this question. You could provide additional prompts by telling students that the answer is given in the last three paragraphs of the text.

ANSWER:

1

Recognizing stance

4 This task requires a sophisticated understanding of nuance in the author's choice of language. You can provide additional help with this task first of all by asking students to identify the sections of text in which each topic is covered (i.e. the Doha trade round is discussed in paragraph 1, the EU and NAFTA in paragraph 6; and Japan's big idea and Fred Bergstein's plan in paragraph 2). When this has been done, ask students to identify the words the author uses to describe each item and whether or not the writer's stance is generally positive or negative / critical in each case. You could demonstrate the task by highlighting some of the key language in the first paragraph (e.g. *gardens neglected*) and asking students to identify whether this has a positive or a negative meaning.
Monitor closely while students do the task, providing plenty of help and additional input as needed. Next, give students a few minutes to compare answers in pairs, before going through the answers on the board. Use the text on the board to highlight relevant areas for discussion.

ANSWERS:

1 the Doha trade round: when gardens are neglected (a metaphor for the Doha talks), withering (continuation of the metaphor, with negative connotation), predictably (this adverb indicates how the writer views the consequences of the talks' breakdown, i.e. the 'weeds' of unworkable grand plans), more political puffery than economic substance (again critical)
2 the European Union and NAFTA: regionalism's only big successes are the EU and the North American Free Trade Agreement (a clearly stated argument in favour of these two groupings)
3 Japan's big idea and Fred Bernstein's idea: these schemes are 'no magic bullets' (a metaphor for a quick, effective solution), in other words Japan's big idea is not an effective solution

5 Be prepared to recap the meaning of *to defy* (to resist or contradict), *moribund* (no longer effective and not likely to continue for much longer), *to dog* (to follow, especially in a hostile way) and *sui generis* (of its own kind). Draw students' attention to paragraph 6 and ask them to highlight the language that conveys evaluation or stance. If this is too challenging, use closer questioning to guide students, e.g. *What does the writer say about the belief that faster progress can be made in regional groupings?* (it defies evidence to the contrary) *How does the writer describe APEC's dreams of freeing trade in the Pacific rim?* (they remain dreams, and are therefore not likely to be realized). Encourage students to use their own words to paraphrase or express the writer's ideas. Monitor intensively and provide additional help and input.

ANSWERS:

Paragraph 6 contains a lot of evaluation, all of which contributes to the writer's sceptical stance towards the concept of regional groupings: *also defies abundant evidence to the contrary; remain dreams; are moribund; South America's Mercosur is in trouble, as are its talks …; Disputes … have dogged …; South Asia's plans for a customs union look like a joke; Regionalism's only big successes are the EU and the North American Free Trade Agreement – and the former is too sui generis to be replicable.*
This language includes evaluative words (e.g. *moribund*) and arguments which are essentially the writer's opinion.

Discussion

6 This final activity provides an opportunity for students to discuss their responses to the text. You can provide additional help by using guiding prompts.
For example, in question 1 you could ask students to specify the kind of person that reads the *Financial Times* (people in the financial services sector, executives, traders, politicians, etc.).
For question 2, you could ask your students to pick out some examples of fact and opinion, e.g. in paragraph 1 *the growth of preferential bilateral deals* is probably a fact, whereas asserting that this growth *generates more political puffery than economic substance* is a value-judgement, especially since 'puffery' suggests empty rhetoric.
For question 3, either ask students to recap the main arguments presented or input them yourself, e.g. bilateral trade agreements don't work; protectionism is damaging to international trade; regional trade organizations can be more effective than the WTO; the best solution is to unilaterally remove trade barriers. These topics will provide the basis of the discussion.
Monitor while the groups discuss the questions and make notes of language points for later attention. Take whole-class feedback.

SUGGESTED ANSWERS:

1 Educated, with a lot of world current affairs knowledge, very interested in trade, commerce and politics.
2 With close reading, it is reasonably manageable to work out what is evidence and what is evaluation. The writer is presenting a particular argument, which is closely connected to his stance on free trade. It is important to recognize stance because it is not actually fact and the reader does not have to agree with it.
3 Student's own answers

8.2 Grammar

Phrasal and prepositional verbs

This module tests and revises a range of phrasal and prepositional verbs.

Internet research

The suggested keyword search could be usefully set as a homework task prior to this lesson. If this is not possible, you could allocate 20 minutes at the start of the lesson for this. Divide the class into two groups and assign each group one of the topics. Then pair students from each group to share their information. It would be useful for students to have this background information on GATT and the WTO when they do the cloze activity in exercise 1.

Did you know?

The list of verbs and particles can be incorporated into a range of brainstorming activities. For example, create a table on a sheet of A4 paper, similar to the following:

come	around
go	away
put	back
get	down
take	in
turn	into
run	off
bring	on
look	out
cut	over
	through
	up

Distribute a copy to groups of three in the class. Explain that their task is to generate as many sentences as possible (orally) using combinations of the verbs and particles. They should keep a tally of each sentence they generate, adding one point to their score each time. Set a time limit of two to three minutes. When the time is up, ask each group to tell you their score. Ask the group with the highest score to share their sentences with the class. Ask other groups to challenge any which they think are incorrect and to provide correct versions.

Another activity using these word combinations is the 'round robin' brainstorming technique. Copy one verb plus all the particles onto sheets of A4, as follows:

	around	away
	back	down
	in	into
come	off	on
	out	over
	through	up

Do this for each verb. Give one sheet to each pair of students in the class so that each pair has a different verb sheet. Set a time limit of one to two minutes and ask the pairs to write down as many sentences as they can using the verb and particles. After one or two minutes stop the activity and ask the pairs to pass their sheets along to the pair to their right. Each pair will now have another verb + particles sheet. Again, set a time limit and ask the pairs to write out as many sentences as they can. Repeat this process until the pairs get their original sheets of paper back again. Now ask each pair to feed back on the sentences generated by the class. Provide remedial correction and clarification as needed. You could display the sheets on a classroom notice board for reference. Finally, draw students' attention to the information in the *Did you know?* box.

Focus on frequent verbs

1 Pre-teach or elicit the following words from the text: controversial /ˌkɒntrəˈvɜː(r)ʃ(ə)l/ (debatable; not generally agreed), *in the wake of* (following; as a consequence of), *conquest* /ˈkɒŋkwest/ (the act of conquering), *an advocate* /ˈædvəkət/ (a supporter or defender), *in the face of* (when confronted with), *widespread* /ˈwaɪdˌspred/ (covering a large area) and *to grow out of* (to evolve from).

Although students' earlier Internet research work will have provided them with useful background information on GATT and the WTO, it might also be useful at this stage to elicit / input some background information on Genghis Khan and Adam Smith.

Give students a few minutes to read through and complete the text. Provide an opportunity for students to compare in pairs, then take whole-class feedback. Once the answers have been checked and clarified, you could check students' comprehension of the text, e.g. *What happened in the 13th century?* (free trade took off between Europe and Asia) *What benefits did Adam Smith believe free trade would bring?* (increased wealth to the nations involved).

ANSWERS:

| 1 go | 2 took | 3 turn / look | 4 put | 5 brought |
| 6 get | 7 came | 8 cut | 9 ran | 10 look |

2 For this activity you might find it useful to adapt the answer key into a synonyms list for the phrasal verbs used, e.g. *to go back to = return to (a time or place)*. You could incorporate the list into a matching activity or a sentence transformation activity, with an opportunity for pairwork practice. An example transformation activity would be:

1 *It's necessary to return to the economic theories of the early 20th century.*

 go

 It's necessary to _____ the economic theories of the early 20th century.

An example pairwork activity would be for students to test each other, e.g.

A: *return*

B: *go back to*

ANSWERS:

1 go back *return*
2 took off *became popular*
3 turn / look to *direct your attention to*
4 put forward *propose, offer, suggest*
5 brought about *caused*
6 get across *communicate*
7 came up with *initiate, think of*
8 cut down on *reduce*
9 ran into *encounter, meet*
10 look for *search, seek, investigate*

3 This exercise tests students' knowledge of phrasal verbs. As the verbs are out of context in this exercise, it would be helpful to provide some example sentences for each of the verb + particle combinations, e.g. *Most commentators agree on how the financial crisis came about.* Be prepared to provide some definitions as well, e.g. *to come about* (to occur). Beware, also, that in number 2, the answer given is that *go from* is incorrect, but you could say, for example, *the situation has gone from bad to worse.* However, *go from* is not strictly speaking a phrasal verb as it does not have an idiomatic meaning.

As with the introductory activities described in the *Did you know?* section above, you can make the activity more interactive by getting students to work in threes to orally produce as many examples as they can, ticking each verb and particle as they do so, e.g. *The housing sector went through a tough period last year, but has now come through it.* Set a time limit of two to three minutes and conduct oral feedback at the end. Finally, go through the exercise with the class.

ANSWERS:

The following cannot be used
1 come behind   2 go from   3 put for   4 get against
5 take above   6 turn under   7 run above
8 bring past   9 look without   10 cut about

Focus on frequent particles

4 This is a challenging text that provides excellent revision for students with a very high level of proficiency. With very high level classes you could set the exercise as prescribed in the Student's Book. With lower level students you may need to approach the task differently. One suggested way is to present the text in its complete form. Read the complete text aloud to the class, as though you are actually giving the presentation (students have their books closed). Ask students to listen and to make a note of the theme and purpose of the presentation (*theme: a new strategy to deal with new trading conditions; purpose: to outline the background to the situation and the challenges facing the company*). Next, read the presentation through again and ask students to note down the phrasal verbs they hear, but not to worry about spellings at this stage. Once you have read through the text again, ask students to compare the words they have noted down in pairs. Next, ask students to read through the text itself on page 99 and to check for the verbs and to add in the particles. Go through the answers with the class.

ANSWERS:

1 around   2 back   3 over   4 up   5 in   6 out
7 away   8 on   9 off   10 down   11 through   12 into

5 Ask students to work again in pairs to guess the meaning of each phrasal verb according to the contextual clues provided. Do the first as an example, using guiding questions: *kick around: What does the manager want to 'kick around? (a few new ideas); What would you normally expect to do with ideas in a meeting? (discuss / brainstorm); So what might 'kick around' mean in this context? (to discuss / brainstorm).*
Monitor while students work on deducing the meanings from context. When they have finished this task, elicit suggestions from the class, but do not provide any definitive answers yet. Next, refer students to the list of synonyms and ask them to match them to the phrasal verbs. Check through with the class. Finally, ask students to test each other in pairs, e.g.
A: *kick around*
B: *discuss*

ANSWERS:

1 kick around = discuss
2 claw back = recover
3 gloss over = ignore
4 weigh up = assess
5 take in = absorb
6 bail out = rescue
7 do(ne) away (with) = remove
8 focus on = concentrate (on)
9 tail off = dwindle
10 nail down = finalize
11 get through = survive
12 buy into = accept

Listening

6 and **7** 2.33 Set the scenario as described in the Student's Book. Play the extract through once and ask students to make notes of the main points while they listen. Allow a few moments for checking in pairs and then elicit the main points from the class. Play the extract again, but this time ask students to note down all the phrasal verbs they hear. Again, allow a few moments for checking in pairs before eliciting the list to the board. If necessary, play the extract again for the class to add items to the list. Now isolate the 10 phrasal verbs for exercise 6 and direct students' attention to the gapped summary text. Tell them to complete the cloze text using the list of verbs provided. Let students check in pairs, then take whole-class feedback.

ANSWERS:

6
1 commence   2 erode   3 continue   4 enter   5 diversify
6 produce   7 protecting   8 initiate   9 dilute
10 surrender

7
1 commence – kick off
2 erode – eat into
3 continue – crack on with
4 enter – break into
5 diversify – branch out
6 produce – come up with
7 protect – shore up
8 initiate – start up
9 dilute – water down
10 surrender – bow to

8 This continuation of the previous exercises presents / reviews a further seven phrasal verbs. Students will already have noted the phrasal verbs during the listening stage. If students struggle to supply meanings for the phrasal verbs, supply the meanings yourself in random order for students to match to the phrasal verbs. Be prepared to provide some extra examples to reinforce the meaning and usage of the verbs. As a final round-up of the listening exercises, set up a short pairwork practice for students to test each other. The phrasal verbs can be incorporated into progress tests later in the course.

ANSWERS:

focus on (concentrate on)
conjure up (produce)
go in (x2, enter)
get in (enter, arrive)
build up (increase)
calm down (relax)
stand by (remain with)

RECORDING SCRIPT

 2.33

Dave: Well, as Lawrence says it's tough out there. We've got to all be tough ourselves, first of all. I think we should kick off with a review of the trading laws in South-east Asia …

Jin: Another review? That's the last thing we need. They last forever and it would eat into our valuable time.

Sara: Hey Jin, we should at least listen to each other's proposals and not just ignore them without discussing them.

J: OK Sara, but we've got to crack on with the real strategy – what the heck is our best way into the new Asian markets?

S: Asian markets? We can't break into them yet – what about our own domestic market?

D: Thank you Sara. As I was saying, we've got to focus on getting a review …

J: Wait. It's no use putting all our eggs in one basket. Our own market's tiny first of all. As the boss says, at last we can branch out into our competitors' comfort zone. It's a whole new era with these new trade laws. That's where the real gains are going to be – the free market's massive now.

S: OK, but what's your plan?

J: Well that's why we're having this meeting – to come up with one. I can't just conjure up a plan from thin air. These are unchartered waters. Our priority at the moment has got to be finding the best way into Asia and then maybe at a later date we can head west and see what we can do with the Americas.

D: Asia again, and America! They're massive. I say we shore up our home market first, and then …

J: Yeah, we know what you say. Words are not what we need, it's action. It's time to start up the strategy. How about a multi-market-wide blitz for starters? Japan, China obviously, and a few of the other main countries in the region, you know, Korea, Malaysia and all that. Go in big, all guns blazing. Grab their attention before the whole market gets saturated. Get in there first, before the big players. Or should that be the new players from those emerging markets? Although why they call them 'emerging' I don't know – most of them actually 'emerged' years ago.

S: Have you quite finished? That approach is just typical of you. And risky. You always talk about different markets as if they're all just one and the same. They might be in the same geographical area from your perspective but each one behaves differently. The cultures are different. Anyway, your plan would cost a fortune. I say we should test the market, don't go in big but start small, get a feel for things. And then we can build it up from there.

J: As usual you're trying to water down my proposals before we even discuss them.

S: Calm down. We don't even know the market – how can we go in big? Where's all the support and investment funding going to come from?

D: Quite right. We must bow to the inevitable and stop talking about all these grand expensive ideas. I stand by my original idea. How about a quick review of …?

J and S: No, no more reviews …

This module focuses on ways of creating new words. This topic is dealt with in a humorous, fun and engaging way and provides opportunities for students to practise creating new words.

Internet research

As the internet research box suggests, a search for *new words* will return sites that list newly invented words. This activity could be done for homework prior to the lesson or at the start of the lesson.

Reading for gist

1 Begin by introducing the topic of the unit and of the reading text (forming or creating new words). Provide one or two examples of such language yourself, e.g. *broadband is a combination of broad + bandwidth.* Ask students to work in pairs or small groups and either to brainstorm new words they have encountered or those they garnered from the Internet research activity. Elicit the words and put them on the board. Pre-teach / elicit the meaning of the following words from the text: *affix* (an element of a word), *open the floodgates* (to suddenly make it possible or easier for a lot of things to happen), *to raid* (to attack or invade in order to seize property), *mortar* (a building material made by mixing lime, cement and water) and *lifeblood* (an essential life-giving force).

Draw students' attention to the text and ask them to read to identify the purpose of the article. Check their answers. Ask students to read through quickly, highlighting all the new (i.e. italicized) words mentioned. Next, elicit these from the class and ask students to briefly discuss the meanings. Then ask students to identify the 10 ways of creating new words. Elicit the categories and write them on the board in tabular form, e.g.

acronyms	attaching letters	combining words and affixes	blends

Next, ask students to provide an example of each from the text and write these in the correct columns.

ANSWERS:

1 The article aims to give a light-hearted overview of how new words can be created, with contemporary examples from a business and commerce context.

2 acronyms, e.g. *BRIC*; attaching a letter, such as 'e' for *electronic*, to existing words, e.g. *e-commerce*; combining old words and affixes to create new words, e.g. *offshoring*; blends, e.g. *globaphobic*; raid words from other contexts, e.g. *guru*; shortened words, e.g. *max (from maximum)*; change the part of speech, such as phrasal verb to noun, e.g. *stopover*; rhymes, e.g. *clicks and mortar*; combine two words in a novel combination, e.g. *swarm businesses*; metaphors, e.g. *glass ceiling*

Vocabulary

2 Dictate the list of items from the Student's Book and ask students to write them down. Encourage students to compare in pairs. Ask students to turn to the list on page 101 to check against their lists. Now ask students to work in pairs to decide in which category each word belongs. Once students have discussed this, elicit their answers and write the words into the suggested columns on the board. These classifications will be open to interpretation, encouraging discussion and debate. Once the table has been completed, ask students to discuss the meaning of each new word. Keep this stage brisk and go through the answers with the class. Get students to test each other on the meanings.

SUGGESTED ANSWERS:

acronyms: B2B, NAFTA, ASEAN
attaching a letter: e-signature
combining old words and affixes to create new words: presenteeism, downsize
blends: Coca-colonization, infonomics, blog, agflation
raid words from other contexts: (marketing) crusade
shortened words: dotcom
change the part of speech: dollarize, Google(d), bookmark(ed)
rhymes: al desko, get rich click, brandalism
combine two words in a novel combination: angel investor, marketing crusade
metaphors: cappuccino / goldilocks / tiger (economy), angel (investor)

B2B = business to business; NAFTA = North America Free Trade Association; ASEAN = Association of South East Asian Nations
e-signature = electronic signature
presenteeism = being present at work but effectively absent due to long hours and low productivity;
Coca-colonization = coca cola + colonization; infonomics = information + economics; blog = web + log; agflation = agriculture + inflation; downsize = through economic necessity reduce the workforce and assets of a company
crusade = an aggressive (marketing) campaign
dotcom = company which does its main business over the web
dollarize = to get rid of a country's local currency and go for the dollar; Google(d) = to google / search for something; bookmark = to (electronically) add a bookmark
al desko = eating at your desk (rhyme: *al fresco*), get rich click = get rich by means of the Internet (rhyme: *get rich quick*);
brandalism = defacing public buildings with corporate slogans and advertising (rhyme: *vandalism*)
angel investor = a helpful individual who invests in a start-up company
cappuccino economy = an economy like the coffee – frothy on top, flat underneath; goldilocks economy = not too hot, not too cold, just right; tiger (economy) = a fast-growing economy which is dynamic like a tiger

Blends

3 Dictate the six items to the class and ask them to write them down. Elicit the words, put them on the board and check spelling. Ask students to tell you the meaning of *Oxbridge*, if they know it, and to highlight the two components making up the word (i.e. **Ox***(ford)* + *(Cam)***bridge**). Now ask students to repeat this process with the remaining words in the list. Please note that 'genericide' may cause particular difficulty as it uses two Latin terms (*generic* and the suffix *-icide*), so you may need to provide additional examples and explanations (e.g. *homicide* and *regicide*). Encourage students to discuss their answers in pairs before going through with the class.

ANSWERS:

1 Oxbridge = Oxford and Cambridge (universities)
2 wikinomics = wiki + economics
3 flexicurity = flexibility + security, as in the Danish jobs market
4 genericide = generic + -icide, i.e. killing brands by becoming the word for all products in that category, e.g. aspirin, iPod
5 stagflation = stagnant (growth) / stagnation + inflation
6 philanthopreneur = philanthropist + entrepreneur

Combining words

4 Check students understand the meaning of the following words: *virtuous, anorexia, catalyst, venture* and *spin*. Before students attempt the sentence completion task, ask them to combine the words on the left with those on the right to create as many meaningful combinations as they can. Provide an example or two to get the ball rolling, e.g. *venture coach: someone who trains you to become a risk-loving investor; corporate-proof: something that cannot be taken over or bought by corporations.* Allow several minutes for this, then elicit suggestions from the class and discuss. Now ask students to read through the gapped sentences and to select possible combinations of words to fill the gaps. If students find this too difficult, you could provide the combinations in advance for them to slot into the sentences. Alternatively, put the first word of each combination into the appropriate gap and ask students to select a suitable second word for each.

ANSWERS:

1 venture catalyst
2 corporate anorexia
3 virtuous cycle
4 future proof
5 spin journalism
6 career coach

Creating new words

5 This fun activity provides an opportunity for students to be creative with language to produce new words out of existing words. Emphasize that there are no right or wrong answers and that students should try to create as many words as they can in each case. For example, a *metrosexual* could also be a *heteropolitan*.
Collate students' answers and put them on the board. Have a class vote on the best, funniest or most effective words.

SUGGESTED ANSWERS:

1 womenomics
2 cleantech
3 lifestreaming
4 upcycling
5 rightsizing
6 metrosexual (has also led to retrosexual, technosexual, heteroflexible)
7 CXOs
8 Wal-Mart effect

8.4 Management skills

Leading the team

This module explores the characteristics of effective teams and the roles played by team members, and culminates in a roleplay to actively engage learners with the topic.

Preparation

Copy the roles and definitions from the table on page 102 onto pieces of card for a matching activity as outlined in the instructions for exercise 2.

Also, copy the 'Leadership checklist' (page 117) onto an OHT or IWB to display during the leadership evaluation activity at the end of the module.

Internet research

This is an amusing angle on the topic, and as the search box suggests the keywords *meeting behaviour cartoons* and *boss cartoons* will return lots of funny examples. Download and print your favourites to bring to class.

Discussion

1 The discussion questions can be dictated to the class or displayed on the board. Give students a few minutes to prepare their answers before starting the discussion. Be aware, also, that some of the class may be team leaders themselves and so question 2 will be asking them to discuss their own strengths and weaknesses. Once students have noted down their answers to the questions, ask them to discuss the questions in pairs. After the pairwork, conduct a whole-class discussion of the questions. For question 3 you could elicit the qualities of the ideal team leader and put them on the board, then ask students to work in pairs and rank the qualities in order of importance. Ask each pair to discuss their rankings with another pair and to agree a new ranking. Try to reach a class consensus on the top five most important qualities of an ideal team leader, e.g. *integrity, vision, commitment, empowering others, leading by example, motivating, striving for excellence, communication, generosity, adapting, growing.*

Reading

2 Pre-teach or elicit the following vocabulary: *optimal* /ˈɒptɪm(ə)l/ (most desirable, best, ideal), *to weigh up* /weɪ ʌp/ (to evaluate or assess), *morale* /məˈrɑːl/ (confidence or well-being, happiness), *to defuse* /diːˈfjuːz/ (to reduce the danger of something) and *concrete* /ˈkɒŋkriːt/ (real or actual).

The reading text can be broken down into a series of matching tasks. First of all, the roles can be matched to their characteristics. This can be done on cut-up cards, e.g.

| Shaper | Drives the team to overcome obstacles and perform. |
| Implementer | Puts ideas into action. |

Distribute one set of cards to each pair in the class and ask them to match the roles to their definitions. Go through the answers. Next, write the headings *Action-Oriented Roles, People-Oriented Roles, Thought-Oriented Roles* on the board and ask the class to categorize the roles accordingly. When students have done this, draw their attention to the table on page 102 to check. Now ask students to match the responsibilities a)–i) to the roles. Ask students to check in pairs and then go through the answers with the class. Finally, ask students to discuss questions 2–4 in pairs, then take whole-class feedback.

ANSWERS:

1 a) specialist b) resource investigator c) coordinator d) shaper
  e) monitor-evaluator f) team worker g) implementer
  h) completer-finisher i) plant
2 and 3 student's own answers
4 suggested answers: by recruiting and delegating when necessary, defining responsibilities, empowering team members in particular areas, motivating, encouraging and coaching team members to take on new roles, taking on missing roles themselves

Listening

3 🔊 2.34–2.39 Play the extracts through once and ask students to take notes on the general points being discussed. Give students a few moments to check in pairs before eliciting points from the class. Check students understand the meaning of *to coach* (to train), *to take on* (to employ), *to empower* (to give power or authority to somebody), *constructive criticism* (criticism or advice that is useful or helpful). Ask students to read through the six functions and to match them to what they heard in the recording. If necessary, play the recording through again for students to check. Pick out the language in the extracts that provide the answers, e.g. in 1 the speaker mentions *research* (investigation) and says *go ahead* and *you decide* (empowering).

ANSWERS:

coaching a completer-finisher: 3
taking on a specialist: 6
empowering a resource investigator: 1
giving constructive criticism to a plant: 5
delegating to a shaper: 2
motivating a monitor-evaluator: 4

4 Ask students to complete as much information as they can from recall and the notes they made during the listening. Encourage students to work in pairs to combine their ideas and then play the extracts again to check. Next, ask students to discuss what they think the phrases mean in these contexts. Go through the answers and clarify the meanings. Next, drill the sentences for pronunciation, stress and rhythm.

ANSWERS:

1 go ahead, follow up on 2 keep me in the loop
3 along the same lines 4 take ownership of
5 huge strides, keep up the good work 6 keeping on top of
7 let him get on with it 8 help us out

5 This task requires students to grade the requests according to the degree of delegating, supporting, etc. given by the speaker. This is a challenging task, as the function of each request is not always transparent. There is therefore plenty of scope for interpretation and discussion.

Ask students to work in pairs to assign values to the requests. Copy the rating scale to the board and collate students' ratings on the scale to find agreement and divergence of opinion.

SUGGESTED ANSWERS:

1, 5 participating / supporting   2, 8 delegating / observing
3, 4, 7 selling / coaching   6 telling / directing

RECORDING SCRIPT

 2.34–2.39

1 Chris, I know you've already done some research on possible distributors in Vietnam. I think you should go ahead and follow up on those contacts, don't you? Just keep me in the loop on what you decide, would you?

2 Paula, do you remember the Japanese market study we did

together last year? I wonder if you could get Jack and Ella to do something along the same lines for China? I'm pretty tied up with the partnering discussions at the moment, but I'm sure you can handle it. We'll see how far you've got, say, at the end of the month? Is that OK?

3   You did a great job on the Hong Kong project, Soo-Hyang. I never thought we'd finish it in time, but you really came through! I really appreciate being able to rely on you to get things past the finishing post. This time round, I'd like you to take ownership of the whole logistics side of things – do you feel ready for the challenge?

4   Listen, Henry, you really shouldn't worry about it. I was extremely happy with ninety-nine per cent of your report, and I think you can feel very satisfied with a job well done too. Not picking up on just that one ratio was of no real significance, and it wouldn't have changed our decision in any way. You're a really valuable asset to the team – I don't know where we'd be without you! You've made huge strides in the last six months, so let's just keep up the good work, all right?

5   Just one other thing, Karen; I know you're brilliant at coming up with new ways to improve processes, and I really do appreciate your input – but don't you think that keeping on top of foreign exchange is really Phil's baby? Clearly he doesn't have your creativity, but he does have a lot of experience in his specialist area, so perhaps we should just let him get on with it, what do you think?

6   The thing is Max, until Ling gets back from maternity leave, the team's a bit short on negotiating skills: so if you were able to help us out, I'd really appreciate being able to call on your skills, especially as you've got first-hand experience of working with the Chinese.

Roleplay

6   Ask students to work in groups of four to five students and to read through the background to the roleplay. Ask one or two comprehension questions, e.g. *Who do you work for? Who are your target customers? What is the purpose of your meetings today?*

Ask students to read through the agendas for each of the three meetings and tell you what the objective of each meeting is (1 = decide the best business partners for the US and Canadian markets; 2 = decide the best type of event for a promotional tour; 3 = decide the best media for an advertising campaign). Assign each student in each group a role card and tell them to read through their roles carefully. Check all students understand what they have to do. Once you are satisfied all students know what they have to do, ask them to hold the first meeting. Set a time limit of seven to eight minutes for this. Monitor and note any language points for later attention. Also provide additional help and support as needed. Once the first meeting is finished, ask the groups to discuss the roles each person played.

Next, if you made a copy of the 'Leadership checklist' onto an OHT or IWB, display this to the class. If not, refer students to the checklist on page 117. (Note: the items on the checklist relate to the topics covered in the other 'Management skills' modules in units 1–7 of the Student's Book. If your class has been together throughout the book, you could ask students to work in small groups and brainstorm the points they think the checklist will contain). Read through the first point on the checklist with the class and give students time to individually consider their evaluation of their team leader. Next, ask the students to discuss this first point in their groups and to provide feedback to their team leaders. Repeat this process with each item on the checklist. Conduct a brief whole-class discussion with the groups. Repeat this process with meetings 2 and 3.

8.5 Writing
Formal invitations

This module presents the key language of formal invitations and provides practice in using the language productively.

Preparation

Bring some example invitations to class to use as realia and sources of authentic language in use. Prepare sets of cards for the matching task (exercise 4, page 104) and make enough for each pair of students.

The jumbled words and phrases task (exercise 8, page 105) could be prepared on cut-up cards for students to assemble into sentences. Alternatively, the words and phrases could be incorporated into a 'drag and drop' computer-assisted language learning (CALL) exercise or into draggable text boxes on an IWB. If you do not have the time or facilities to do this, copy the exercise from the Student's Book onto an OHT or scan it onto your IWB.

Discussion

1   Dictate / write the following on the board:
Have you ever …
… been to a formal business lunch / dinner?
… been to the opening of a new building?
… entertained an important visitor to your company / institution?
… organized a formal event?
Select a student from the class and ask him / her one of the questions. If he / she replies 'yes', follow up with a 'Wh-' question, e.g. *When was this? Where did the event take place? Who else was there? What did you have to eat and drink?*
Explain to students that they should interview each other in pairs, using 'Wh-' questions to find out more details.
When the personalization activity is complete, draw students' attention to the discussion questions on page 104. Tell students that they are to organize each of the events listed and are to make notes under the headings provided (i.e. *venue, food and drink, guests, tickets, dress code*). Note: if time is short, ask the pairs to select one of the events to plan. Ask each pair to share their ideas with the class.

Analysis

2   Draw students' attention to the three invitations on page 104 and ask them to read them and identify the event being held in each case. You may like to extend this slightly by asking students to identify the venue, food and drink, ticket requirements and dress codes as well.

ANSWERS:

1   Talk on 'The Price of Trade'
2   Dinner and dance celebrating of the opening of a computer laboratory at Amir College
3   Retirement function

3   Read through the phrases with the class and give students a few minutes to add them to the invitations. Ask students to compare in pairs, the take whole-class feedback.

ANSWERS:

1 e   2 d   3 a   4 f   5 b   6 c

Style

4 If you prepared a set of cut-up cards for this, distribute one set to each pair of students and allow a few minutes for students to match the phrases to their explanations. Go through the answers together. Next, ask students to test each other in pairs, e.g.

A: *Dinner jackets preferred, i.e. formal evening dress: suit with matching trousers.*
B: *Black tie.*

ANSWERS:

| 1 h | 2 c | 3 d | 4 b | 5 a | 6 g | 7 f | 8 e | 9 i | 10 j |

5 Write the six categories of information on the board. Ask students to work in pairs. Explain that you are going to read out some phrases and that students should decide which category each phrase belongs to. Read the first phrase and give students a few seconds to discuss the category it fits into. Elicit suggestions from the class. Repeat this process with each item. Next, ask students to complete exercise 5 on page 105, confirming or modifying their answers. Go through the answers with the class. Finally, ask students in pairs to discuss the relative formality of each phrase. You could ask students to decide whether a phrase is formal, semi-formal or informal. As a follow-up ask students to add one or two extra phrases to each category.

ANSWERS:

Naming yourself: Ms Annie Foulkes (*semi-formal*), Dickens and Associates (*formal*)
Inviting: Join us to celebrate (*informal*), Mack Corporation cordially invite you to (*formal*), share with us the celebration of (*semi-formal*), would like you to come to (*informal*)
Stating purpose: a get-together (*informal*), Tim's 50th birthday (*informal*), an evening of fashion and food (*formal*)
Time: on Saturday evening (*informal*), from 20.00 to 23.00 (*formal*), around 7p.m. (*informal*)
Dress: black tie optional (*formal*), business attire (*formal*), smart casual fine (*informal*), evening wear (*formal*)
Replying: Please let us know if you can come (*informal*), contact: F. Patterson (*formal*), Replies to Gabriella di Marco (*semi-formal*)

6 This exercise requires students to identify the inappropriate expressions for formal invitations and to reword the phrases accordingly in a suitably formal style. Ask students to work through the sentences, making the modifications they think necessary. Next, ask students to refer back to the sample invitations on the previous page and to find expressions that carry the same meaning as those in sentences 1–5 and to compare with their own re-wordings. Ask students to compare their answers in pairs, then take whole-class feedback. As a follow-up, you could ask students to test each other in pairs to transform informal expressions to formal, e.g.

A: *You'll be able to park your car.*
B: *Parking available.*

SUGGESTED ANSWERS:

1 John and Maria Shaw request the pleasure of the company of Anna Maria Martinez at their party.
2 Please join us at a reception to celebrate the launch of the new …
3 Cocktails (etc.) will be served.
4 Regrets only.
5 Plaza Hotel Ball Room. Admission by ticket only.

RSVP / Replies

7 2.40 Ask students to close their books. Explain the idea of etiquette when replying to invitations. Ask students to work in groups of three. Read aloud the first statement from the list 1–8 and ask students to note down whether they think it is true or false. Next, ask the groups to discuss whether they think the statement is true or false and why. Elicit opinions from each group. Repeat this process with each statement. Next, ask students to read through the statements in their Student's Books. Play the recording through once and ask students to check whether their answers were correct according to what Wendy and Yun Joo say. Allow a moment or two for students to compare in pairs and play the extract again if necessary.

ANSWERS:

1 False: in writing, in black ink
2 False: handwritten in black ink
3 True
4 True
5 False: it isn't necessary
6 False: only the date
7 False: the person should be named; if not, always ask the host; you should only take a partner to a wedding if you are engaged to that person
8 False: you can reply by email

RECORDING SCRIPT

2.40

Wendy: Oh, by the way, have you sent your reply for the black tie event at the government offices yet? The deadline's tomorrow.

Yun Joo: Sent a reply? I was going to call them later today. I've been rushed off my feet with work. Can't I just pick up the phone? Look, there's a number here on the invitation.

W: Oh no, you can't do that. This is going to be a really formal occasion. In this country if you receive a written invitation you should send a written reply.

Y: Oh! But surely from a practical point of view – you know, catering and so on – then it's just a question of numbers. As long as I tell them whether or not I'm coming, surely it doesn't matter if I email, call or send a text message.

W: Sure, but etiquette doesn't work that way. It's much more about courtesy.

Y: So I have to type up and print out a letter, then?

W: Ah, well, actually, no. Your reply should be clearly hand written, in black ink and ideally on headed paper, although that isn't essential, and in the third person.

Y: You are joking I hope! This is so old-fashioned!

W: Well, there is some good news, actually. There isn't a 'correct' way of wording a reply. Instead, there are preferred styles, but I'd say that the golden rule is to reply in the same manner as the invitation. So this means, for example, using the same layout, and the same spacing, centering the text, you know, mirroring the invitation. And of course you should also specify the dates, time and place.

Y: You mean, repeat all that on the reply?

W: Yes, that's right.

Y: OK. It seems a bit unnecessary to me, but if I have to then I will. But, you know, not all formal invites include this RSVP on them. In this case, can I call them?

W: Well, yes, probably. It means it's less formal, so it's probably acceptable.

Y: 'Acceptable'? It's sounding like I wouldn't want to go to any of these events in any case!

W: Well, be that as it may … Now, about declining invitations, do you know what you need to do if you can't go?

Y: Yes? Is that easier?

W: Well, you don't have to go into details about why you can't go. It's important, though, to include the date of the event.

Y: So I can just write, something like, 'Sorry, Jerry won't be able to go'.

W: Er, yes, sort of. It's probably easier to use the standard wording, like 'So-and-so regrets he or she is unable to attend', and then name the event or date, or 'he declines with regret'.

Y: Oh, I see. And the opposite is ... I suppose ... 'accepts with pleasure'?

W: Exactly. Perfect!

Y: And what about taking along other guests? My girlfriend would love to come to the party tomorrow night. It's OK to bring her, right?

W: No. Many invitations will include your name and then 'and spouse' or 'partner' – so, you can take anyone along, although never take a child. That's an absolute no-no, unless they are specifically included. If it's a wedding invitation, you can always contact the host, and ask if you can take someone along, but you are expected to be either engaged to that person, or at least they should be your partner. You're not supposed to just take along a friend.

Y: It's so strict; there are so many rules!

W: Well, obviously rules are made to be broken, but make sure you know the host or hostess before you break too many of them!

Y: Oh, just one last thing. What if I get an email invite? Surely I don't need to send a written reply to that. Will an email do?

W: Oh, yes of course. And they're becoming increasingly more common these days.

Y: Thank goodness for that!

W: Oh, and, if your invitation carries the message 'regrets only' at the end, then you really only have to reply if you can't go.

Y: Well at least that's simple. Thanks for all your help, Wendy! I'd better get off and write my reply for the party tomorrow night!

8 If you had time to make cut-up cards for this activity, distribute a set of cards to each pair in the class and allow several minutes for them to reconstruct the sentences. If you copied the exercise onto an OHT or an IWB, display the first jumbled sentence on the board and ask students in pairs to reconstruct it by writing it out on paper. You could make this into a race, with a point for the first pair to get the sentence ordered. Repeat this process for each sentence. Finally, refer students to the exercise as it appears in the Student's Book, for reference.

ANSWERS:

1 Gerrard Stein, Head of Faculty, and guest would be delighted to attend the Festival Celebratory Lunch at the Grand Hotel, on Sunday 12 August at 12.45 pm.

2 Mr Fernando Cabrera regrets he is unable to accept the kind invitation of Dr and Mrs Albert Casey for Saturday 18th December.

3 Gerhard Pohl thanks the Dean and his wife very much for their kind invitation to the Senate dinner on December 9th at Graduation Hall, New Street, and has much pleasure in accepting.

9 Ask students to choose one of the events from the three sample invitations on page 104 (or the authentic examples you have provided yourself) and to write a short but appropriately formal reply following the models provided.

Writing

10 The final activity in this module provides an opportunity for students to write a formal invitation using the language presented throughout. Students could prepare for the writing in pairs. Ask students to read through the information about the three events and to choose one for which to write an invitation. Once students have chosen an event, ask them to brainstorm additional details under the following headings: *venue, food and drink, guests, tickets, dress code, contact details.*

When the details have been decided, set a time limit of 15 to 20 minutes for students to write their invitations. Collect for correction. As a follow-up in a subsequent lesson, you could distribute the invitations to other students in the class and ask them to write replies.

SUGGESTED ANSWERS:

1

Sir Reginald Hall, Chairman of the Campaign for Pan-European Economic and Political Cooperation, cordially invites you and your partner to a gala dinner-dance in celebration of the first annual summit meeting.

Saturday, 16th August 2008

Walthorpe Manor

Dinner served at 8.00p.m.

Business attire

RSVP: Mrs Josephine Scott j.scott@cpeepc.org

2

Venturia Plc requests the pleasure of your company at a reception in honour the UK's top two Formula One drivers.

Place: Cheshunt House, Pall Mall, London.

Saturday, June 21st 2008, 2.30-5.30p.m.

Champagne and canapés will be served on the terrace.

Dress: smart-casual

Invite only.

Reply to: formula1@venturia.com

3

Congreve Associates request the pleasure of your company at an evening of dining and musical entertainment in honour of Paul Krafflezwitzer, in celebration of the recent and highly acclaimed premiere of his piano concerto, Heaven.

Wednesday May 14th 2008

Peacock Restaurant

Four Seasons Palace

London

Dinner will be served at 8p.m., Aperitifs at 7p.m.

Black tie (optional)

RSVP to Congreve Associates, 77B Jessop's Court, Berkeley Street, London W1 6TT.

Tel: 020 7884 6336 email: events@congreve.co.uk

8.6 Case study

The cartel

This module provides free speaking practice in the context of a case study of two companies vying for control of the lucrative global market in hologram video technology.

Internet research

As suggested, a search for *cartels* and *antitrust laws* will return lots of sites covering these topics. You could divide your class into two groups and assign a topic to each group to research. Then pair students from each group to exchange information.

Discussion

1 Write the words *monopoly*, *duopoly* and *oligopoly* on the board and ask students to define them (monopoly = when a market is controlled by a single seller or firm; duopoly = when a market is controlled by only two sellers or firms; oligopoly = when a market is controlled by a small number of sellers or firms). Ask students to work in groups of three to brainstorm as many examples of each as they can. An Internet search for these terms will provide a source of current examples. Finally, ask groups to discuss and brainstorm the advantages and disadvantages of duopolies / oligopolies for companies and consumers. This information could be collated to a table, e.g.

For the company		For the consumer	
Advantages	Disadvantages	Advantages	Disadvantages

Elicit ideas, put them on the board and discuss.

SUGGESTED ANSWERS:

For companies:
Advantages: a few companies control the market, prices and profits. They can enjoy stable market share and cash flow, and invest in development with minimum risk.
Disadvantages: companies are vulnerable if a competitor decides to cut prices. It is difficult to raise prices without collusion with other firms. Innovation may be retarded. A lot of energy may be spent on monitoring competitors' activities.
For customers:
Advantages: all products on the market are likely to be of similar, good quality. Encourages global technological standards. Companies are encouraged to make product or marketing improvements in order to differentiate themselves. Prices may be lower if manufacturers have used their dominant position to reduce costs.
Disadvantages: price levels are significantly higher than in a competitive market. Innovation may be retarded. Companies may be able to exert excessive political influence.

Reading

2 Explain to the class that they are going to read about the hologram video market. Ask students in pairs to brainstorm everything they know about hologram videos, elicit ideas and put them on the board.
Dictate the following vocabulary and ask students to write it down: *lucrative* /ˈluːkrətɪv/ (profitable), *vinyl* /ˈvaɪn(ə)l/ (a type of plastic), *slug it out* (fight or battle it out), *to roll something out* (to spread or distribute more widely), *to pick up steam* (to gather pace; speed up), *to come on stream* (to begin regular operation), *watertight* (impossible to defeat), *me-too* (copying the designs or ideas of rivals and competitors), *to join the fray* (to join the battle), *stakes* (rewards), *to slash margins* (to cut or reduce dramatically), *to be slated* (to be expected). Ask students to compare their lists in pairs and to discuss possible meanings. Then ask students to scan through the text to locate the words to check spellings. Elicit the words, put them on the board and check meanings. Drill for pronunciation.
Next, draw students' attention to the reading comprehension questions 1–5 and allow a few minutes for students to note their answers and to compare with a partner.

ANSWERS:

1 The 'holo pioneers' are Holoplay PLC and ThreeD-Vision Inc. They are the two protagonists in the format war for the lucrative new hologram video market.
2 'There can be only one' refers to previous format wars between audio and video technologies where a single technology always becomes the dominant standard, making its competitors obsolete. There is also a cultural reference to the *Highlander* film and TV series.
3 Initially supply was limited, so prices were high and demand was low. Demand is now growing in spite of the current $3,000 price tag. When greater production capacity means that supply exceeds demand, analysts expect that prices will fall.
4 The duopoly is expected to continue because Holoplay and ThreeD-Vision hold watertight patents for their respective technologies, and because of the uncertainty over which format will become the standard.
5 The article suggests that one of the two players will have to reduce its margins significantly in order to acquire a dominant position in the global market, especially in Asia.

Listening

3 🔊 2.41 Ask students to listen to the conversation between the two employees and to make notes of the key points and then to compare notes in pairs. Ask students to briefly summarize the information they heard. Next, ask students to read through the true / false statements and to answer *T*, *F* or *D*. Again, allow an opportunity for students to compare in pairs. Play the recording through again for students to check.

ANSWERS:

1D – she suggests he's not working, but in fact she knows he is attending a meeting.
2T – 'You're not supposed to know about that, young Toby! Don't even think about mentioning it to anyone else, or we can both kiss our careers goodbye!'
3D – Jasmin says it's completely above board, but Toby suspects it's illegal.
4F – 'you can't sell at the same price in India or Africa as in the US'
5T – 'I expect they'll be carving up territories between them'
6T – 'At the moment we can sell everything we can produce. But that won't last.'
7F – 'Toby, use your loaf! It's in everybody's interest – including yours!'

RECORDING SCRIPT

 2.41

Toby: Oh, sorry, did you want to use the copier?

Jasmin: It's OK, you go ahead and finish, I'm in no hurry – my boss is off gallivanting in Paris, the lucky devil!

T: Oh yeah, he's at the meeting with ThreeD-Vision, isn't he?

J: You're not supposed to know about that, young Toby! Don't even think about mentioning it to anyone else, or we can both kiss our careers goodbye!

T: Don't worry, my lips are sealed. But I don't understand why they're meeting our only competitor.

J: A full and frank discussion of mutual interests is the phrase, I believe.

T: You mean fixing prices and production levels, that sort of thing? But that's illegal, isn't it?

J: Now let's not go jumping to conclusions! Yes, cartels are illegal in most countries, but this meeting is to set up an industry trade group, it's completely above board.

T: Hm. So they won't be fixing prices, then?

J: I expect they'll share their ideas on what retail prices should be recommended in different markets: obviously you can't sell at the same price in India or Africa as in the US, so it helps to know what the other side are thinking …

T: Huh! Price fixing in other words. And I expect they'll be carving up territories between them, sharing out the major markets, or even agreeing to share profits …

J: Toby, I think we're going to have to keep our voices down: it's a very sensitive matter.

T: Sorry. But it just seems very dodgy. Anyway, I don't understand why a company would want to take that kind of risk!

J: Toby, use your loaf! At the moment we can sell everything we can produce, and at a very good price. So can ThreeD. But that won't last: very soon we'll be competing directly for the same customers, and there'll be a price war. Unless there's a, well, let's call it a gentlemen's agreement; it's in everybody's interest – including yours!

T: Hm.

Discussion

4 You may find it useful to display the charts on the board to draw attention to pertinent data during the discussion. Show the data to the class and ask a few gist questions, e.g. *Which continent has the lowest price forecast? Which has the largest population?*

Next, ask students to work individually to consider the two discussion questions and to make some notes. You may want to prompt students to think about volumes, margins, prices, quotas and resources. Then ask students to discuss the questions in small groups. Hold a brief class discussion on the points discussed.

SUGGESTED ANSWERS:

1 This is open to debate: the main point is the strategic choice between volume and margin. Both companies will probably want to claim as big a share as possible of the developed markets (Europe, North America, Oceania) before targeting much larger volumes but lower margins in the rest of the world.

2 Possible strategies might include agreeing to keep prices reasonable for the consumer, agreeing to develop cross-format compatible applications, agreeing on a policy of transparency on technical developments and specifications, collaborating on R&D to provide more choice and versatility for the consumer and agreeing to put an equal percentage of profit into R&D.

Negotiation

5 Explain the situation to the class, i.e. that students are going to act as representatives of Holoplay PLC and ThreeD-Vision Inc. to negotiate an agreement. Draw students' attention to the Agenda on page 107 and make it clear that these are the points they will need to agree in the negotiation. Divide the class into two groups, A and B, and distribute the role cards on pages 115 and 117. Ask students to read through their role cards. Monitor and deal with any queries. Next, arrange the class into groups of four (two from group A and two from group B) to carry out the negotiation. Set a time limit of 15 to 20 minutes for the negotiations. Monitor and note language points for post-correction. When the negotiations are complete, ask the groups to report back to the class on the agreements they reached.

Review 7 and 8 answers

Review 7

(page 108 in the Student's Book)

7 Investment

1

1 maximizing
2 promoting
3 limiting
4 investing
5 creating
6 assisting

2

1 Should a counter-bid be launched we are going to have to raise our offer.
2 What I would like to do in the next session is draw up a long-term investment plan.
3 Had we been told that ours was the only bid, we could have offered less.
4 Under no circumstances may the sealed bids be opened before the closing date.
5 Were we in a stronger position financially we might be able to increase our bid.
6 The candidate we have appointed is Maurice D'Arby.
7 No sales executive has performed better than Sandra Notham.
8 The issue that most concerns me is lack of professional discipline.

3

1 premium priced product
2 risk-averse
3 put all your eggs into one basket
4 blue chip companies
5 diversified portfolio
6 boost revenues
7 market volatility
8 the herd instinct
9 lack of transparency
10 bricks and mortar

4

1 out of the **running / equation**
2 a make or break **factor**
3 it stands to **reason**
4 out of the **equation / running**
5 the be all and end **all**
6 the figures speak for **themselves**
7 it's pretty black and **white**
8 it's an open and shut **case**

5

1 carving
2 stepping
3 generate
4 underpinned
5 forecasting
6 beaten
7 trading
8 boosted

Review 8

(page 109 in the Student's Book)

8 Free trade

1

1 liberalization
2 barriers
3 round
4 protectionism
5 goods
6 reform
7 progress
8 agreement

2

1 tail off
2 get through
3 take in
4 go in / weigh up / come up with
5 claw back
6 kick around

3

1 implementor
2 investigator
3 empowering
4 delegate
5 coordinator
6 coach

4

1 d
2 a
3 e
4 b
5 c
6 h
7 i
8 j
9 f
10 g

5

1 b
2 e
3 d
4 f
5 a
6 c

Grammar and practice answers

1 Personal development
(page 118 and 119 in the Student's Book)

1

1. to build
2. intend
3. be
4. 've been learning
5. 've learnt
6. don't envisage
7. to take
8. has suggested
9. smarten up
10. put
11. 'm
12. to watch

2

1. looked
2. haven't risen
3. had
4. are getting / have been getting
5. drawn up
6. are
7. was
8. 've asked
9. 'm waiting
10. Have you written
11. need
12. didn't advertise
13. have been running
14. 're looking

3

1. LT
2. F
3. AN
4. AN / LT
5. RN
6. AN
7. LT
8. F / RN
9. RN
10. F

4

1. reached / reaches
2. ask / (were to ask)
3. 're passing by OR pass
4. sit down
5. had known
6. had left / given [note: 'given' shares the same 'had' as 'left' – both are past perfect]
7. had listened
8. were , 'd have been hit
9. had been
10. hadn't been

5

1. a great deal of research has been done
2. persist
3. do many employees believe
4. employees who have achieved a specific degree of success
5. employees may want such rewards
6. Intrinsic motivation plays a major role
7. is not affected by external rewards
8. can help themselves

2 Corporate image
(page 120 and 121 in the Student's Book)

1

1. meet
2. are expected to focus mainly on
3. is set to ask for
4. is likely to seek
5. leaves
6. can tackle
7. could significantly worsen
8. would be lost
9. move
10. take
11. should have
12. 'll see

2

1. c
2. a
3. b
4. b
5. c
6. a

3

1. e)
2. h)
3. a)
4. f)
5. c)
6. g)
7. d)
8. b)

4

1. must
2. won't
3. should
4. shouldn't
5. must
6. Shall
7. ought not to
8. may
9. shall
10. could

5

1. There is little doubt that the plan will fail.
2. It is widely believed that the causes of inflation are rising commodity prices, but it's not that simple.
3. I would argue that we need our customers to love us more.
4. You might / may want / wish to consider talking to him about it.
5. She may well have got the sums wrong.
6. They'll be / they must be working on it now.
7. It's highly unlikely that he'll ever convince the CEO to change our logo.
8. There is no real possibility that the outcome will be positive.

6

1. a This is more objective, while the other two choices are subjective, i.e. the opinion of the speaker.
2. b This is less certain than the other two choices.
3. b This is significantly more likely than the other two choices.
4. c There is no contrast in this choice, unlike the other two.
5. a This is less likely than the other choices.
6. b Choice 'c' paraphrases 'a', while this choice has a different meaning.
7. c This choice is much stronger than the other two, which are more tentative.

3 Supply chain
(page 122 and 123 in the Student's Book)

1

1. costs
2. allocation
3. business
4. information resources
5. allocation issues
6. problem
7. optimisation model
8. cost reduction

2

1. a rival product
2. supply chain success
3. the most innovative solutions which are implemented successfully
4. an innovative approach called 'from the shelf back',
5. an unavoidable rise in operating costs
6. an ever-increasing range of size formats
7. all the different size variations of tea or rice sold at your local store.
8. this principle of size variation is applied to
9. The alternative approach adopted by the massive container shipping industry
10. one of the most challenging issues facing supply chain managers

3

1. that we should adopt / which is the most viable / I've decided on
2. that would be best for the job / I believe would be an outstanding leader / who I think is the strongest candidate for the post
3. where transport links are optimally sited / that has the strongest transport links
4. whose vision is aligned to ours / that never lets us down / I have always admired / who builds long-term relations with companies
5. I won't be able to meet the deadline / why she failed to inform you / which I was given

4

1. What, where, why
2. Why
3. what, how
4. That
5. Who, what

5

1. d
2. c
3. a
4. e
5. b
6. g
7. f
8. i
9. h
10. j

4 Managing conflict

(page 124 and 125 in the Student's Book)

1

1 nor (b)
2 but (e)
3 yet (c)
4 so (f)
5 and (a)
6 or (d).

2

1 because
2 While
3 in order to
4 Whenever
5 so that
6 in case

3

1 so that
2 unless
3 While
4 whenever
5 Granted
6 except to

4

1 b)
2 c)
3 c)
4 a)
5 c)
6 b)
7 a)
8 c)
9 a)
10 b)

5 Strategic marketing

(page 126 and 127 in the Student's Book)

1

1 for
2 of
3 throughout / through
4 in
5 on / upon
6 without
7 until
8 by / from / to
9 during
10 before

2

in _____ for: *exchange, return*
in the _____ of: *form, course, case, face, light, region, wake*
with _____ to: *regard, reference, respect*
in _____ with: *accordance, common, compliance, conjunction, connection, contact, keeping, line*
on _____ of: *behalf, account*

3

1 in the light of
2 On behalf of
3 With reference to
4 in accordance with
5 in line with
6 in the wake of
7 in the region of
8 in the face of

4

1 down to
2 irrespective of
3 owing to
4 subject to
5 contrary to
6 together with
7 such as
8 as for

5

1 <u>from</u> outside the company (d)
2 <u>to</u> the intended recipient (a)
3 <u>by</u> then (e)
4 just <u>before</u> the final whistle (h)
5 <u>except</u> to escape in emergencies (f)
6 <u>in the light of</u> what you just said (c)
7 <u>for</u> better or for worse (g)
8 <u>in</u> playing the saxophone (b)

6 and **7**

*Wh-*Questions: 2 What are you looking *at*?
Passive Forms: 6 I know his work is being looked *after* by a temp while he's away. What I want to know is, who's the temp being looked *after by*?
Relative Clauses: 3 The subject I want to talk to you *about* today is …
Exclamations: 5 What a terrible situation she's ended up *in*!
*Wh-*Clauses: 4 What I would like to focus *on* this morning is…
*To-*Clauses: 1 He's very difficult to work *with*.

8

1 barring
2 considering
3 amid
4 versus
5 pending
6 akin to
7 notwithstanding
8 regarding

6 Risk management

(page 128 and 129 in the Student's Book)

1

1 In terms of finance, the whole project has been a disaster – we've lost about $60,000 so far.
2 As far as ethics are concerned, we will need to make sure there is no conflict of interest.
3 From the point of view of the company the plan looks great, but from a (purely) personal perspective / point of view I would question it – it means I've got more responsibility but no extra money.
4 Technologically speaking, the harbour bridge is an amazing feat of engineering, but they certainly broke the bank in building it.
5 To put this into a / its historical perspective, we would be the first company ever to have such a far-reaching policy in place.
6 If we (could) look at this from a cultural point of view / perspective, it's a risky proposition – just look at all the differences in behaviour, appearance, values, you name it.

2

1 b)
2 a)
3 f)
4 d)
5 e)
6 c)

3

1 Please note that *only* the latest 100 transactions can be displayed or printed.
2 It is *admittedly* / *Admittedly* it is a high-risk course of action.
3 *Hopefully* nothing should go too badly wrong.
4 The target consumers are *definitely* not going to pay that sort of money for our software.
5 *Regrettably* the files containing personal data have / The files containing personal date have *regrettably* been temporarily mislaid.
6 *Without doubt* It is / It is *without doubt* the best decision for maximum growth.
7 You have *certainly* tried hard. But you *actually* haven't achieved a satisfactory level of success.
8 *To my mind* they should never have allowed it.
9 *In my view* it won't work.
10 *Apparently* they've got the legal side all taken care of.
11 *In actual fact* it's a pretty good plan.
12 I'll *definitely* back you up should you need me.

4

1 Considering the issues involved
2 In my view
3 Incidentally
4 such as
5 perhaps

5

1 immediately / the minute [it happens] / as soon as [it happens] / without delay
2 overall / on the whole / all in all
3 In other words / To put this another way / If I may put this another way.
4 Also / In addition / What is more
5 Honestly / In all honesty / To be perfectly honest

6

Adverbials that cannot be used:
1 Definitely
2 Thus
3 overall
4 so
5 totally
6 basically
7 Next
8 ultimately

7 Investment

(page 130 and 131 in the Student's Book)

1

1 I have no complaints with their service <u>whatsoever</u>.
2 I am <u>utterly</u> appalled that they should let you down in this manner.
3 You have made an extremely useful contribution <u>indeed</u>.
4 Had I known about his directorship at the time, I would <u>scarcely</u> have trusted him.
5 We were <u>even</u> more impressed with their level of service than their reasonable fee.
6 This project is <u>rather</u> more challenging than the previous one.
7 The share price ended up doubling, <u>somewhat</u> to my surprise.
8 Merely tracking the all-share index is an <u>absolutely</u> unacceptable policy, given their high management fees.

2

1 The reason why I oppose his approach is that he concentrates on tiny details rather than the broader picture.
2 It is not his punctuality but his aggression that is the problem.
3 What is at stake is nothing less than the company's future wellbeing.
4 Only by resorting to underhand tactics would we be able to win – and we're not going to stoop that low.
5 Under no circumstances should you put more than 10% of your assets into that fund.
6 Where I would make changes would be in the areas of responsibility and accountability.
7 Rarely have I witnessed such firmness in the teeth of such opposition.
8 How I would approach the problem is irrelevant – it's your department and your responsibility.
9 Should they not respond, we do have a secret Plan B.
10 The product is what we need to focus on, not the process itself.

3

1 to
2 Not
3 to
4 do
5 what
6 to

4

1 Also clearly significant is the dip in consumer confidence.
2 Should you ever need any further assistance, please do not hesitate to contact us.
3 Never again will I go to so much trouble for so little gain.
4 Not only did he fail to turn up on time, but neither / nor did he apologize.
5 Far more serious appears to be the inflationary risk.
6 Had I caught my flight I would not have missed the meeting.
7 At no time can you claim expenses without a receipt.
8 Were a solution to be found, we would implement it.

5

1 f
2 b
3 e
4 a
5 c
6 d

6

1 I
2 I
3 A
4 A
5 A
6 A
7 I
8 A

7

1 In recent years
2 Not only have we
3 but also
4 what we now need is
5 Most of all,
6 were such investment not to be implemented
7 the person to manage
8 should I agree
9 legitimately be accountable for all aspects of the new strategy.
10 Lastly,
11 can scarcely be

8 Free trade

(page 132 and 133 in the Student's Book)

1

1 out
2 across
3 over
4 with
5 up to
6 out
7 up
8 for
9 apart
10 down
11 on
12 over
13 out
14 out

2

1 Most of the time I get on pretty well with my boss.
2 Give us a break and stop going on about how hot it is in here will you?
3 About the conference next week, could you just firm up the refreshment arrangements with the caterer?
4 Demand should really take off in the months ahead.
5 Your brainstorming session won't work – call it off.
6 I suggest we put off that staff away-day we've been talking about until things have settled down a bit.
7 OK, now get into small groups and come up with three innovations we can all buy into.
8 I know we've come up against a lot of problems recently, but we do need to put all this behind us and move forward.
9 Now come on / Come on now everyone – it's time we did away with all our checks and balances and just trusted each other to just get on with the job.
10 I've just thought of the perfect idea – work on your language skills, then we can do away with our translator.
11 Lay down the procedure, spell out exactly what we have to do, and then they won't have any more reason to make out it wasn't clear.
12 Stressed? Can't deal with it? Talk to Madeleine and she'll sort it all out for you.

3

1 down on
2 up to
3 behind with
4 away with
5 round to
6 down with
7 up to
8 up for
9 off against
10 up for

4

1 You know, I reckon we ought to <u>branch out</u> into whatever areas which are going to <u>go up</u> the fastest.
2 Not now, that discussion would <u>eat into</u> our valuable time – we've got a lot of items to <u>get through</u> this afternoon.
3 So many issues <u>came up</u> from that session – there's just too much for me to <u>take in</u> right now.
4 First, <u>weigh up</u> the issues, then <u>put together</u> your plan.
5 Don't <u>give in / up</u> – <u>soldier on</u> until the job's done.
6 Time to <u>call off</u> Plan A and <u>kick off</u> with Plan B.

5

1 b)
2 d)
3 a)
4 c)
5 e)

6

1 f)
2 a)
3 c)
4 d)
5 b)
6 e)

Additional activities

Speaking: Interview questions

Type of activity: Interview. This activity is best done before or after module 1.3 Vocabulary: Behavioural competencies and setting goals.
Preparation: Make a copy of the interview questions for each student.

1 Put students into pairs and give a copy of the interview questions to each student. Explain that these are interview questions written in phonemic script.
2 Elicit and model each question with the class, paying special attention to stress, intonation and specific lexis (eg, *initiative* and *intervention*).
3 Ask students to write out the questions under the phonemics. Monitor and help with difficult spellings as required.
4 Ask students to compare their written answers.
5 Tell students that they are now going to interview each other using the questions provided.
6 Tell students to work with a new partner and roleplay the interview. Make sure every student has an opportunity to be both the interviewer and interviewee.
7 Take whole-class feedback on the outcome of the roleplays and give any relevant feedback on language use.

ANSWERS:

Questions in plain text
1 When was the last time you showed personal initiative?
2 How important is written communication to good management?
3 Where do you see yourself in a year's time?
4 Can you describe a situation that required your personal intervention?
5 How has your education prepared you for your career?
6 What qualities should a successful manager have?
7 How do you feel about taking direction from your superiors?
8 How well do you handle criticism?
9 What sort of people do you find it difficult to work with?
10 Are you good at working as a member of a team?

Reading: Behavioral interviews – A job candidate's toughest obstacle

Type of activity: Comprehension and discussion. This activity is best done after module 1.3.
Preparation: Make enough photocopies of page 122 for each student.

1 Introduce the topic by describing your interview for your present position. Ask students to work in pairs or groups of three and share their experiences of job interviews. Students read the text and then work in their groups to discuss how behavioural interviews differ from traditional ones.
2 Ask students to read the text again and answer the questions. Give students sufficient time to complete the task and compare answers in their groups, before class feedback.

ANSWERS:

2 a Job candidates often give hypothetical answers that sound good but are not a real reflection of what they would do in reality.
b The basic premise is that past performance is the best indicator of future performance.
c The interviewer is listening for names, dates, places, the outcome and the individual's role in achieving that outcome.
d Candidates can prepare for behavioral interviews by identifying specific examples for each of the behavioral competencies.
e Interviewers trained in behavioral interviewing will investigate the answer given by asking further questions and if the story is false, inconsistencies are likely to occur.

3 Put students in groups of three to discuss questions 3 and 4. Get some whole-class feedback.

Speaking: Interview questions

Interview questions

1 /wen wɒz ðə ˈlɑːst taɪm juː ʃəʊd ˈpɜː(r)s(ə)nəl ɪˈnɪʃətɪv/

_____

2 /haʊ ɪmˈpɔː(r)t(ə)nt ɪz ˈrɪt(ə)n kəˈmjuːnɪˈkeɪʃ(ə)n tə ɡʊd ˈmænɪʤmənt/

_____

3 /weə(r) duː juː ˈsiː jə(r)ˈself ɪn ə ˈjɪə(r)z taɪm/

_____

4 /kæn juː dɪˈskraɪb ə ˌsɪtʃuˈeɪʃ(ə)n ðæt rɪˈkwaɪə(r)d jɔː(r) ˈpɜː(r)s(ə)nəl ˌɪntə(r)ˈvenʃ(ə)n /

_____

5 /haʊ hæz jɔː(r) ˌedjʊˈkeɪʃ(ə)n prɪˈpeə(r)d juː fɔː(r) jɔː(r) kəˈrɪə(r)/

_____

6 /wɒt ˈkwɒlətiːz ʃʊd ə səkˈsesf(ə)l ˈmænɪʤə(r) hæv/

_____

7 /haʊ duː juː fiːl əˈbaʊt ˈteɪkɪŋ daɪˈrekʃ(ə)n frɒm jɔː(r) sʊˈpɪərɪə(r)z/

_____

8 /haʊ wel duː juː ˈhænd(ə)l ˈkrɪtɪˌsɪz(ə)m/

_____

9 /wɒt sɔː(r)t əv ˈpiːp(ə)l duː juː faɪnd ɪt ˈdɪfɪk(ə)lt tə wɜː(r)k wɪð/

_____

10 /ɑː(r) juː ɡʊd æt ˈwɜː(r)kɪŋ æz ə ˈmembə(r) əv ə tiːm/

_____

Behavioral Interviews -
A Job Candidate's Toughest Obstacle

By Damir Joseph Stimac

The interview begins like any other, exchanged pleasantries and then the interviewer starts asking really strange, specific questions. 'Give me a specific example of a time when you didn't meet a deadline.' Your mind races for an example which answers the question and then turns that failure into a success as suggested by your highly regarded interviewing book. Unfortunately, your outdated book taught you how to interview for traditional interviews – not behavioral (competency-based) interviews.

The questions are often hypothetical or theoretical. Job candidates often end up giving hypothetical answers that sound great but aren't a true representation of what they would do in real situations.

An example of a traditional question may be: 'How would you deal with an angry customer?' You end up saying something like, 'I would politely ask them to tell me the problem, then I would offer my assistance in solving the problem.' That doesn't sound too bad. The problem is that your answer is theoretical. It doesn't represent what you would actually do in that situation.

An interviewer using behavioral techniques would ask the same question this way: 'Give me a specific example of a time when you had to address an angry customer. What was the problem and what was the outcome?' Your mind races and you come up with an answer.

'The basic premise behind behavioral interviewing is that your past performance is the best predictor of future performance. In essence, if you ask behavioral questions, you're asking questions that must be answered based upon fact,' says Hewlett-Packard's Bill Smith. The interviewer determines the knowledge, skills, and behaviors (often referred to as competencies) that are essential for success in a position. Competencies may include assertiveness, clarification, commitment to task, dealing with ambiguity, decision-making, interaction, leadership, management skills, communication effectiveness, organizational orientation, problem solving, team building and others. Each competency contains various questions that are designed to determine to what extent the candidate has performed successfully in previous situations similar to those they will encounter in the position for which they are interviewing.

'With a behavioral question, you're looking for results. You're not just looking for an activity list. So you're listening for things like names, dates, places, the outcome and especially what the individual's role was in achieving that outcome,' says Smith.

Candidates can prepare for behavioral interviews by identifying specific examples for each of the above competencies. When preparing, identify an unsuccessful example for each competency because you will probably be asked to give examples of when things didn't work out as planned. One way to end an answer to a negative probe is to say something like, 'the mistake caused me to delay the project, but it helped me to develop a project tracking system to minimize the chance of that happening again.'

Remember, mistakes help us learn. Don't make up an answer either, because interviewers trained in behavioral interviewing techniques will probe deeply into your answer. You will have a hard time keeping your story straight if you start making things up. Inconsistent answers will cause you to be assessed negatively.

Preparing for behavioral interviews can significantly help you in traditional interviews because you can give traditional interviewers specific answers to theoretical questions. Example:
Interviewer: 'How would you address an angry customer?'
Applicant: 'I can give you a specific example. I was the manager of the department when a really irate customer came in yelling at everyone. He was upset because .... I invited him to my office and ... He apologized for his outburst and bought the top-of-the-line air compressor.' When you give specific examples to interview questions, you establish credibility and believability, and that can ultimately translate into a job offer.

---

1 Do you have personal experience of job interviews? Tell your partner about any job interviews you have attended. How do you think behavioral interviews differ from traditional interviews?

2 Read the text to find the answers to the following questions:

a   Why were traditional interviews sometimes ineffective in finding the right candidate for the job?
b   What is the basic premise behind behavioral interviewing?
c   What is an interviewer listening for when he or she asks a behavioral question?
d   How can candidates prepare for behavioral interviews?
e   Why is it not advisable to make up an answer to a question?

3 Do you think nerves would be an issue for you at interview? What techniques might you employ to combat these?

4 What would be your ideal job?

Article by Damir Joseph Stimac, author of **The Ultimate Job Search Kit** and Career Talk host. For additional interviewing tips, visit Career Talk on the Internet. http://www.careertalk.com

2 Corporate image　Teacher's notes & answers

Speaking: Corporate social responsibility

Type of activity: Negotiating, arguing a case and reaching a group consensus. This speaking activity ties in with the theme of module 2.3 and provides an opportunity for students to engage with the topic of corporate social responsibility through roleplay and negotiation.

Preparation: Make enough copies of page 124 for each group of four students. Cut out the four role cards so that each student has a role card.

1 Explain to the class that they are going to take part in a meeting between staff members of a large supermarket, to discuss and decide on the most suitable proposal for a CSR initiative. Ask the groups to read through the scenario (this can be displayed on an OHP / IWB or distributed as a photocopy). Check the groups understand what they have to do.

2 Ask students to work in pairs and brainstorm useful phrases for putting forward ideas, arguing a case and reaching agreement.
You may want to provide the following examples to help students get started:
Putting forward ideas
X is the best because ...
This is more deserving because ...
If we give it to X, we will be able to ...
It would be better to raise funds for X because ...
Tactfully disagreeing
I think one of the drawbacks with that suggestion is ...
I see your point, but ...
That might be true, but don't you think ...
Agreeing
OK. That's agreed then.

3 Elicit phrases from students and put them on the board. Correct and drill as necessary.

4 Distribute the role cards to students to read through. Give students five minutes to prepare a two-minute presentation of their ideas to their groups. Monitor and provide help as needed.

5 Tell students to present their ideas to their groups and to then discuss the ideas and to reach a decision on which idea to adopt. Set a time limit of 20 minutes for this.

6 Once the negotiations are complete, ask the groups to feed back to the class on the proposals they chose and then ask students to forget about their roles and to discuss which proposal they really think is the best, or whether they have other ideas for ways in which the company can promote its image as being socially responsible.

Reading: Ethical MBAs: A search for corporate social responsibility

Type of activity: Multiple matching. This task should be done in conjunction with module 2.3. It would work well before module 2.3, to develop students' awareness of the topic of Corporate Social Responsibility; or could be used immediately after module 2.3 to provide further development of the topic.

Preparation: Make enough copies of page 125 for each student.

1 Lead in: Explain to the class that they are going to read an article on courses in CSR offered at universities. Ask students in pairs to discuss whether or not they have taken / are planning to take any such options as part of their studies, and to discuss the reasons why such courses are now being offered.

2 Matching task: students work individually to match the comments to the names. Set a time limit of 10 to 15 minutes. Then give students a few minutes to compare in pairs / threes before going through the answers with the class.

ANSWERS:

1 d　2 f　3 a　4 f　5 b　6 e　7 c

Scenario

You work for a large supermarket chain in one of the company's largest and most prestigious stores. The company management are looking for ideas to promote the company's image as being a company with Corporate Social Responsibility. You have been asked to take part in a meeting to pool ideas and to reach a decision on the best idea.

Work in groups of four. Your teacher will give you a role card, specifying your job within the company and the CSR idea you most favour. Your task is to persuade the other members of your group to adopt the idea you put forward. Remember, though, that this is a negotiation and your group must reach a unanimous decision on the best idea.

Role card 1
No plastic bag week

You are a nutritionist working in the company's Research & Development unit. You are keen on environmental issues and believe the company could do more to help the environment. Suggest that the company implements a 'no plastic carrier bag' week, in which customers are not given carrier bags with their groceries. Instead, customers are asked to purchase a cheap cotton bag with their shopping. Before you put forward your idea, note down the advantages of this idea (e.g. protection of wildlife, cut down on waste, raise customers' awareness) and ways in which it can be implemented (e.g. posters in stores advertising the event).

Role card 2
Local arts for local people

You are a marketing assistant. You are very keen on the arts and believe the company could do more to sponsor arts in the local community. Suggest that the company implements a 'local arts for local people' campaign, in which a percentage of the profits from sales of some of your leading 'own brand' products is given to a local arts organization (e.g. a local theatre group or a local arts centre). Before you put forward your idea, note down the advantages of this idea (e.g. it will encourage more local art, raise customers' awareness) and ways in which the idea can be implemented (e.g. labels on products to inform customers of how their purchase will help the local community).

Role card 3
Shop against poverty

You are the union representative. You are very concerned about economic inequality in society and you believe that the company could do more to help combat poverty in the world. Suggest that the company implements a 'shop against poverty' week, in which customers are asked to donate points from their loyalty cards and for every point donated the company will give 2p to a designated anti-poverty charity. Before you put forward your idea, note down the advantages of this idea (e.g. helping to fight poverty and raising customers' awareness of poverty issues) and ways in which it can be implemented (e.g. posters in store advertising the event, check-out leaflets explaining how the scheme works; briefing staff on how to promote the scheme).

Role card 4
Resources for schools

You work in the Human Resources Department. You believe very strongly that state schools should be given more funding to help them provide the best education for young people and that the company could do more to help schools in disadvantaged areas. Suggest that the company implements a 'resources for schools' campaign, in which customers are given a voucher for every £5 that they spend. Customers can then give the vouchers to local schools, which can then use them to buy resources (e.g. books, computers, classroom equipment). Before you put forward your idea, note down the advantages of this idea (e.g. raising the profile of education) and ways in which the idea can be implemented (e.g. briefing staff on how to promote the scheme, mailing existing customers).

Ethical MBAs: A search for corporate social responsibility

BY PETER BROWN, TUESDAY, 6 MAY 2008

Business schools have embraced the idea of corporate social responsibility and there are many courses on offer. Several years ago, a combination of
5 the Enron scandal and global warming shook up the business environment. Business schools started to introduce modules onto their MBA courses that looked beyond the profit motive – or,
10 at least, recognized fresh dangers to the bottom line. Ethics began to be taken seriously. David Vogel, of the Haas School of Business at the University of California, Berkeley has called this the
15 "market for virtue". For the ethically-minded prospective student, it can be more like a maze. The London-based Association of MBAs (AMBA) now insists that accredited MBA programmes
20 address social and ethical issues, but does not specify how.

MBAs with Corporate Social Responsibility

Corporate Social Responsibility (CSR) modules come under a range of different names. Some are core courses,
25 though most remain electives. Students, therefore, must decide what approach they feel comfortable with. Michelle Akande, 27, had no doubts. She worked for Sightsavers International, which
30 combats blindness and promotes the rights of disabled people in developing countries, before deciding on an MBA. She opted for the MBA in corporate social responsibility at Nottingham
35 University Business School. "What swung Nottingham for me was the

International Centre for Corporate Social Responsibility, which has a diverse range of well-known people and
40 knowledge. The course has given me the theoretical and practical framework and the arguments to convince people that there are different ways of doing business – like more sustainable energy
45 production." In fact, all seven core MBA courses at Nottingham have ethics embedded into them, says Bob Berry, the programme director.

The elective in CSR goes deeper
50 into the issues at the module stage and that is reflected in the name of the degree. Three years ago, Lancaster University Management School went a little further, converting a CSR elective
55 into a global society and responsible management module, which all MBA students must take in the second term. At Warwick Business School, on the other hand, the Corporate Citizenship
60 module is still an elective – but lectures are always packed, says Professor David Wilson, deputy dean.

"You can't force ethics down the throats of mature students, so you
65 have to create an environment where all students have to think about what stance they'll take," says Professor Rosa Chun. At Oxford, the Saïd Business School runs an MBA elective
70 on CSR and ethical marketing, which looks at the complexities of balancing stakeholder interests while protecting reputations. And at the Judge Business School in Cambridge a new CSR elective
75 is being introduced.

Henley Management College takes a different approach. "We've baked CSR into the MBA," says Marc Day, director of studies. "For example, I teach
80 supply chain management, where food miles are an issue. Both CSR and lean management involve reducing waste and the impact on the planet."

World wide trend

The message has spread across Europe.
85 The SDA Bocconi School of Management in Milan has just introduced a corporate citizenship course in response to demand from both employers and students. Reims Management School in
90 France has a new chair in management for non-profit organisations and social business. In the US, and now also in London, the University of Chicago Graduate School of Business
95 offers an ethics module taught by the controversial Nobel laureate, Robert Fogel. At Nottingham, Akande accepts that there is a certain amount of scepticism about CSR among her peers.
100 "But I think that's because they don't understand the bottom-line business case for it. They see it as some sort of philanthropy. Part of the problem with business is that it's very short-termist."
105 Some commentators believe that with the downturn in the markets after the credit crunch companies might simply drop CSR. But Henley's Marc Day sounds a warning. "In the short term
110 they may think they can drop ethical responsibility. It might come back to bite them."

Pre-reading

1 Why do you think MBA courses are now including courses in Corporate Social Responsibility (CSR)?

Reading

2 Match the questions 1–7 with the people a–f. You will need to use one of the names twice.

a) David Vogel
b) Michelle Akande
c) Bob Berry
d) Professor David Wilson
e) Professor Rosa Chun
f) Marc Day

1 Who says that although one of their CSR options is very popular, it's still not compulsory?
2 Who argues that ignoring CSR in the short term may create longer-term problems for companies and businesses?
3 Who has coined a new phrase to express the fact that corporate social responsibility is now a serious business?
4 Who provides an example of the way in which CSR is integrated into the various modules of the MBA course?
5 Who says that many MBA students do not fully understand the fundamental business sense of CSR?
6 Who makes the point that it is better to encourage students to think critically about CSR issues rather than making them adopt an ethical position?
7 Who states that the study of ethical business practices is now a component of all the courses at their university?

Speaking: Communicative crossword

Type of activity: Vocabulary definitions and explanations. Revision of collocations relating to supply chains and logistics.

Preparation: Make one copy of page 127 for each pair of students. Cut the page in half so that each student has Part A or Part B.

1 Explain to students that they are going to complete a crossword puzzle by explaining the answers to each other. In order to do this, they will need to use paraphrasing, relative clauses and definitions. You might want to feed in the following useful expressions:

This is a These are	process(es) tool(s) machine(s)	(that)	companies businesses organizations	use	to + infinitive for + verb + ing
Companies Businesses Organizations	employ use	these this	machine(s) tool(s) process(es)	to + infinitive for + verb + ing	

3 Elicit further suggestions from the class.
4 Distribute the crosswords and give students time to prepare their clues and to check / clarify meanings.
5 Tell students to work in pairs, facing each other, but stress that they must keep their crosswords concealed from their partner's view.

Alternative method: If you have the facilities, your students can do this exercise in Internet chat rooms. You would need to set up an individual chat room for each pair. Alternatively, pairs can create a private chat area for this purpose.

Reading: Ten Ways To Go Greener

Type of activity: Matching headings to paragraphs and using the task as a springboard for discussion of business and eco-awareness. This activity could be done after module 3.3.

Preparation: Make enough copies of the text and questions for each student.

1 The class discusses the lead-in questions about pollution and logistics in small groups. Explain the meaning of *carbon footprint* if this is a new term for anyone in the class.
2 Tell students to work individually and set a time limit for them to match the headings to the paragraphs. Allow them to compare in pairs, then take whole-class feedback. Note: the WEEE directive and *idling* are explained in the text so should not need clarification before the matching exercise.

ANSWERS:

1 f   2 a   3 h   4 e   5 b   6 j   7 d   8 i   9 c   10 g

3 Follow up with a brief discussion of big business and environmental issues, comparing attitudes in different cultures and countries.

3 Supply chain Speaking

Student A

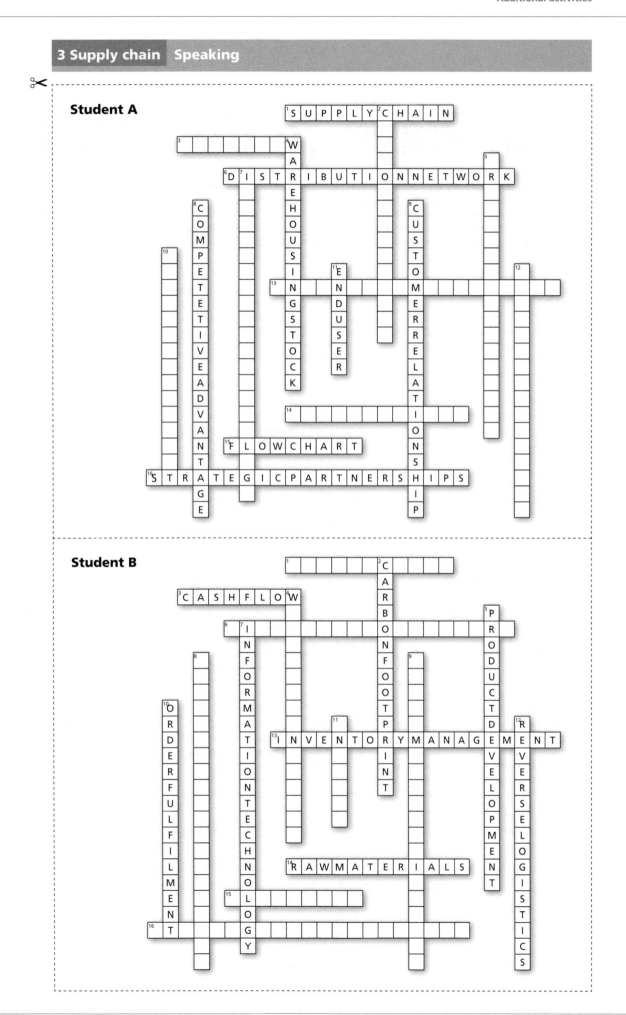

¹ S U P P L Y C H A I N
³ ...... ⁴ W
⁶ D I S T R I B U T I O N N E T W O R K
⁸ C ⁹ C
¹³ ...... ¹¹ E
¹⁵ F L O W C H A R T
¹⁶ S T R A T E G I C P A R T N E R S H I P S
¹⁴ ......

Student B

³ C A S H F L O W
⁶ ......
¹³ I N V E N T O R Y M A N A G E M E N T
¹⁴ R A W M A T E R I A L S

The Business Advanced Teacher's Book © Macmillan Publishers Limited 2009. This page may be photocopied and used within the class.

Ten Ways To Go Greener

Competition among retailers and manufacturers is intensifying as brand reputation and consumer loyalty have become a valuable by-product. But what are the true costs of "going green" and does this mean that profits have to take a dip into the red to reach this status?

A recent survey by Boston-based AMR Research found that reducing energy consumption had two clear benefits; significant reduction in operating costs and simultaneous lowering of carbon dioxide emissions. Reducing a company's carbon footprint at the same time
5 as improving the bottom line is certainly an achievable goal and the supply chain is one area that should be a core focus for every organisation. Here are ten tips on getting the most out of a greener supply chain:

1 _____: integrating material handling and warehouse management systems allows manufacturers and
10 distributors to move and touch products fewer times, and reduce the use of forklift trucks. This leads to lower handling costs and helps to cut energy consumption and emissions.

2 _____: advanced
15 warehouse management systems help companies to make their warehouse processes more efficient. Goods received in can be distributed out to stores without the need to hold stock in the distribution
20 centre. Supplying to demand helps minimise inventory and increase product turns. With more stock flowing through the warehouse, companies can manage their business with smaller distribution centres – which require
25 less space and consume less energy.

3 _____: a good distributed order management system allows companies to route orders to the closest fulfilment location. This reduces overall mileage and
30 helps cut down on the number of empty hauls in the movement of goods, while also requiring less fuel.

The level of visibility that such a system provides across an entire supply chain also
35 enables a business to ship incoming products directly to their destination, allowing them to bypass the distribution centre altogether. A good distributed order management system typically produces a ten per cent reduction
40 in miles travelled. According to United Parcel Service, for a company that ships 100 million parcels, that ten per cent improvement would reduce the company's carbon emissions by 210 tonnes.

45 **4** _____: the rise in fuel costs and constant scrutiny of carbon emissions is applying more pressure to UK companies. Sophisticated transport management systems are being used to find the best way to ship
50 goods, whether it is by road, train, boat or plane – or a mixture.

A typical five-axle, European specification, 40 tonne truck, doing 80,000 miles a year will use around 55,000 litres of fuel, costing
55 about £60,000. Over a generous ten year life that 40 tonne truck will deliver goods worth some £100 million and cost nearly £850,000 to run. For a fleet of 50 trucks, the annual fuel bill will probably be around £3 million, making
60 transport management a top priority.

5 _____: best-of-breed planning, forecasting, and replenishment helps to drive efficiency in manufacturing and distribution operations by reducing the
65 amount of inventory required in a given supply chain network to support fluctuating customer demand. This results in reduced energy and materials consumption and improved operational efficiency.

70 **6** _____: a good warehouse management system will allocate the right units to pick and then select the correct size and type of container for the order and advise the workers how to use the space
75 in each box most efficiently. Getting the packaging right can reduce cardboard use in a warehouse by more than 20 per cent. Once all the manufacturing, shipping and disposal processes are included, taking one pound
80 of paper out of the supply chain reduces a company's carbon emissions by a pound, too.

7 _____: replacing manual, paper-based processes with technology, such as radio frequency identification, bar codes
85 and voice-picking, improves warehouse efficiency and reduces paper consumption.

8 _____: much of the fuel consumed and emissions produced by trucks come from drivers idling their trucks
90 to keep the heat and air conditioning going at shipping and receiving docks. Comfort stations can substantially reduce idling, lower maintenance costs and enhance driver safety. Combined with "No Idling" policies
95 at the dock, companies can quickly achieve an improvement in costs, emissions and community relations.

9 _____: companies can further reduce their fuel consumption and
100 environmental impact by selecting more streamlined tractor profiles, employing automatic tyre inflation systems, implementing wide-base tyres, incorporating hybrid power-train technology and instituting
105 comprehensive driver training.

10 _____: with landfill sites full to bursting, the WEEE directive came into force for UK companies on 1st July 2007 forcing producers, distributors and retailers
110 of electronic goods to take their share of responsibility for the recycling of household electronic equipment. As a result, the ability to manage the reverse logistics process efficiently has become a critical factor
115 for business success. Companies need to manage the physical process of collecting products, and also record which product has been taken where.

---

1 Work with a partner: Can you think of any ways in which a supply chain could be made more environmentally friendly? Do you try to buy products produced locally in your country? Do you worry about a product's 'carbon footprint' when you are shopping?

2 Read the text and match the paragraph headings below (a–j) to the numbered paragraphs (1–10).

a De-stock the DC
b Synchronise supply and demand
c Improve fleet aerodynamics
d Cut paper use
e Choose the right transport

f Get hands off stock
g Take care of WEEE
h Know where stock is
i Reduce idling
j Size up the packages

3 How important are green issues to businesses in your country?

4 Managing conflict   Teacher's notes & answers

Speaking: Discussion

Type of activity: Discussing and hypothesizing to resolve sources of conflict at work. This activity links with Module 4.4, Management skills and assertiveness techniques.
Preparation: Make one copy of page 130 for each student in the class.

1   Ask students to work in groups of three to brainstorm some possible causes of conflict at work. Elicit responses.
2   Explain to the class that they are going to read about and discuss six conflict situations at work. Their job is to work as a group in order to decide on the most appropriate course of action in each situation.
3   Distribute the texts and give students a few minutes to read through to check they understand each situation. You may find it useful to ask the following gist questions:
    Which text is about ...
        ... possible theft? (C)
        ... conflict between colleagues? (F)
        ... staff-client relationships? (D)
        ... employees with family problems? (C and E)
        ... religious issues? (B)
        ... absenteeism? (A)
4   Now ask students to make a note of the action they would take for each situation, e.g.

Situation	Action to take
A	To begin with I would approach the employee and politely say 'Good evening.'

5   Monitor the class and provide help and guidance where needed.
6   Once students have made a note of their ideas, get them into groups of three to discuss each situation. Stress that it is important for the groups to reach a consensus on the best course of action.
    Option: At this stage you could elicit useful phrases for this type of discussion, e.g.
    In this situation I'd ...
    I certainly wouldn't ...
    I think it might be an idea to ...
    I agree that would be the best course of action.
7   Set a time limit for the groups to complete the discussion. As the discussions take place, monitor and make a note of language points for post-correction and feedback.
8   Once the discussions are completed, ask each group to feed back to the class on their solutions to each problem. Where appropriate, throw these open to whole-class discussion.
9   Conduct feedback and post-correction based on the notes you made during the discussions.

EXTENSION ACTIVITY

If there is time, or during a subsequent lesson, students could roleplay some of the situations, taking the part of the manager and employee in each case.

Reading: Which Management Style to Use

Type of activity: Comprehension, discussion and multiple matching. This activity could be done after module 4.1 or module 4.3.
Preparation: Make enough copies of the text and questions for each student.

1   If working through the book consecutively this lead-in will provide the opportunity to recycle management qualities discussed in module 1.4, but this time as nouns. Otherwise, the nouns can still be written on the board and drilled for stress and pronunciation.
2   Students do the prediction activity then read the first part of the text to check their predictions. Elicit the summaries from different class members then move on to the multiple-matching activity.
3   Set a short time limit for the scanning activity and allow students to compare in pairs, then take whole-class feedback.

ANSWERS:

Directing: 6, 4
Supportive: 1, 8
Coaching: 3, 7
Delegating: 5, 2

4   Read the text to the class, or select students to read a paragraph each. Note and drill any pronunciation difficulties. Elicit answers from the class. Then ask students for their opinions on the content of the article, and encourage them to relate any personal examples of good or poor management they have experienced.

ANSWERS:

Student's own answers

Situation A

As the manager of a small team working on an urgent project, you have been presented with a doctor's note explaining a key member of your team's five-day absence due to depression. It is Friday night and as you push your way to the bar you notice your employee drinking and laughing with friends in a corner of the bar. He appears to have a very good suntan. What do you say and do?

Situation B

You work as the manager of a hair and beauty salon. One of the applicants for a vacancy that has arisen is a Muslim lady wearing a headscarf. She has a lot of relevant hairdressing experience, but it is usual for your stylists to display their hair and you are unsure about how your customers and other hairdressers will react. What do you do?

Situation C

A colleague of yours, with whom you have a good personal relationship, is experiencing serious financial difficulties. She has recently been left by her husband and is struggling to raise a small child alone. At close of business one day you notice a discrepancy in the accounts. A small sum of money is missing from the petty cash and only you and your friend have access to these funds. What do you say and do?

Situation D

You work as the Director of Studies at a private language school. It is school policy that relationships between teachers and students must remain strictly professional. However, on leaving the school one day you catch sight of one of the teachers in a passionate embrace with a student. What do you say and do?

Situation E

One of the most junior members of staff has been repeatedly arguing with his parents and has threatened to leave home as a result. On arriving at work early one morning you notice a sleeping bag in the corner of your office. On further investigation you discover he has been sleeping at work for the past three nights. How would you handle the situation?

Situation F

You work for a small company. You have a colleague who joined the company at the same time as you and you are of equal seniority in the organization. However, as a result of your performance and feedback from customers, your boss decides to promote you to a management position. You find that you are now your colleague's line manager. However, your colleague refuses to acknowledge your promotion. She refuses to cooperate when you ask her to do things and she starts taking days off work without permission and without giving any reasons why. How would you deal with this situation?

 Photocopiable

4 Managing conflict Reading

Which management style to use

A manager is generally responsible for a project or a team of people and, essentially must be able to communicate, negotiate and influence. However, these skills can be performed in different ways. A key component of job satisfaction is the relationship between managers and their staff. This, in turn, is influenced both by the people and management styles involved.

Four basic styles

Management styles do not always fit into nice, neat, recognised definitions. However, management writer, Ken Blanchard narrows management down to four basic styles: directing, supporting, coaching and delegating.

Directing

Directing is telling someone how and when to do something. Most managers find this style easy to use. It works best when tasks are straightforward and when the manager is better informed and more experienced than the member of staff. This style also works well when decisions have to be made immediately, when risks cannot be taken or when a task has to be performed to a given specification. Directing is also suited to situations where commitment from staff is irrelevant and where perhaps large numbers of staff are involved in completing a task. This style, however, does not come easily to everyone.

Supportive

A supportive style is appropriate for staff who have ability but need motivation or more confidence. A manager who uses this style needs to be a good listener but also needs to be able to provide encouragement to staff who may be reluctant to recognise their own achievements. A manager using this style works alongside staff as a colleague and offers honest praise and encouragement when appropriate in order to raise motivation levels. Supportive management is about finding out how the other person feels (e.g. ask "how do you feel that task went?") and giving constructive feedback. Managers should ask themselves questions such as: Do I acknowledge success and build on it? Do I analyse set-backs, identify what went well and give constructive guidance to improve future performance? Do I show those who work with me that I trust them or do I surround them with unnecessary controls? Do I provide adequate opportunities for training and retraining if necessary? Do I encourage each individual to develop his or her capacities to the full? Do I recognise the contribution of each member of the team and encourage team members to do the same?

Coaching

Coaching uses a combination of directing and supporting. It requires good two-way communication between staff and managers and is used as a vehicle to enable staff to develop their skills and competence. Relationship building is crucial. Coaching opportunities often arise during normal day-to-day activities and managers can informally coach staff as the need arises. Some organizations employ professional coaches. Coaching works on the premise that the person doing the coaching has confidence that the person being coached will succeed.

The stages involved in coaching include: identifying the areas of knowledge, skills or capabilities where learning needs to take place; ensuring that the person understands and accepts the need to learn; discussing with the person what needs to be learnt and the best way to undertake the learning; getting the person to work out how they can manage their own learning while identifying where they will need help; providing encouragement and advice; providing specific guidance as required; agreeing how progress should be monitored and reviewed.

Delegating

Of the four basic styles delegation is perhaps the most challenging. Some managers tend to have a reluctance to let go of a task and often end up supervising rather than delegating. Other managers delegate and disappear, failing to check on how the delegated task was completed or failing to carry out progress checks. Often delegation fails as a management style because of poor communication about the delegated task. Delegation works when agreement is reached on the nature of the delegated task, deadlines for completion are agreed, it is decided how potential problems will be addressed and the right person is chosen for the task.

Staff who are delegated a task need to be respected for their knowledge and skills. They should be involved in the decisions about how progress on the delegated task will be monitored. Because delegation is not abdication by a manager, the person to whom a task is delegated should be aware of the lines of accountability for the delegated task.

1 What qualities does a good manager need? Would you make (or are you) a good manager? Why / why not?

2 The text describes four commonly recognized management styles (Directing, Supportive, Coaching and Delegating). What do you think characterises each style? Read the text and check your predictions.

3 Scan the text again and match the following statements to these management styles:

Directing	Supportive	Coaching	Delegating

1 This style is appropriate if you need to develop confidence in your staff. (_____)
2 In this style it is necessary to agree on a time for completion of the task. (_____)
3 This style requires the manager to believe their staff will succeed. (_____)
4 This style is appropriate when it does not matter how committed your staff are. (_____)
5 This style works best when the most suitable person is selected for the job. (_____)
6 This management style is most effective for rapid decision making. (_____)
7 In this style manager and staff need to agree on a system for checking progress. (_____)
8 This style requires the manager to acknowledge how every team member contributes. (_____)

4 Discussion
1 Which of the management techniques described in the article have you experienced?
2 Which management style most appeals to you? Why?

Speaking: Presentations

Type of activity: Presenting brands. Peer assessment of presentations. This activity explores the concept of 'cool brands' and can be used in conjunction with modules 5.1 or 5.3.

Preparation: Make one copy of the background text on page 133 for each student in the class. Prepare a copy of the 'CoolBrands Official Results 2007/2008' text for display on an OHP or an IWB. You may also want to obtain copies of the logos for each of the 20 brands listed. These could be used for illustrative purposes and may also be used by students in their presentations.

1 Write the words *CoolBrands* on the board. Ask students to work in pairs or threes to discuss the following questions (these may be dictated or written on the board):
Which brands do you think are 'cool' and why?
Which two brands do you think are the coolest?
What do you think makes a brand cool?
Which brands are definitely not cool? Why not?

2 Tell the students that they are going to read about the process of selecting CoolBrands. Put the following questions on the board or an OHP:
   1 *How many brands are submitted to the CoolBrands Council?* (just under 1,200)
   2 *Which brands are council members not allowed to score?* (those with which they have a direct association or with which they are in direct competition)
   3 *How many consumers take part in judging the brands?* (3,265)
   4 *How many brands finally achieve 'CoolBrand' status?* (500)
   5 *What are the six key criteria for judging a cool brand?* (how stylish, innovative, original, authentic, desirable and unique the brand is)

3 Distribute the background text 'CoolBrands Selection Process 2007/08' to each student in the class and ask them to read it quickly to answer the five questions. Let them compare quickly in pairs, then take whole-class feedback.

4 Note: Depending on the size of the group, the next stage can be done individually, in pairs or in small groups. Give each student or pair / group a brand from the top 20 list on page 133. Also give them the six judging criteria: Stylish, Innovative, Original, Authentic, Desirable and Unique.

5 Give students twenty minutes to prepare a short (five-minute) presentation on why their brand is the coolest based on the six criteria given.

6 Ask students / pairs / groups to deliver their presentations to the class. Explain that the object is for the class to vote on which is the coolest brand according to the quality and persuasiveness of the presentations.

7 Finally, give students the top 20 list to see the actual ranking of CoolBrands. If there is time, you could conduct a short open-class discussion on student reactions to the rankings, how they would change them and which rankings they agree / disagree with.

Reading: Actions speak louder than words

Type of activity: Matching and discussion. This reading activity should be done in conjunction with module 5.4.
Preparation: Make enough copies of the text and questions for each student.

1 Ask students in pairs to discuss the lead-in questions and to scan the text quickly to check their answers. This may be a good opportunity to pre-teach the words *furrowed*, *empathy*, *reticence*, *blink*, *gaze* and *fidget*.

2 Students work individually to do the matching activity and then compare their answers in pairs. Go through the answers with the class and clarify any points that arise.

3 Ask students to practise the short roleplay in pairs, using body language to enhance their communication. With small groups you could get students to act out their dialogues after they have practised them.

ANSWERS:

1 Student's own answers
2 1 i   2 j   3 g   4 h   5 f   6 d   7 a   8 e   9 b   10 c
3 Student's own answers.

5 Strategic marketing Speaking

CoolBrands: Official Results 2007/2008

1	Aston Martin: Automotive – Supercars	11	Ferrari: Automotive – Supercars
2	iPod: Technology – General	12	Ducati: Automotive – Motorbikes
3	YouTube: Online – General	13	eBay: Online – General
4	Bang & Olufsen: Technology – General	14	Rolex: Fashion – Accessories, Jewellery, Watches
5	Google: Online – General	15	Tate Modern: Leisure & Entertainments – UK Attractions & The Arts
6	PlayStation: Leisure & Entertainment – Games & Toys	16	Prada: Fashion – Designer
7	Apple: Technology – General	17	Lamborghini: Automotive – Supercars
8	Agent Provocateur: Fashion – Lingerie	18	Green & Black's: Food
9	Nintendo: Leisure & Entertainment – Games & Toys	19	iTunes: Online – General
10	Virgin Atlantic: Travel – General	20	Amazon: Online – Retail

Background text
CoolBrands Selection Process 2007/08

Independent researchers use a wide range of sources to compile a list of the UK's leading CoolBrands. From the thousands of brands initially considered, an extensive list of just under 1,200 brands is forwarded to the CoolBrands Council.

The independent and voluntary council considers the list and members individually award each brand a score from 1–10. The score is intuitive, but Council members are asked to bear in mind how stylish, innovative, original, authentic, desirable and unique each brand is. Council members are not allowed to score brands with which they have a direct association or are in direct competition to. The lowest-scoring 50 per cent of brands are eliminated at this stage.

A nationally representative panel of 3,265 consumers is surveyed by YouGov, the UK's most accurate online research agency. These individuals are asked to vote on the surviving 625 brands which remain after the Council has scored.

The surviving brands are ranked based on the combined score of the CoolBrands Council (70 per cent) and the consumer panel (30 per cent). The lowest-scoring brands are eliminated while the leading 500 brands are awarded 'CoolBrand' status and are invited to join the CoolBrands programme. Criteria Experts and consumers were given the following guidelines when considering the brand list:

	'Cool' is a subjective and personal. However, over the years, our research has shown there to be six key factors inherent in a CoolBrand:
1	Stylish
2	Innovative
3	Original
4	Authentic
5	Desirable
6	Unique

When selecting which brands you consider to be 'cool', please bear these six factors in mind.

(source: http://www.superbrands.uk.com)

Actions speak louder than words

ACCORDING to research, more than 50% of our communication is conveyed by body language alone. Therefore, it is vitally important when trying to clinch that all-important sale that you are aware of the body language of your potential client. For example, you may ask a question and receive a 'yes', but if your prospect has a furrowed brow or you are failing to make eye contact, then it may be time to take a coffee break and recommence the hard sell later. This article provides you with a few tips on the key areas of body language that you can focus on, to help you 'read' the real feelings of the person you are selling to.

There are many dimensions to body language, but the key areas are our facial expressions, our posture and the way we position our arms and legs. So, let us take each of these in turn, to assist you in knowing what subconscious messages are being sent out, so you can gain a greater understanding of what your next move should be.

Let's look first of all at the way we communicate using our face. If you have really connected with a customer upon first meeting, then you should notice a rapid raising of the eyebrows. However, if you fail to notice this, then maybe you need to work harder to establish this initial contact that leads to empathy. Also, look out for widening or narrowing of the pupils and blinking too much. Widening of the pupils is usually a positive sign, whereas narrowing may indicate reticence or even active dislike. Excessive blinking may be a sign of insecurity or a fear that the customer's doubts or concerns are not being taken seriously. Pay attention to the eyes when reading if a smile is really felt, as a genuine smile should light up the whole face and cause wrinkling around the eyes. When you are pitching your sale, again pay particular attention to the eyes. They should be gazing up, which indicates consideration of an offer or proposal, or centred, which might indicate that the other person is focusing on what you are saying. Wandering eyes, on the other hand, might signal that you have lost the interest that you need to maintain in order to effect your sale. Maybe boredom is setting in and you need to change topic or reformulate your pitch.

Posture is also a useful indicator of what your prospect may be thinking or feeling. If they are resting their cheek on their hand, this is a positive sign as they are probably giving a lot of thought to what you are saying. The position of the torso is also important. Leaning back in the chair shows a relaxed attitude whilst leaning slightly forward signals interest in a proposal. If they have their hands interlocked behind their head this may show that they are very secure and open to ideas.

One easy guideline to remember is that a closed posture may represent a closed attitude, whereas an open posture reveals a more receptive and open attitude.

Finally, we can also interpret the body language of the arms, legs and lower body. Look at the way your interlocutor uses their arms and hands. If they keep their arms folded across their chest, they are being defensive and most probably disagree with what you are saying. If they start tapping their fingers or fidgeting, this may indicate nervousness or boredom or even that they are growing impatient because they have something to say. Sitting with the legs slightly open is a relaxed comfortable position. Just as with folded arms, if the legs are crossed this may be interpreted as a defensive, closed position, but the crossing can take many forms. If the ankles are crossed with legs tucked under the chair, there may be an attempt to conceal anxiety. When one leg is crossed so that the ankle rests on the other leg's knee, there may be an implied challenge or rejection of what the client is listening to. A more relaxed crossing of the legs at the knee is a more positive sign, but be careful if the knee starts bouncing up and down as this can be a sign of impatience.

1 Pre-reading

Work with a partner. Imagine you are in a sales negotiation with a client. What signs of body language might indicate the negotiation is going well? What signs might indicate it is going badly? (Think about eye contact, facial expression and posture.) When you have finished, read the text quickly to check your ideas.

2 Reading

Read the text again and match the examples of body language to their meanings:

1 narrowed pupils
2 blinking a lot
3 eyes looking up
4 wandering eyes
5 leaning slightly forward
6 hands interlocked behind the head
7 arms folded across the chest
8 tapping fingers or fidgeting
9 ankles crossed with legs tucked under the chair
10 one leg is crossed with the ankle on the other knee

a) your client disagrees with you
b) your client may feel anxious
c) your client may reject what you're saying
d) your client is open to ideas
e) your client has something to say
f) your client is interested in your proposal
g) your client may be considering an offer or proposal
h) you have lost your customer's interest
i) your client does not particularly like you
j) your client may feel insecure or afraid

3 Post-reading

Work in pairs. One of you is a sales person, the other a client. You are selling and buying a car.
Client: Respond with negative body language.
Sales person: Mirror the client's negative body language and try to steer your client into a more positive frame of mind and more positive body language.

6 Risk management   Teacher's notes & answers

Speaking: Asking for and giving information: Discussion.

Type of activity: Information exchange. Ranking.
Preparation: Photocopy enough case studies from the eight provided on page 136 for your students to have at least one each. With very small classes, more than one case study can be given to each student. Create a table as follows with a row for each (up to a maximum of eight rows) on an A4 size sheet of paper and make enough photocopies for each student in your class.

Company(ies) involved	The PR disaster	The final outcome

1 Write *PR blunder* on the board and elicit / explain the meaning of the term. Tell students that they are going to read some short texts about PR blunders.
2 Distribute the reading texts and information grids to each student. Explain that as they read their texts they should make notes about the PR disaster and the final outcome in the first row of the information grid.
3 Give students enough time to read their texts and to complete the first row of the grid. Monitor and provide help and input as needed.
4 Once all students have made notes about their PR disasters, tell them they must now move around the classroom to tell their classmates about their PR disaster and to find out about those of their classmates. As they do so, they should make notes in the grid. Monitor and note any language points for post-correction.
5 Once students have finished collecting the information about the various case studies, provide feedback and remedial correction based on the points noted in the previous stage.
6 Next, ask students to form pairs or groups of three. Explain to the class that each pair / group should now rank the PR disasters according to the severity of the impact on the companies involved. Ask students to consider:
   • the financial impact;
   • the impact on the companies' reputations;
   • the impact on the individuals involved.
7 Conduct a full class discussion based on the groups' rankings. If you have time, ask the class to reach a consensus on which was the most serious and least serious blunder.

Reading: Reputation Management

Type of activity: Comprehension and discussion. This reading activity could be done in conjunction with module 6.4.
Preparation: Make enough copies of the text and questions for each student.

1 Ask students in pairs or threes to discuss the lead-in question about how to avoid a potentially damaging public crisis. Elicit suggestions from the class and then ask students to skim read the text quickly to compare their own ideas with the advice given.
2 Ask students to work individually to answer the true / false questions and then to compare their answers in pairs.

ANSWERS:

a) F (Your point person should be a senior person who has the credibility, authority, and courage to make decisions fast, without time-consuming, widespread consultation).
b) T (Bring in an experienced crisis/reputation management adviser to provide objectivity and an external perspective).
c) T (A prerequisite of crisis management is brutal honesty with yourselves).
d) F (Formulate your key messages quickly, and stick to them. Make the case clearly and simply).
e) T (Continue to monitor and measure public perceptions long after the immediate crisis has passed).

3 Ask students, without referring back to the text, to orally summarize in pairs the key things to avoid in a crisis. Finally, ask students to note down the key points then to check against the text.

SUGGESTED ANSWERS:

Don't panic; avoid indecision from the top, or slow or late responses to the media; avoid apportioning blame; don't be distracted by the media clamour; don't allow a communications vacuum to occur; never lie.

1 Hoover's flying fiasco

Hoover's free flights promotion in 1992 offered two round-trips to Europe for any customer that spent more than £100 on Hoover products. The offer was later extended to include transatlantic flights, leading to massive consumer demand. £100 for a round-trip to the USA seemed too good to be true for customers, and over the next 21 months the company found itself utterly overwhelmed. The marketing debacle, initially intended to offload a backlog of washing machines and vacuum cleaners, cost the group £48m. Hundreds of customers took Hoover to court. The company was hauled into court rooms up and down the country for six years.

2 Shopping's a riot

In 2005, 6,000 frenzied shoppers stampeded on the midnight unveiling of Britain's then-biggest Ikea store. It closed just 40 minutes later leaving 20 in need of hospital treatment. One woman was said to have been threatened by a man with a mallet, and another waiting in the checkout queue was 'mugged' for her cut-price sofa. The 45 security guards were reported to have fled the scene as police were called and a fleet of nine ambulances ferried people to hospital with heat exhaustion and crush injuries. The huge crowd had gathered for the opening of the Swedish furniture store in Edmonton, north London, and had been entertained by fire eaters, stilt walkers and music.

3 Foster's wobbler

To celebrate the arrival of the new Millennium, a striking new bridge was built across the Thames, joining St Paul's Cathedral in the City with the Tate Modern on the South Bank. Londoners and tourists alike flocked when it opened to the public on June 10, 2000. Its popularity came as no surprise to the distinguished design team – architect Lord Foster, sculptor Sir Anthony Caro and engineers Arup – but the fact that it wobbled did. The bridge was closed after just three days, and finally reopened two years later after extensive work to make it more robust. Lord Foster said he would throw himself off the bridge if it wobbled again, but luckily for him it didn't. Despite the new-found sturdiness, eight years on it is still affectionately known as 'the wobbly bridge.'

4 Persil not-so bright

The 'soap-wars' between Unilever's Persil and Proctor & Gamble's Ariel saw the launch of Persil Power in 1994. Much ado was made of the product's newly developed manganese-based catalyst that would help clean clothes at lower temperatures. However, shortly after the launch it emerged that in some cases the new-fangled catalyst would attack dye on fabrics and damage clothes beyond repair. Pictures began to circulate of 'rotting' clothes that had been tainted by the powder. Unilever eventually withdrew the product from the market after strenuous attempts to keep a new and improved version on the shelves.

5 Branded a turkey

Sales of poultry products fell across the country in February 2007, as the last of the 24 lorry-loads of turkey carcasses drove away from the Bernard Matthews farm in Holton, Suffolk, following an outbreak of the H5N1 bird-flu virus. It took less than 24 hours for Bernard Matthews to cull its 160,000 turkeys, but much longer for the company's brand to recover. The maker of once-popular turkey twizzlers, the school dinner staple, Matthews plummeted to the second-least-liked brand in Britain, behind McDonald's, YouGov's BrandIndex reported at the time. More damaging were the ructions overseas. South Africa, Ukraine, Japan, Russia, South Korea and Hong Kong stopped importing all UK poultry because of the outbreak and countless other countries considered partial bans.

6 Wembley's extra time

Wembley, England's new national football stadium, was finished a year late and £400m above the original estimate. It was supposed to open its doors in time for the FA Cup final in May 2006, but Liverpool and West Ham were forced to cross the border and play at Cardiff's Millennium Stadium instead. Wembley finally opened its doors to full capacity a year later, when Manchester United met Chelsea in the 2007 FA Cup clash. As the saga of Wembley Stadium unfolded relations soured between the Football Association and the stadium's Australian builders, Multiplex, and a legal battle ensued.

7 The Millennium Doom

Tony Blair had hoped that the Dome would be a showcase for New Labour. Instead it turned into a £1 billion white elephant, attracting just over half the 12 million visitors originally forecast by the then Dome minister Lord Falconer. It closed its doors to the public on New Year's Eve in 2000 exactly a year after its disastrous launch when VIPs were forced to queue at rail stations to obtain their tickets to what was supposed to be the UK's all-singing all-dancing celebration of the new Millennium. Its failure came at a huge cost to taxpayers, as it was funded primarily by lottery money.

8 Ford's tyred new look

In 2000 Ford advised owners of its Explorer utility vehicles to replace their Firestone tyres as a result of safety fears. The recall followed up to 200 deaths and hundreds of injuries in the US after accidents involving vehicles with Firestone tyres. The recall alone cost Ford almost half a billion dollars. But it also knobbled the brand. According to research carried out by Interbrand, a UK branding consultancy, Ford's brand value plummeted from $36.4bn (£18.7bn) in 2000 to $30.1bn in 2001 as a direct result of the controversy. That's $6bn (£3bn) for using a supplier's flawed products. Firestone fared equally poorly: its North American division paid Ford $240m (£122m) in compensation and its net profit in the half-year following the controversy almost halved.

Reputation Management

by Roger White

Integrity and reputation are the only real assets held by partners in professional services firms; when one is lost, everything else follows. For that reason, every firm must develop a plan to prepare for the day its corporate integrity is threatened.

A problem becomes a crisis when the media amplifies it and matters escalate rapidly out of your immediate control. It affects the everyday life of the organisation, with real and lasting risks to the firm's image and reputation. When, where, and how the crisis is resolved is entirely in your hands.

Would you know what to do if a problem at your firm were to evolve into a genuine crisis? Having navigated through a variety of crises, I have learned a number of hard lessons, culminating in the following "top 10 tips" for managing in a crisis.

1. Don't panic! Stay calm, think clearly, and act fast. Remember to look at issues from an external – not an internal – viewpoint.

2. Manage the response early and from the top. Your CEO or senior partner should stand up and be the voice of the firm. Find agreement on your crisis strategy, get the commitment of top management, and then provide decisive leadership. Indecision from the top, or slow or late responses to the media, will make you a bigger target.

3. Put someone clearly in control of managing the crisis. Your point person should be a senior person who has the credibility, authority, and courage to make decisions fast, without time-consuming, widespread consultation. Establish an effective communications network to enable the fast flow of information both internally and externally.

4. Form a small but dedicated multi-disciplinary crisis team, including advisers, communications specialists, lawyers, risk managers, technical specialists, and seasoned hands. Bring in an experienced crisis/reputation management adviser to provide objectivity and an external perspective.

5. Conduct a very fast SWOT analysis of the problem. Your analysis will be key to how you go forward, possibly for years ahead. A prerequisite of crisis management is brutal honesty with yourselves; if you are less than open with each other, the crisis will control you. It is important to avoid apportioning blame. Accept that you are accountable as a firm, and take collective responsibility. Try to keep in mind that the media is not the problem; be cooperative and don't be distracted by the clamour.

6. Formulate your key messages quickly, and stick to them. Make the case clearly and simply, ensuring that it is understood both inside and outside the firm and that everyone is singing from the same songsheet. Look to identify positive messages as well as responses to the negatives.

7. Handle the media sensitively, professionally, and with an understanding of their agenda. The media will have three questions: What happened? Why? And, what are you doing about it? Don't allow a communications vacuum to occur. Nature abhors a vacuum and so does the media. If you don't tell them anything, there are plenty of others who will fill the void, and you can be sure they will not be on your side.

8. Listen to your stakeholders and the public. Research what people are really thinking about your firm. Don't base your strategy solely on what the media are saying, but find out what impact the crisis is having on clients, employees, and other key audiences. Then, craft your tactics to get the real messages through to the people that matter.
Continue to monitor and measure public perceptions long after the immediate crisis has passed.

9. Use direct communications with your stakeholders. The media has the widest impact but it is uncontrolled. Take advantage of your "narrow cast" channels to get specific messages to identifiable audiences.

10. Never lie! Outright untruths – as well as lies by omission – can only serve to exacerbate your problem. Great crisis management is a critical part of great reputation management. The leadership of a professional services firm, and the partners in it, must manage their reputation as aggressively as they manage costs or any other management responsibility.

1 What advice would you give to senior managers on how to avoid a potentially damaging public crisis?

2 Decide whether the following statements are true or false according to the text:

a) During the crisis it is advisable for senior management to follow standard consultation procedures when making decisions.
b) It is a good idea to employ the services of outside consultants to advise you on how to manage the crisis.
c) It is essential for the management of a company in crisis to be absolutely honest with themselves.
d) During a crisis it is advisable to create detailed messages informing the public about the situation.
e) Once the crisis is over, it is advisable to carry out continuing research in order to evaluate the company's reputation.

3 Summarize what, according to the article, are the key things to avoid during a crisis.

Speaking: Discussion

Type of activity: Evaluating and selecting. This activity provides additional practice in decision making and can be used as a follow-up to module 7.4.

Preparation: Make copies of Text A 'Background information' and Text B 'Applications for arts sponsorship' on page 139 for each student in the class.

1   Ask students to discuss the following questions in pairs or small groups:
    Can you think of any examples of companies having sponsored the arts?
    For what reasons might a company decide to sponsor an arts event or arts organization?
    Do you think it is a good idea for companies to sponsor the arts? Why / Why not?
2   Elicit student responses to the questions and, if appropriate, discuss in open class.
3   Explain to students that they are going to work in small groups to select an arts group or event for sponsorship.
4   Distribute copies of Text A to all students and ask them to read through. Use the following questions to check comprehension:
    What is your job in this task? (PR officer)
    Where are you based? (the southwest of England)
    How much money do you have available for sponsorship? (£10,000)
    How many groups are you allowed to sponsor? (only one)
5   Distribute a copy of Text B to each student and give them enough time to read through each application. Monitor and help with vocabulary as necessary.
6   Ask students to briefly note down what they see as the benefits and limitations associated with sponsoring each of the applications.
7   Ask students to work in groups of three and explain that they must now discuss the relative strengths and weaknesses of each application. The following guiding questions may help students to structure their discussion:
    What would be the benefit of sponsoring this application ...
        ... to the community?
        ... to the organization itself?
        ... to our company?
    Are there any limitations associated with sponsoring this application?
8   Allow groups enough time to reach agreement on which event to sponsor. Monitor and note language points for post-correction.
9   When groups have finished, ask a spokesperson from each group to tell the class which application they sponsored and why. This will provide an opportunity for the groups to compare their outcomes.
10 Provide feedback and correction based on the notes you made while monitoring the discussions.

Reading: The Investment Column: Costain steers clear of construction woes

Type of activity: Comprehension and discussion. This reading activity could be used as a supplementary activity for module 7.5.

Preparation: Make enough copies of the text and questions for each student.

1   Ask students to work in pairs or threes and discuss the lead-in questions about which investment options they think would be the best and why. Elicit suggestions from the class and then ask students to skim read the texts quickly to compare their own ideas.
2   Ask students to work individually to answer the comprehension questions and then to compare their answers in pairs. Go through the answers with the class.

ANSWERS:

1   Banking
2   Costain doesn't build houses, so its share price has not been so badly affected.
3   Underground gas storage and rail infrastructure.
4   Because of the impressive rise in stock (up by 24%) and revenues (up by 183%).
5   Higher-than-expected costs on acquisitions.
6   Because the company claims to offer a 'single technology platform' as well as 'implementing multi-channel solutions'.
7   Because it is so closely connected (inextricably linked) to the banking sector.

3   Ask students in pairs or threes to discuss which company shares they would buy and why. Elicit ideas from the class.

Text A

Background information

Linking your logo with a cultural event makes a lot of business sense. UK businesses gave £153.4 million to the arts in 2005–2006. You and your partners work as public relations officers for a small law firm in a city in the southwest of England. You must decide how to use the £10,000 available for arts sponsorship in the region. You have been instructed that the money cannot be divided between the groups, as having only one recipient would maximize the resulting beneficial publicity.

Text B

Applications for arts sponsorship

1 **'Opera for Everyone'** has a reputation for innovative and sometimes controversial productions. They tour the Southwest trying to expand the audience for this art form by encouraging new talent and experimenting with new interpretations of the classics. The sponsorship package includes brand and logo identity on marketing and promotional materials, tickets and corporate hospitality.

2 **'Make some Noise'** is a music-making project that works with young people at a social or economic disadvantage. They aim to reach youngsters in challenging circumstances who are drawn to music-making activities and would benefit from such opportunities. They provide singing lessons, musical instrument tuition and ultimately the opportunity to release music downloads which would carry the sponsor's logo.

3 **'Crafts Creation'** runs workshops and evening classes in silverwork, ceramics and jewellery making for the elderly. Through the provision of state-of-the-art facilities and expert tuition, the over-65s are encouraged to produce work for exhibitions which can be displayed on your business premises.

4 **'The Weybridge Literature Festival'** aims to provide a showcase for the finest international literary and journalistic talent. This annual event is guaranteed to attract media attention through a series of readings, poetry recitals and book signings. The festival boosts tourism in the region by attracting an international audience and the sponsor's name will be prominently displayed on all publicity materials and on a banner in the main hall.

The Investment Column: Costain steers clear of construction woes

By Alistair Dawber, *Tuesday, 14 October 2008*

Costain

Our view: Hold for now
Share price: 20.75p (+1.5p)

Investors are often accused of acting as part of a herd at best, at worst a mob. When one construction group suffers – and the sector is second only
5 to banking in the toxicity league tables in recent months – those holding the shares of others in the sector have tended to abandon ship too.
Buyers with a bit more about them
10 have noticed that Costain is a bit different, however, notably because it does not build houses, meaning that its shares have fallen by less than most. Those buyers are now being rewarded.
15 The stock soared by 7.8 per cent yesterday as an improving market was treated to an upbeat trading statement, which said that the group's order book, at £2bn, is at record levels and expected
20 profit numbers are on track. Its chief executive Andrew Wyllie says that the group's strategy of targeting blue chip private and public sector clients for big projects such as underground
25 gas storage and rail infrastructure developments is paying off. Only if the world falls apart, says Mr Wyllie (and he concedes that this is not as ridiculous as it once sounded), will
30 Costain really suffer.
Analysts at Finncap argue that the price is appealingly cheap and that that "value will emerge at the end of the day" for Costain investors. Long-term
35 buyers in Costain should do well, but in the short term, because the market has a habit of acting as one, things could still be a bit hairy. Hold for now.

YouGov

Our view: Hold
Share price: 54.25p (+10.25p)

Buyers that have kept faith with the
40 polling and market research group YouGov in the past year can finally afford to give themselves a well-earned slap on the back following an impressive 24 per cent rise in the stock
45 after the group yesterday announced its full year numbers. Revenues were up 183 per cent to £40.4m, with operating profits in markets such as the UK up by double-digit percentages.
50 If there was a fly in the ointment, it was disappointing news on profits. Pre-tax earnings were down by 29 per cent due to higher-than-expected costs on acquisitions. House broker Numis says
55 that it expects to downgrade YouGov's 2008-09 figures, but still expects the share price to hit 110p in the next 12 months.
That might be a tough ask. The
60 truth is that, while the company is operationally sound and Numis's downgrade is down to unexpectedly high investment costs, good news has been hard to come by for punters with
65 the stock falling by more than 70 per cent in the 12 months before yesterday. YouGov is a solid group and its model, of using internet panels representing a cross-section of society, has a proven
70 track record. Investors should wait to see, however, how well it can ride out the predicted recession still to hit the economy. Hold.

Focus Solutions

Our view: Cautious hold
Share price: 30p (+1.5p)

Reading sections of Focus Solutions'
75 website is like looking at a dictionary of management doublespeak. Aside from offering organisations "an integrated whole office solution through a single technology platform", the group
80 also claims to have "a successful track record of implementing multi-channel solutions across a broad range of financial services products to thousands of end users".
85 The company says that interim numbers will show an increase in sales, profits and cash, but nervous buyers in these markets (is there any other type?) will rightly point out
90 that the group is inextricably linked to the banking sector and given the troubles of the likes of Royal Bank of Scotland, HBOS, Lloyds TSB, et al, Focus Solutions' shares are inevitably
95 doomed. They have a point. Why would anyone buy stock in an industry that is likely to serve fewer customers offering fewer products?
Its chief executive Richard Stevenson
100 says that the software is inspired by FSA regulation and, with more of that on the way, Focus Solutions is on to a winner, especially as banks might need to offer a greater number of products to
105 spread risk. With a price earnings ratio of 3.7 times, the group is undervalued, he adds, saying that it is beyond him as to why the shares are so poorly rated. The reason is that investors are unlikely
110 to touch anything related to banking with a barge pole for sometime. Cautious hold.

1 Pre-reading

You are going to read about share performance in a construction company, a market research company and a financial software company during a period of recession. Which do you think would be the best investment choice and why?

2 Reading

1 Which sector of the economy is described as being worse than construction at the time of the report?
2 In what way is Costain 'a bit different' from other construction companies?
3 Find two examples of the types of projects Costain is involved with.
4 Why can buyers of YouGov shares 'give themselves a well-earned slap on the back'?
5 What has brought about the drop in YouGov's pre-tax earnings?
6 Why does the author accuse Focus Solutions management of 'doublespeak'?
7 Why do buyers think Focus Solutions shares are 'inevitably doomed'?

3 Post-reading

If you were an investor with money to invest, which of these three companies' shares would you buy and why?

8 Free trade   Teacher's notes & answers

Speaking: Discussion

Type of activity: Arguing for and against the topic of free trade. This can be used as a supplementary speaking exercise with module 8.1.

Preparation: Make copies of Text A 'For free trade' and Text B 'Against free trade' on page 142 for each pair of students in the class.

1 Explain to students that they are going to discuss the pros and cons of free trade. Put the following table on the board and ask students to copy it.

Arguments for free trade	Arguments against free trade

2 Tell students to work in pairs and brainstorm some of the arguments for and against free trade, and to make notes in the table.

3 Elicit students' ideas and write them on the board in the columns provided. This provides a good opportunity to gauge students' knowledge of and familiarity with the topic.

4 Distribute texts A and B to half the class respectively. Give students enough time to read through the statements about free trade. Monitor and help with vocabulary as necessary.

5 Tell students that they are going to hold a 'for and against' debate with one of their classmates, using the arguments on their task sheet. Stress that it is important that they argue the points as best as they can, even if they do not actually agree with the opinions. The objective is to provide controlled practice in arguing a point of view.

6 Display the following exponents on the OHP or IWB:
   Useful phrases for giving opinions
   Yes, but don't you think that ...
   I agree with you up to a point, but ...
   I'm sorry I can't agree with you there.
   I see what you mean, but surely ...
   Yes, but on the other hand ...
   No. I'm afraid I must disagree, because ...

7 Drill each exponent, paying particular attention to stress and intonation.

8 Explain to students that when arguing their points about free trade, they should use each of the exponents in turn (Note: there are six exponents and six arguments).

9 Tell students to form new pairs to conduct their debates. Set a time limit for this. Monitor and note language points for post-correction.

10 When the debates are finished, take the opportunity to provide remedial correction of any language points arising in the previous stage.

11 Explain to students that they are now going to discuss the pros and cons of free trade again, but this time using their own opinions and views on the topic. Again, set a time limit and ask students to use the exponents on the board. Monitor and note language points for post-correction feedback.

12 Finally, take whole-class feedback to find out if the class are on the whole more for or against free trade.

Reading: Fairtrade profits rise, but is the small farmer missing out?

Type of activity: Comprehension and discussion arising from the text. This activity could be done after module 8.3.

Preparation: Make enough copies of the text and questions for each student.

1 Bring in some products displaying the Fairtrade logo, or advertisements for supermarkets stating their commitment to stock Fairtrade goods. The following definition could be read quickly as a dictogloss (students note down the key words, then working as a whole class, build up the definition on the board, one acting as secretary).
   'Fair Trade is a trading partnership, based on dialogue, transparency and respect, that seeks greater equity in international trade.'

2 Students work individually to answer the comprehension questions then compare answers in pairs.

ANSWERS:

a) £217 million

b) They have promised to make all of their retail range Fairtrade by 2009.

c) They have been accused of charging the consumer more than finds its way to the producer ('profiteering') and stocking these goods in an attempt solely to appear more socially aware.

d) Because only farmers who operate as cooperatives are eligible to participate in the Fairtrade system.

e) Increased income by a third, paid for school fees, and health care costs, had bridges built, leaf collection centres upgraded and founded a centre for orphaned children.

3 Finally, students discuss the availability of Fairtrade goods in their countries and their personal willingness to purchase these in preference to other brands.

Text A

For free trade

1 It's a violation of human rights to say that if I labour to produce something, I can only trade it with people in my own country.
2 Free trade limits the power of the state and gives more importance to the power of the individual.
3 Free trade brings communities together across borders, culturally and in other ways. For example, the Internet and mobile phones are tools of friendship, not just of business.
4 Free trade leads to a higher standard of living, a stronger middle class and greater freedom.
5 Free trade fosters peace. It makes war more expensive because war disrupts trade.
6 Free trade is beneficial for the poor in society, because everyone can trade in goods, not just the wealthy elite.

Text B

Against free trade

1 Free trade leads to higher unemployment in our native countries, as the workers cannot compete with cheaper goods produced abroad.
2 Free trade would mean that money is leaving our country, which will lower our GDP (gross domestic product).
3 National security depends on the protection of certain key industries (e.g. the defence industry, steel and oil).
4 Other nations may exploit their workforce. Free trade encourages this exploitation by buying cheaper goods from those countries.
5 Other countries may 'dump' their goods in another country in an attempt to drive local producers and manufacturers out of business, so that they can then gain a monopoly and raise their prices.
6 Free trade may lead to greater damage to the environment because of carbon emissions from the transportation of goods.

Fairtrade profits rise, but is the small farmer missing out?

By Susie Mesure and Steve Bloomfield in Kenya
Sunday, 24 February 2008

Once, people laughed at the notion that fair trade could infiltrate the profit-hungry world of retail. Yet new figures from the Fairtrade Foundation will reveal tomorrow that UK consumers take the issue very seriously, spending half a
5 billion pounds on Fairtrade-branded products last year.

However, the rush to fair trade is prompting questions about how "fair" it really is to small farmers in developing nations. The rate of sales growth rocketed during 2007, up 80 per cent on the previous year as companies from Sainsbury's
10 to Virgin Atlantic stepped up their commitment to fairly traded goods. The total value of Fairtrade sales hit £490m, up from £273m in 2006.

Sainsbury's move to stock only Fairtrade bananas meant the supermarket chain almost tripled the value of its
15 Fairtrade sales to £140m. Its tea, coffee, hot chocolate and sugar brands will be next to get the Fairtrade badge, helping to put the Fairtrade Foundation, which licenses the mark to products sold in the UK, on course to quadruple its annual sales to £2bn by 2012.
20 Speaking ahead of Fairtrade fortnight, which starts today, the Fairtrade Foundation's executive director, Harriet Lamb, said: "People laughed when we first started talking about fair trade [in 1994]. But now it is an increasing part of consumers' shopping habits."
25 With a recent poll showing that more than half of UK shoppers recognise the Fairtrade logo, even the big brands are waking up to the selling power of the black, green and blue symbol. Tate & Lyle this weekend became the biggest company yet to carry it, promising to make all of its retail
30 range Fairtrade by the end of 2009.

It isn't just Sainsbury's giving Fairtrade products more shelf space: the Co-operative Group has switched all its own-brand hot beverage drinks to Fairtrade; Waitrose only sells Fairtrade bananas and Marks & Spencer is expanding the
35 Fairtrade clothing range to its fashionable Limited Collection.

Cynics claim their devotion to the cause is less than altruistic, however, pointing to the higher profit margins some Fairtrade products enjoy and the fact that the goods provide a useful marketing tool as supermarkets attempt to
40 paint themselves a greener hue.

Tim Harford, author of *The Logic of Life*, who first highlighted that some chains were profiteering from Fairtrade, said: "At the UK consumer end, some companies have charged a far higher mark-up on Fairtrade products
45 than ever goes to producers. Fairtrade is about a promise for fair value to the producer, not a fair price to the consumer."

Research this month by the consumer group Which? found that Fairtrade products were 9 to 16 per cent more expensive per gram than their non-Fairtrade equivalents. Philip Booth,
50 at the Institute of Economic Affairs, a free-market think tank, said: "How much of that higher price finds its way back to the grower?"

Douglas Holt, L'Oréal professor of marketing at Oxford's Saïd Business School, said the extra amount that Fairtrade
55 producers received was "nice but relatively trivial". He added: "Until you have the whole value chain, especially retailers, buying into Fairtrade and taking lower margins so they can pass on as much profit as possible, Fairtrade can never make more than a marginal difference."
60 Other critics go further, claiming the Fairtrade system leaves unaccredited farmers worse off. A new report from the Adam Smith Institute criticises the movement's core stipulation: that farmers must belong to co-operatives to get the Fairtrade premium.
65 Even Tate & Lyle's move will help only those farmers supplying the retail branded side of its business, not its bigger ingredients arm. Claire Melamed, head of trade and corporates at ActionAid, said: "Fairtrade is still essentially a niche product. The challenge is to get all trade conducted
70 according to much fairer principles."

Where it works, though, the fair-trade movement is much feted. For more than 6,000 farmers on the Iriaini tea plantations in Kenya's Central province, Fairtrade has increased their income by about a third, paying for school
75 fees and healthcare costs that for generations have been beyond them.

"Fairtrade is not just about the money. It changes the people's attitude. [It also] creates a better product," said Matthew Nd'enda, the unit manager of the Iriaini plantation.
80 Bridges have been built, leaf collection centres upgraded and a centre for orphaned children has been established.

That's the image UK shoppers will be buying into when they next buy a Fairtrade product.

---

1 Have you heard of Fairtrade products? Would you recognize the logo?

2

a) What was the increase in sales of Fairtrade goods in 2007?
b) What have Tate and Lyle pledged to do?
c) Why have the retailers who stock Fairtrade goods been criticised?
d) Why has the Adam Smith Institute criticised the Fairtrade system?
e) What are some of the positive effects of the Fairtrade system in Kenya?

3 Are Fairtrade products widely available in your country? Will you buy them in the future, if you can?

Macmillan Education
Between Towns Road, Oxford OX4 3PP
A division of Macmillan Publishers Limited
Companies and representatives throughout the world

ISBN 978-0-230-02152-5

Designed by Keith Shaw, Threefold Design Limited
Cover design by Keith Shaw, Threefold Design Limited

The authors and publishers are grateful for permission to reprint the
following copyright material:
Bizhelp24 for an extract from "Find the right finance for your
business" copyright © www.bizhelp24.com;
Career Talk for an extract from the article "Behavioral Interviews - A
Job Candidate's Toughest Obstacle" by Damir Joseph Stimac, author
of The Ultimate Job Search Kit and Career Talk host. For additional
interviewing tips, visit Career Talk on the Internet. http://www.
careertalk.com;
Independent News & Media Ltd for extracts from "Fairtrade profits
rise, but is the small farmer missing out?" by Susie Mesure and Steve
Bloomfield published in The Independent 24 February 2008; "Ethical
MBAs: A search for corporate social responsibility" by Peter Brown
published in The Independent 6 May 2008; and "The Investment
Column: Costain steers clear of construction woes" by Alistair
Dawber published in The Independent 14 October 2008 copyright ©
The Independent 2008;
Centaur Media plc and Manhattan Associates for an extract from
"Ten ways to go greener" by Allen Scott, UK Managing Director at
Manhattan Associates published in Logistics Manager 1 May 2008
www.logisticsmanager.com, reproduced with permission of Centaur
Media plc and Manhattan Associates;
The Pharmaceutical Journal for an extract from "Which management
style to use" by Ruth McGuire The Pharmaceutical Journal, Vol 275,
10 September 2005, reproduced with permission;
Superbrands (UK) Ltd for a text extract and the table 'Top20
CoolBrands" from CoolBrands: Official Results 2007/2008 survey
www.superbrands.uk.com, reproduced with permission;
Newsweek for an extract from "New! Improved! It's School!"
published in Newsweek 26 November 2007, www.newsweek.
com copyright © 2007 Newsweek, Inc. All rights reserved. Used
by permission and protected by the Copyright Laws of the United
States. The printing, copying, redistribution, or retransmission of the
Material without express written permission is prohibited;
Jaffe Associates, Inc. for an extract from "Balancing Life and Practice"
Reputation Management by Roger White. November 2003 published
on www.lexisone.com copyright © Jaffe Associates, Inc.

These materials may contain links for third party websites. We have
no control over, and are not responsible for, the contents of such third
party websites. Please use care when accessing them.

Although we have tried to trace and contact copyright holders before
publication, in some cases this has not been possible. If contacted
we will be pleased to rectify any errors or omissions at the earliest
opportunity.

Printed and bound in Hong Kong

2013 2012 2011 2010 2009
10 9 8 7 6 5 4 3 2 1